In Search of Personality

In Search of Personality

Christianity and Modern Psychology

Peter Morea

SCM PRESS LTD

0 334 02682 2

First published 1997 by
SCM Press Ltd
9–17 St Albans Place London N 1 0NX

Typeset at The Spartan Press Ltd,
Lymington, Hants
Printed in Great Britain by
Biddles Ltd,
Guildford and King's Lynn

Contents

For Sally

Introduction:
Materialist Psychology and
Christian Theories

... that behind the cotton wool is hidden a pattern; that we – I mean all human beings – are connected with this; that the whole world is a work of art; that we are parts of the work of art.
    (Virginia Woolf, *A Sketch of the Past*)

Just when I seemed about to learn!
Where is the thread now? Off again!
The old trick! Only I discern –
Infinite passion, and the pain
Of finite hearts that yearn.
    (Robert Browning, 'Two in the Campagna')

For twenty-five years I taught psychology at Middlesex Polytechnic (now Middlesex University). Students on my 'Personality' course often expressed appreciation for the understanding of themselves and others which they had gained from Freud, Jung, Rogers and other personality theorists. But some students went on to say that these were still not the answer, while admitting that they were not quite sure what the question was. I eventually realized what sort of questions such students were hoping to find answers to: Who am I? What am I? What should I do to be happy? Does my life have meaning? Death? In traditional religious terms, these students were looking for God.

In the past hundred years the personality theories of Freud, Rogers, Maslow and others have increased our insight into ourselves. We now have greater knowledge and understanding of the unconscious, sexuality, aggression, the self, personal relations, childhood and its influence, morality, guilt, dreams, human needs, the effects of the environment on personality . . . and many other areas. But modern personality theory has little or nothing to say about any need for God. In modern accounts of personality, with the exception of Jung, God for the most part is dead.

Religion tries to provide answers for the questions which seemed to concern many of my students. Such questions have always troubled humans, which is one reason why, as anthropologists confirm, religions exist in most human societies. What we need nowadays is to abandon an outdated confrontation between science and religion. When it comes to personality, we need to combine insights of scientific psychology and religion.

The following chapters outline six accounts of personality from a specific religious tradition, namely, Christianity. The chapters attempt to relate these Christian accounts to modern scientific psychology. Christian and scientific theories of personality have much in common, often overlap, and even complement each other. The six Christian theories are not given in a historical order, nor is any historical development of ideas explored; each account is presented as a significant theory in its own right, relevant now.

Augustine of Hippo, among the most eminent of Christian thinkers, was born in North Africa in AD 354. His *Confessions*, the most accessible of his writings to a modern audience, is still widely read. In this autobiographical account of his early life, he often achieves a fusion of emotion and religious thought which approaches poetry. The psychological analysis in the *Confessions* and other writings at times anticipates Freud, especially in the emphasis given by Augustine to the influence on personality of bodily needs such as sex. But while Freud seems to regard humans as not really free, Augustine holds that a degree of freedom usually remains possible for human beings. He saw such freedom as originating in part from mind. In the importance which Augustine gives to mind, evident in his emphasis on the significance of human language, he resembles modern cognitive psychology. Augustine sees personality as human spirit restless for God, imprisoned in the body, made free by God's grace. He views human life as a troubled pilgrimage from a condition of homelessness and exile on earth to the eternal city of God. He died in AD 430.

Søren Kierkegaard, born in 1813, was Danish and lived most of his life in Copenhagen, where he died in 1855. The modern age has stressed the importance of intellect, reason and thought in human affairs. Kierkegaard liked irony; it was an irony, and one he was aware of, that a man of such intellect should stress the limits to the usefulness of reason in human life. He argued that the critical problems of the human condition, such as life's meaning, are in the last resort to be solved not by intellect but by decision, not by thinking but by commitment, not by reason but by choice. He saw that the despair which he detected at the core of the human self could not be cured by thought alone. Such despair is cured only by choice, by the decision to open and commit oneself to God. Regarded as the founder of modern existentialism, Kierkegaard has been described as the greatest of Christian psychologists.

Thomas Merton was born in France in 1915; his father came from New Zealand, his mother was American. In the United States, after becoming a Christian, he entered a Trappist monastery. He wrote extensively on a variety of subjects, poetry as well as prose. His writings, at times hauntingly beautiful, often in thrilling prose, incorporate modern and ancient thought of East and West. He expressed in his life and writings the Christian paradox that though the arts, nature and the beauty of life are to be celebrated, they eventually leave humans unsatisfied; only God will satisfy the longings of personality. Influenced by existential psychology, Merton sees a terrifying void at the centre of human experience. The only solution, and one by which we become truly human and ourselves, is the alternative terror of discovering God. Merton sees personality in terms of a search for identity and of a movement from a false to a true self, found only in God. The search for God and for our true self are one and the same. Merton died in 1968.

Blaise Pascal was French, born in 1623, and made significant contributions to science and mathematics. He began writing what he intended as an argument for the reasonableness of belief in God and, specifically, of Christian belief. The work was never completed and is now known as the *Pensées*, a collection of thoughts providing a fresh psychological perspective on Christianity. In fragments of wit, epigrammatic force and striking image, exciting even in translation, Pascal describes personality as a contradiction of greatness and wretchedness. Though Pascal's tone is often amusing, he is in no doubt as to the seriousness of the issue. The *Pensées*, in their tragic analysis of the human condition, anticipate twentieth-century existentialism. But Pascal maintains that human beings are wretched and fill their lives with distractions only because their lives are without God. If humans reach out with their hearts as well as their heads, the hidden God will eventually appear. Pascal died in 1662.

Teresa of Avila, born in 1515, was a Spanish Carmelite nun. During a life with many mystical experiences, she remained an active practical woman until her death in 1582. Teresa often describes our relationship with God as a friendship between equals. In *The Interior Castle*, using the castle as an image of the soul, she gives an account of an inner journey to a centre where God is. Aware that the way to God remains in the last resort inexpressible, she uses image and symbol to try to describe the journey. Her description has many resemblances to Carl Jung's psychological account of personality development. Teresa sees the journey in two stages – in the first the individual does things for God, and in the second God does things to the individual. In a way that seems modern, though in Christian tradition it goes back to Augustine, she saw that the finding of God is also a discovery of our true self. Teresa stressed that one immediate outcome of the journey to God is to make us return, perhaps reluctantly, to our responsibilities in this world, especially those to other people.

Karl Rahner was German, born in 1904; he became a member of the Jesuit Order, and died in 1984. Among his extensive and influential writings he proposed a view of humans as the species which asks questions. Influenced by modern existentialism, he saw that the starting-point for our questions is always the material world in which we live. But Rahner differs from secular existentialists in asserting that we exist in more than the material order. He argues that in the everyday, as well as in exceptional moments, we reach through the material world to the experience of something beyond, which is the experience of God. The difficulty lies in recognizing it as such. Human personality exists orientated to the divine, longing for God, and already in God's presence – if we did but know it. At a deep level we do. We are aware, in everyday and exceptional moments, of a mysterious something in our experience which the material world cannot account for. This implicit awareness in our experience is of a Mystery traditionally called God.

Throughout history, humans have looked for a God. But scientific psychology ignores, or explains away, any suggestion that humans seek something beyond the material world, or that there is anything beyond the material world to seek. Modern psychology has adopted materialism. Traditional materialism holds that only matter exists; this matter is the stuff of commonsense experience and of classical physics. In the materialist account of modern psychology, a human being is material body and brain, nothing else.

But materialism is an assumption. And when it comes to personality, materialism poses problems. One obvious problem is that of free will. The material world is characterized by cause and effect; but humans seem, within limits, to be free. If humans are free, and the material world is characterized by cause and effect, how can humans be only matter? Christianity makes other assumptions. Christian accounts of personality assume that God exists. Christian accounts of personality assume that there is more to human personality than the material body and brain of traditional materialism; this second assumption proposes that something non-material like soul exists or that matter is different from what common sense or classical physics suggest.

In Chapter 7, we examine the similarities and differences between scientific and Christian theories of personality, such as in their analysis of the self. In Chapter 8, we consider the materialist assumptions behind scientific theories, and in Chapter 9, the final chapter, we examine the assumptions of Christian accounts. We argue that the assumptions behind Christian theories are as reasonable as the materialist assumptions of science. But in spite of differences between scientific materialist and religious accounts, the task of relating them has already begun with existential and humanistic psychology.

In the past, psychology has also adopted scientism. The position of scientism is that only the methods of the natural sciences, such as physics, are appropriate for studying humans. But existential and humanistic psychologies have abandoned scientism. Existential and humanistic psychologies hold that when it comes to personality much else besides the methods of the natural sciences is needed. Philosophy, the arts, theology and religion have much to say about personality. Certainly the view that personality reaches beyond experience and the material world is found in philosophy down the ages, and is present in literature and other arts in past and modern times. The view is expressed in the literature of science fiction, which developed in the twentieth century as the influence of religion declined in the West and that of science grew. Science fiction often describes humans attempting to go beyond present material reality to a utopian future.

In older science fiction of the utopian kind, human beings remain recognizably human and the promised future often resembles nothing more than a pleasant summer school. Though the summer school is enjoyable, lasts for ever, and is usually in the arts and sciences, there seems little in the way of bliss or ecstasy to be had there. In a different strand of science fiction, the future may promise happiness, ecstasy, joy, but its human inhabitants seem more than human. In Arthur Clarke's *Childhood's End* new capacities emerge, the older state of the human species becomes extinct (hence the title), and a new stage of development begins in which human beings become one extraordinary collective consciousness – though seeming to lose their separate identities in the process. In the kind of utopian science fiction of which Clarke's *Childhood's End* is an example, the human condition not only improves but changes dramatically and becomes super-human, even God-like.

What the utopian strand in science fiction seems to express is that humans do not find their present existence satisfying and hope that it is not the last word; they long for something better. The intention of such science fiction is rarely religious; its thrust is mostly scientific, since the better future envisaged is usually the result of technological progress or further evolutionary development. But such science fiction resonates with the hope and longing found in Christian thought. In the New Testament, St John declares: 'My dear people, we are already the children of God, but what we are to be in the future has not yet been revealed.' Christian accounts of personality express the view that the final end of human personality is to exist in union with God. In such accounts, we participate in God's life while retaining our separate identities.

Towards the end of the nineteenth century Nietzsche announced the death of God; and modern personality theory, acting on Nietzsche's report, has denied or ignored the validity of any search for God. But it has seemed to me – I may be wrong and have misread the situation or interpreted it incorrectly – that the search for God was very much alive in the personalities of many of the students I taught. If the report of God's death is premature, then religious accounts of personality need to be used to complement modern materialist theories. A sense of incompleteness, a feeling of unrealized potential, a restless awareness of something lacking in one's life, a hope for something better, a longing for fulfilment, are a core human experience – as existential and humanistic psychologies confirm. And so does much of science fiction, the arts and religion. In Christian thought, this core human experience is seen as the expression of our need for God.

In the Christian theories of personality which follow, the assumption is that the need for the divine is central to human personality and that only God will satisfy this need. These Christian accounts are abstracted from a larger body of each writer's published work. Though theories of personality, and the world-views they express, are influenced by the contemporary state of knowledge, the older accounts of personality which follow are not included for historical interest. They are presented here as being as contemporary in their relevance as Freud, Rogers, Jourard, Maslow or any other modern personality theorist.

My thanks go to staff of Heythrop College, University of London, for their help with the following chapters.

I

The Passionate Pilgrim: Augustine of Hippo's Restless Path

A certain odour on the wind,
Thy hidden face beyond the west,
These things have called us; on a quest
Older than any road we trod,
More endless than desire . . .
    ('The Song of the Pilgrims', Rupert Brooke)

You made us for yourself and our hearts find no peace until they rest in you.
    (*Confessions*, St Augustine)

The *Confessions* were written by Augustine at the request of friends who wanted to know more about his life. But he wrote also, like Milton with *Paradise Lost*, to 'justify the ways of God to men'. Completed about AD 401, the *Confessions* give a history of Augustine's early years and his conversion to Christianity. In the *Confessions* and other works, Augustine in his deep psychological analysis of human motivation anticipates Freud. In his emphasis on mind, Augustine resembles contemporary cognitive psychology. Like Freud, he stresses the influence of body on human behaviour; like modern cognitive psychologists, he stresses the importance of mind. But in Augustine's view, on the pilgrimage to God, it is mind, broadly conceived, which takes us on our way; on the path to God, body is as much a hindrance as a help.

The psychological self-analysis which characterizes the *Confessions* is familiar to us in our post-Freudian age. In Book 2, where Augustine tells how as a youth he stole pears from an orchard, what concerns him is that the pleasure of stealing, and not hunger, motivated him. He is puzzled and troubled by what seems a love of wrong-doing; such perversity, he concludes, has its origins in childhood. In the *Confessions*, Augustine dismisses the idea that infancy is a time of passivity and innocence. He observes that babies are passionate, envious, demanding and angry when their demands are not met. He comments on how babies cry to get what they want, work themselves into a rage, and strike out when they do not get what they want. On the basis of his observation he concludes (*Confessions* 1,7): 'This shows that, if babies are innocent, it is not for lack of will to do harm, but for lack of strength.' Fifteen hundred years later Freud, by submitting the activity of childhood to a more thorough scrutiny, was to lay the foundations for psychoanalysis.

Augustine believed, as Freud did, that the child is not an innocent taught bad ways by the environment. Both believed that humans are wilful and motivated by self-interest from birth. In Freud's view, this was because of innate instincts collectively referred to as the id, with sexuality and aggression being particularly dangerous. Freud saw this grasping biology, constantly demanding gratification, as the core of human nature. According to Freud's pleasure principle, we want above all to satisfy our instinctual needs. Since others do so as well, we have to exercise restraint and scale down our needs in order to avoid conflict; this is the reality principle. But beneath the veneer of adult restraint, the instinctual id survives – greedy, aggressive, preoccupied with its own needs and not with those of others.

Augustine too regarded humans as dangerous in their natural state; but since he believed in the reality of sin and free will, his explanation differs from Freud's. Sin, implying as it does free choice, is central to Augustine's thought. Freud's position on free will is confused; and where Freud talks of id, Augustine refers to original sin.

In the first chapters of the Old Testament, Adam and Eve disobeyed God by eating fruit from the forbidden tree. This original sin corrupted and inclined them to sin, and in the traditional Christian account humans have inherited from Adam the guilt and effects of the sin. Whereas Augustine believed that the Bible story recorded a historical event, many Christians today regard the disobedience in the garden as a myth. But what the myth attempts to explain is real enough. Humans have good in them, but they also have a tendency to act selfishly and dangerously with regard to others – in short, to sin. Most cultures have tried to account for the origin of such evil inclinations, and the Old Testament does so in terms of this original act of rebellion against God at the beginning of history. However unsatisfactory such an explanation may be, some explanation seems called for. It is clear from Freud, other modern personality theorists, and novelists such as Conrad and William Golding, that in the twentieth century the origin of evil perplexes us still.

One contemporary Christian explanation is that evil and sin are not inside human beings but outside in the environment. In this account, original sin refers to the influence of the immoral structures of society to which we are exposed from birth, and which condition us to act badly. Neither Freud nor Augustine would have had much sympathy with so social an explanation. Both were more sympathetic to an individual psychological account where inclination to wrong-doing is largely innate and a product of our bodies and 'the flesh'. In any nurture-nature debate on social as opposed to genetic explanations of human nastiness, Augustine and Freud emphasize innate nature.

In fact, both Augustine and Freud see society more as a bulwark and defence against our own and other people's violence and sexuality. They believed that society in the form of family, city and state is an influence for the good in restraining our actions; with Augustine, the church particularly is important here. Augustine and Freud believed that human nature was such that, if the institutions of society were too easy and permissive, our bodily inclinations would be let loose. So the social order has to be tough and authoritarian, if law and order is to prevail and we are to live in safety. In their view, society has to be repressive for our own and everyone's benefit, because of the dangerous influence which our bodies have over our behaviour.

Freud came to see human unhappiness as partly the result of society having to repress so much of the gratification of our instincts. Augustine too saw that the need to restrict the demands of the flesh was a cause of pain. But Augustine believed that human unhappiness also has a spiritual cause. Humans certainly seek material and bodily satisfactions, and for Augustine these are rest and refreshment for the pilgrim. But for Augustine what really matters is the goal of the journey, namely, God, who alone can satisfy and is to be found only when our pilgrimage ends.

Another contemporary explanation of human nastiness is that an inclination to evil and sin originates in the damaging experience of early childhood. Such a view is indebted to Freud, and constitutes his acknowledgment that social factors are also involved in human wrong-doing. But however sympathetic the modern temper is to social and environmental explanations, the recent rise of socio-biology indicates that in science the debate between nurture-nature explanations stands very much where it was. This emphasis on the innate is also found in much modern literature. Novelists such as Dostoevsky, Mauriac and Melville appear to hold, like Freud and Augustine, that human nastiness originates largely within human beings. Captain Ahab in Moby Dick regards the whale as an embodiment of all that is evil and sinful. But Melville, the author, seems to suggest that the nastiness which Ahab sees as outside in the whale is a projection, and in Ahab himself.

Both Augustine and Freud emphasize the compulsive and driven quality of human actions. For both, this results from the power which the body exerts on our behaviour. For Freud all human behaviour, even when the result of sublimation, originates in instincts such as hunger, thirst, sex, self-preservation. Freud regards human actions as caused by internal bodily instincts, modified by experience and restrained by society. Seeing human behaviour as determined by biology and childhood experience, Freud did not regard humans as free. In *Parapraxes* Freud states: 'You nourish the illusion of there being such a thing as psychical freedom, and you will not give it up. I am sorry to say I disagree with you categorically over this.' Freud holds that our behaviour is motivated by the id's unconscious desires and past experience. But because such causes of our actions are unconscious, the illusion that we are free persists. Though seemingly a hard determinist, in the end Freud is ambiguous about human freedom. He remains uncertain whether human behaviour is completely caused, or only largely caused with a minimal element of freedom remaining.

Augustine too sees humans as almost overwhelmed by the passions of their bodies, and also by habit. He asserts that in theory

humans have freedom and the potential to choose and to do good.
But, like Freud, Augustine is aware of the power of 'the flesh'. And,
equally importantly, he holds that habits born of past actions have to
be overcome if we are to do good. In his later writings particularly,
Augustine stresses that it is not possible for humans to act freely and
do good without God's help.

Augustine seems to hold that what freedom humans have often
manifests itself at first in wrong-doing. This is how bad habits begin.
These habits subsequently lead to more wrong-doing and further
impede our freedom to do good. When we decide to use our freedom
to do good, we immediately find that our past actions, in the form of
bad habits, constrain us. 'Again I become a prey to my habits, which
hold me fast. My tears flow, but still I am held fast. Such is the price
we pay for the burden of custom!' (*Confessions* 10,40).

For Augustine the power of habit resides in memory, which
affects human actions through the workings of habit. If Augustine
had regarded the power of habit as arising from bodily repetition
affecting our muscles, then the Augustinian concept of habit would
be close to behaviourist theory. But since he sees habit, though
originating in the body, as operating through the workings of mind,
specifically of memory, he resembles Freud. The dynamic nature of
the unconscious was emphasized by Freud, who insisted that our
actions and emotions are affected by thoughts and memories which
are not in the conscious mind. Why on a lovely spring morning does a
certain man feel sad and with no wish to do anything? Because the
warm breeze, the cherry blossom in bloom and the birdsong put him
in mind, without his being consciously aware, of a past spring
morning when his father was buried. And they trigger off the sadness
and apathy he felt then.

Freud's dynamic unconscious can be seen as memories which are
repressed, but which are also remembered and active. Freud saw
that the past affects our present behaviour, and memory is involved.
Augustine's account of memory in the *Confessions* has many
resemblances to the Freudian unconscious. Augustine, with his
almost Proustian preoccupation with remembering the past, sees
memory as the mind holding on to its contents. He regards the
human adult as a vast storehouse of memories. 'The wide plains of
my memory and its innumerable caverns and hollows are full beyond

compute of countless things of all kinds. Material things are there by means of their images; knowledge is there of itself; emotions are there in the form of ideas or impressions of some kind, for the memory retains them even while the mind does not experience them, although whatever is in the memory must also be in the mind' (*Confessions* 10,17).

Augustine saw that many of these memories have an odd status: they exist in an in-between stage since they are not wholly absent from, nor wholly present to, the individual. One is not always aware of such memories, but they must in some way be present, or it would not be possible to recall them. So Augustine holds that there exists this storehouse of memories, of some of which we are only dimly conscious. '. . . there are some things in man which even his own spirit within him does not know. But you, O Lord, know all there is to know of him, because you made him' (*Confessions* 10,5). And the resemblance to the Freudian unconscious increases when Augustine insists that these memories affect our present behaviour. For Augustine, the way in which memories affect our present behaviour and curtail our freedom is through the powerful working of habit.

In Augustine's view, humans are, or become, creatures of habit. What we do, whether it is right or wrong, makes us what we are. We create our personality by the habits which we form. We are not forced to form certain habits, but once formed they cause us to act in certain ways. What we do takes on a momentum of its own through habit. Augustine holds that though our behaviour in the first place is a result of what we choose, habits soon form and become our nature or a second nature. These habits, though originating in our acts of will, become a second will. In the *Confessions* (8,5), Augustine, wanting to do good, finds '. . . I was held fast, not in fetters clamped upon me by another, but by my own will, which had the strength of iron chains . . . For my will was perverse and lust had grown from it, and when I gave in to lust habit was born, and when I did not resist the habit it became a necessity.'

In Augustine's account, habit functions at the level of mind, as a weight or drag upon free action. The pleasure of what we did in the past is recorded in memory; this is what gives habit its permanence. How this actually happens is not clear. But habits exist in the mind and are a product of the workings of memory; and it is memory which gives continuity to human life, and which makes us partly prisoners of the past. For both Augustine and Freud, human freedom is severely curtailed as much by our past as by our bodies. But both also see the possibility of limited freedom, though for different reasons.

In Freud's view, if human freedom exists, it does so because a part of mind is conscious. Freud's position appears to be that what is unconscious is caused and determined, and what is conscious can be free; humans can be free when the mind is conscious. The basic objective of psychoanalytic treatment is to reduce the unconscious and extend the area of the conscious self-aware mind. In this way a person becomes more free. But since Freud regards a great deal of the human mind as unconscious, the extent of human freedom is limited.

Augustine, too, is aware of the need for self-knowledge, if personality is to develop. He seems in part to have written the *Confessions* as an act of therapy. Writing the *Confessions*, he becomes aware how psychologically helpful confessing and revealing oneself can be. This view, implicit in the Roman Catholic practice of confession, is explicit in Freudian psychoanalytic therapy. However, for Augustine, the possibility of human freedom has its origins primarily in God's grace. In a traditional Christian account, grace refers to a supernatural gift and communication of God to human beings, which helps them to avoid sin and to choose good. Augustine, like novelists such as Conrad and Golding, holds that natural virtues like loyalty, honesty, doing one's duty, are inadequate in the face of the human inclination to evil. Augustine concluded that humans can cope with sin and evil only with the help of God. God's grace is necessary for human freedom.

In his later writings Augustine stressed even more the importance of grace. In *The Grace of Christ and Original Sin*, he states that humans can avoid sin only with the help of grace. Our spiritual dependence on God is immense, and the human person can ascend to God only because God has first descended to the human person. In *Enchiridion*, on Faith, Hope and Charity, Augustine emphasizes that both our freedom and our faith are gifts from God. Augustine came to insist on the help that humans needed from God to overcome evil and do good and to win the reward of eternal life. Such help is not merited by humans and is a gift from God. But whatever the extent of the influence of God's grace, Augustine believed that humans ultimately remain free – to choose good or evil.

For Augustine, there is a fundamental reason why humans have the potentiality to be free. For Augustine, free choice is possible because part of the structure of the human person is spirit. Freud does not believe in spirit. Freud, as a scientific materialist, holds that only matter exists and that humans beings are only bodies; humans have a physical organ called the brain, but this has nothing to do with spirit. According to Freud, the human mind is biology alone. But to the extent that Freud holds humans to be free, to that extent he has a problem. The material world is characterized by cause and effect. Since Freud held that humans are only biology, he has to explain how a purely material human can act in a way that is free and not determined by cause and effect. For Augustine, humans have the capacity to act freely because they are spirit as well as body.

Philosophers such as Plato used words like soul or spirit in their explanations of human beings, particularly to explain mind. If the body is a ship, then mind is the pilot. The metaphor of pilot and ship makes clear that mind is different from body, though mind interacts with and controls the body, like the pilot controlling the ship. According to such dualism, two things exist. There is body; everybody knows what body is. And there is something non-material called mind, soul or spirit; though no one knows what this is, according to dualism it is certainly not material and not part of the physical world.

Plato holds an extreme dualism. In his view, the soul or spirit which constitutes mind is not only separate and more important than body but really is the person. Augustine, too, is a dualist. Like Plato, he too believed that this non-material spirit called soul is the real person and that the body is only the container, even the unpleasant prison. Augustine saw soul as something separate, complete and independent in itself, though connected to the troublesome body. In the dualist tradition of Plato, Augustine and (later) Descartes, soul or spirit is agent. Plato's pilot is independent of the ship, presumably could walk off at any port, need not return but could transfer to another vessel. Though Descartes' pilot and ship interact and need each other, they are still different. In all dualist accounts mind, since it is spirit, is different from body. Body is a living organism which the person uses to operate with in the physical world.

Augustine regarded non-material being – whether referred to as soul, spirit or mind – as more important than our physical bodies. In Chapter 27 of *The Morals of the Catholic Church*, he speaks of a human being as 'a rational soul using a mortal and earthly body'. In Chapter 13 of *The Greatness of the Soul*, he speaks of the human soul as 'a substance endowed with reason designed to rule the body'. But Augustine's belief, as a Christian, in the resurrection of the body held him to the view that the human person, whole and entire, consists of both soul and body. And in works like *The Trinity* he approaches closer to the body-mind interactionist position which we now associate with Descartes. Though Augustine came to stress more the unity of a human being, with body and mind interacting, he remained a dualist and still regarded the structure of the person as consisting of two substances. In his later view, though body and soul are still independent of each other, and soul remains the dominant partner, body is now seen as needed for the person to be complete. But even in this later view, Augustine believed that when someone says 'I', it is the soul speaking.

Augustine does not regard soul and mind as the same. He takes mind to be the reasoning, understanding and remembering part of the soul; mind is the soul operating to gain knowledge. With soul and with mind as part of soul, human beings are conscious, purposive, and they have meaning and intentions in their thoughts and actions. Soul gives life to and energizes the body, making it possible for the body to run, stand, talk, walk. While we live, the soul 'rules the body, moves the limbs, guides the senses, prepares thoughts, puts forth actions, takes in images of countless things' (*Exposition on the Book of Psalms*, Psalm 146). In Augustine's account, the dynamic structure of the human person consists in interacting body and soul, with soul dominant, and with mind as the superior part of the soul.

Though Augustine resembles Freud in his account of motivation and influences on human behaviour, when it comes to mind he has resemblances to modern cognitive psychology. Augustine regarded intention, our purpose in doing something, as central to human action. This is why his own motivation in stealing the pears seemed so important to him. But Augustine's dualistic view of humans as made up of soul as well as body is not held by cognitive psychology. Like Freud, cognitive psychologists adopt the position of scientific materialism and attempt to account for human mind as biological brain and nothing else.

Modern psychology adopts the Darwinian position that mind is material and completely part of the natural world. Interestingly, Wallace, who arrived at the idea of evolution independently of Darwin, differed from Darwin on human mind. Wallace held that the material processes of natural selection accounted for the evolution of the body but not of the human mind. Darwin's view, and not Wallace's, has prevailed in science: mind is regarded as part of nature and is held to have evolved by the material processes of natural selection. This view has bequeathed to psychology and the biological sciences the task of providing an evolutionary explanation of human mind. This would normally be done by demonstrating a continuity between the human mind and that of animals. For Augustine, there was no such continuity. Contrary to Darwin and modern psychology, Augustine asserts that humans are significantly different from animals with regard to mind. Language, for Augustine, was an example of a particularly human activity, and modern cognitive psychology agrees with Augustine on the importance of human language.

Thomas Huxley, Darwin's Bulldog, conceded that evolutionary theory failed to explain human language and speech. And the publication of Darwin's *Origin of Species* led to so much conjecture on the origins of language that, in 1866, the Paris Linguistic Society banned papers on the subject. Cognitive psychology assumes that human language has emerged by a process of evolution from the communication of animals. But many cognitive psychologists acknowledge that to say this does not provide an explanation of the origins of human language; it is merely a statement of faith in the possibility of an evolutionary explanation.

In his book *Verbal Behavior* (1957), B.F.Skinner, the behaviourist, argued that human language is just verbal behaviour. Babies make noises, sometimes spontaneously, sometimes in response to reinforcements, and by a process of operant or classical conditioning, language is formed. If the noise a baby makes, such as ma, da, mama, dada, ta or thanks, is rewarded by parents, the sound will be repeated by the baby. Infants start by emitting noises, the appropriate sounds are reinforced, words and sentences eventually emerge, and in this way language is shaped. According to Skinner, external verbal behaviour plus reward, selective reinforcement, generalization, are enough to account for language. And human language, according to behaviourism, can be explained without reference to anything inside humans such as mind. Augustine, like modern cognitive psychologists, would disagree with this behaviourist view that mind is irrelevant to language.

Noam Chomsky attacked such a view in his now famous 1959 review of Skinner's *Verbal Behavior*. Chomsky regarded as inadequate any attempt to explain language and speech without reference to what goes on inside human beings. He contended that human language can only be accounted for by some inborn psychological capacity. The kind of innate capacity which he meant is traditionally referred to as mind.

The behaviourist approach to language has now been discarded, just as behaviourism generally has been replaced by cognitive psychology. In abandoning behaviourism and emphasizing human cognitive processes, modern psychology is, like Augustine, asserting the reality of mind and its centrality for humans. And cognitive psychology, for which Chomsky's 1959 article laid the foundations in giving a more satisfactory account of language, provides an argument for the reality of human mind.

Most sentences in this chapter have probably not been said or written before in the exact form that they are here; but most readers (hopefully) will understand them. The vast vocabulary of human language helps to make it a medium of such versatility that humans can always say something new or something old in a new way. But human language is versatile and creative largely because of the way humans are pre-programmed with respect to language. The pre-programming takes the form of syntax. Syntax is the set of rules which every language has about sentence construction and how words are arranged. Because of our knowledge of syntax we are able to create original sentences every day of our lives. This pre-programming in the rules of syntax also means that listeners or readers can understand these original sentences. Humans, Chomsky contends, are born with a general knowledge of such rules as they apply to all languages. This is part of what we usually call mind.

Further argument for Augustine's and cognitive psychology's assertion of the reality of mind comes from what is known about the acquisition of language. Chomsky points out that children learn language simply by listening or half-listening to adults and other children. By about five or six years of age, the child has acquired human language and, like an adult, is saying sentences which have never been said before. The number of possible ways of combining words into sentences is so large – possibly infinite – that a child could not possibly have heard them all. During this time there is no need for parents to correct a child's incorrect grammar, as every child will subsequently unlearn errors and correct them simply as a result of half-listening to others. Chomsky concludes that children acquire the rules of grammar for themselves simply by listening and talking to others, and in this way discovering what others regard as acceptable.

But the grammar of human languages is complex as well as abstract. For a child to acquire this grammar, and to do so with such ease and speed, is an extraordinary achievement. Such an achievement makes unlikely the behaviourist claim that children start life as blank slates. Cognitive psychologists conclude that children can learn something as complex, abstract and as difficult as language, and can do so with such speed and ease, because the child enters the world with an innate mental capacity for language. Listening to others speak triggers off this inborn capacity and makes it possible for the child to express its thoughts in whatever language is available. Whether a child grows up to speak Russian, French or English depends on the environment. But innate pre-programming (usually called mind) enables the child to cope with the form which the rules of syntax take in any particular language. Chomsky concludes that humans are born genetically equipped with a universal grammar, a common syntax, a set of principles which form the basis of all languages.

So the claims of behaviourists, like Skinner, that language is learned from the environment, and that learning language involves no innate capacity, seems wrong. Human language depends on an innate factor – though the environment of parents and other language speakers is needed. Children from an early age completely isolated from adults, usually as the result of some misfortune, and sometimes being reared by animals, do not learn language. Exposure to language is needed for children to learn language, but exposure is all that is needed. And a child's acquisition of language proceeds in a definite sequence like the bodily changes of adolescence. This unvarying order, the same the world over, is further evidence that the capacity for language is present at birth and that mind exists innately in humans.

The account of language provided by Chomsky and cognitive psychologists returns mind to psychology. Augustine is supported by modern psychology in his assertion of the centrality of language for humans. And cognitive psychology supports Augustine's view of language as a product of mind which is part of human nature or, in modern terms, is innate. But though cognitive psychology has returned language and mind to centre stage in modern psychology, the origin of human language, presumably from the communication of animals, remains a puzzle for evolutionary theory.

Though the origin of human mind generally remains a problem for evolution, language does seem special. Humans could not have invented language in the way they have invented tools, because language made them humans in the first place – and able to invent tools. Linguists such as Chomsky assert that we do not even have the beginnings of an explanation of the origins of human language. Perhaps this is why myths and legends about language abound.

In the Christian account, it was language that broke the silence of the universe. St John's Gospel starts: 'In the beginning was the Word'. Human beings use language to ask questions of the material world in science and religion: 'But what is my God? I put my question to the earth' (*Confessions* 10,6). Language is necessary if one is to ask such questions. Truth and the experience of individuals are ephemeral until they are put into language.

But however language originated, it is now inseparable from humans. What would it mean to refer to pre-language humans? Language implies humans, and humans imply language. The existence of language seems evidence that the human mind is something special. And for Augustine the extraordinariness of human mind, as evidenced by language, demonstrates that mind is not material but soul or spirit. Augustine argued that anything completely material would not be capable of human language. He sees language and other human activities, like free choice, as made possible by the superior part of the non-material soul, called mind.

Augustine holds that there are three levels of nature: the divine, spiritual and bodily; he categorizes all natures according to these levels. He constructs a hierarchy with God at the top. God is at the top because the divine nature is unchanging over time and is unmoving, since it is not located in any place. Bodies are at the bottom, because bodies change in time and place, growing old and decaying, moving or being moved from place to place. Augustine places animals on this bottom level, arguing that, since they lack true minds, they do not have souls but only bodies. Human beings occupy the middle level since they have bodies, which change in time and place, and souls, which change in time but not in place.

This intermediate position of human beings, having a nature between the divine and the bodily, is one cause of the awful tension of the human condition. In Augustine's account, humans on the middle level of the hierarchy can look up or down. Humans can follow the inclination of their souls, look up and try to participate in God and the divine realities; or they can give way to the pull of their bodies, look down and participate in the world of bodies. Augustine holds that whether we look up or down is our choice and a matter of will. We can turn to God or we can turn away from God.

According to Augustine, there is nothing morally wrong with our bodies, though their goodness is inferior to the soul and, of course, to the divine. But Augustine regards 'the flesh' as being as much a hindrance as a help when it comes to finding God. And we cannot look in two directions at once; we cannot look up at God and down at bodies at the same time. If we concentrate primarily on bodies and the material world, it will involve turning away from God and relegating the divine to second place. In Augustine's view, we eventually have to make a choice between the things of God and the material world of bodies. If we choose for God and the heavenly city, we choose eternal life and the divine realities that do not change. If we do not choose for God, we choose what is temporal and material and the earthly city which passes away. What Augustine values above all about bodies is that they can bring us to God.

To understand better these humans on the middle rung, with God above and the world of bodies below, we need to know what innate features they are born with and which features they acquire. But even in modern psychology there is no agreement on this age-old question of nature and nurture. At one extreme, behaviourist psychology takes the position that humans are born with very few innate psychological features; behaviourism stresses the moulding by the environment. At the other extreme, sociobiologists, and to a great extent Freud, believe that innate and unchanging biology is the hard core of human personality and that social influences are slight.

Erich Fromm, a neo-Freudian, distinguishes between nature and nurture by referring to inherited qualities as temperament and acquired qualities as character. Augustine speaks of nature and person to make the same distinction, though the meanings he gives to the terms are not fixed and change. But Augustine frequently uses 'nature' to refer to what is innate and given to human beings at birth. In much of his writings, Augustine regards the 'person' as what we become, partly through shaping by the environment, but also as a result of what we choose to make ourselves. Whereas Fromm sees our acquired character as largely a passive product of external influences, Augustine stresses more the human being's active choice in becoming a person. At the same time, Augustine is aware of the pressures that limit freedom and shape the human being.

In Augustine's account, nature is seen as the answer to 'What am I?', and person as the answer to 'Who am I?'. But there are never any clear-cut and certain answers to 'What am I?' and 'Who am I?' questions. In Augustine's view, our nature has inborn features, and these incline our love and will in certain directions; these innate features, together with the environment and past experience, shape the person. But Augustine holds that persons have choice and partly choose what they love and will. As a person, I can be true to my nature or I can turn my back on my true nature. Augustine's prayer, 'Give me chastity and continence, but not yet' (*Confessions* 8,7), implies choice.

But Augustine goes on to suggest that what may start out as our free choices become habits and make us into creatures of the habits which we have acquired, and into being a certain person. And the person I become, partly through choices, partly through choices becoming habits, partly through the effects of the environment, may be true or false to my nature. But the person I have become and now am – be it aggressive, gentle, caring, inconsiderate – now shapes and directs what I do. In the past I made a series of choices, and though the mind is not totally imprisoned by these past choices, my mind is powerfully constrained by them. The main difference here from Freud's account is in the freedom which Augustine sees as existing in the earlier behaviour. Augustine holds that the earlier behaviour, now become habit, was in part chosen.

Augustine sees this earlier behaviour as being motivated by unsatisfied desire. In regarding behaviour as originating in the attempt to satisfy desire, Augustine anticipates modern drive-reduction theory. A drive is an aroused and tense state of an organism, caused by unsatisfied need. According to the drive-reduction hypothesis, human actions are motivated by the reduction of tension subsequent on the satisfaction of needs. But in *The Trinity*, Augustine stresses that the pleasure, enjoyment, happiness and delight which humans seek is not just physical, but involves relationships with other human beings and God. Augustine's emphasis on relationships in human motivation and his assertion that human life is about relating to self and others, including God – indeed, above all to God – is not surprising. The Christian concept of the Trinity, three persons in one God, postulates a relationship as core to the nature of God.

Augustine's assertion that relationships are central to human happiness anticipates W.R.D.Fairbairn's object-relations view that relationships are primarily what humans seek. Fairbairn, in opposition to Freud's pleasure principle, sees humans as being primarily not pleasure-seeking but relationship-seeking. For Fairbairn, what humans really want is relationships and the experience of other people as ends valuable in themselves. For example, according to the object-relations account of sexual behaviour, what is sought in another human being is a relationship, with sexual pleasure as the product of that relationship.

In Augustine's view, we have no choice about human nature, but a human person is what we become or do not become through the choices we make. My nature does not of itself constitute me as a full human being; nor is it inevitable that I will become one. Augustine, anticipating modern existentialism, regards being human and a person as not given but as something which we have to achieve. He qualifies this existential position by stressing that we do possess a human nature in the first place. And if we choose to ignore our human nature's claims, this God-given nature will continue to call upon the person to respond to its claims. Augustine believed that the responses which we choose to make involve responsibility, guilt, notions of right and wrong, good and bad, sin, regret.

When it comes to the soul part of human nature, Augustine in his mature thought sees mind, the superior part of the soul, as consisting of a trinity of memory, will (or love) and understanding. But mind is not divided into three different structures or functions; all the mind is memory and will and understanding. Augustine holds that the experience of the human person is unified and is so because the human mind is one.

As we have seen, memory, the first part of this trinity, is the mind operating to retain its contents. Though Augustine regards humans as active, propelled by bodily instincts, he also sees them as externally shaped by the environment, and internally by what is stored in memory. If my life is preoccupied with money, then I and my behaviour will be shaped by money, since my memory will be loaded with monetary concerns. Augustine was aware that some memories can be recalled to consciousness easily, while others are difficult to recall. Like Freud, Augustine did not regard all mental life as conscious. And he was puzzled as to where in the mind such forgotten – Freud would say repressed – memories were contained. Both Augustine and Freud saw that these unconscious memories, though not available to the conscious mind, influence behaviour.

The second element in this trinity of mind is will, which decides on and implements behaviour. For Augustine, will is the function of mind involved when a human being is doing something. In Augustine's view, at the core of every desire which motivates human beings and causes the will to act is a desire for happiness. We want to be happy and we have no alternative: wanting to be happy is our nature and the basis for every action of our will. Self-destructiveness does not invalidate this; self-destructiveness reveals our perversity about where we sometimes choose to seek happiness. Like Dostoevsky's anti-hero in *Notes from the Underground*, we may try to find happiness in destroying ourselves psychologically. We have choice about where we seek happiness – in money, sex, art, self-destructiveness, God – but we have no choice about wanting to be happy. The problem arises because, as a result of original sin, at the core of our personality something is now faulty in our will.

Augustine's emphasis on will, and on the choices and decisions which we make with our wills, underlines his existential orientation. In the end it is not intellect, thought, reflection that does anything; it is our will that does. What brings us to God is not intellect, thought, reflection, but the turning of our will to God. Augustine came to hold that the human will was moved by desire or – put another way – by the prospect of delight. We seek and follow delight; and delight is the source of human action. In his account of will and of how the will is moved to seek delight, Augustine is outlining a theory of motivation. According to Freud, it is fundamentally our instincts and the gratification of instincts that cause us to act. According to Augustine, it is the prospect of delight which motivates us.

In his early thinking, Augustine had stressed the role of intellect in human actions. By the time he came to write the *Confessions* he held that it was the promise of positive feeling and affect, what he termed delight, which motivates the will. This delight is not in our control, is not even conscious, is not just intellectual and is certainly not just physical. What we can say is that there exists that which delights the human being; and it is this which we act to obtain. Augustine came to hold, in the way in which Freud did, that feeling as much as intellect is central to human motivation. Similarly, Augustine came to the view that emotional growth and personal insight into feelings are as important as intellect in the development of personality. Freud would also have agreed with him here.

Augustine sees the presence of love in all human existence. The love that moves us is in effect the delight we seek in objects and people. Humans beings are wills. 'We are nothing else but wills,' says Augustine; and the core of human will is love. Human love strives for what it does not have. It is love which moves us, says Augustine, just as weight moves material objects downwards. Everything in life is worthy of love, except sin, but more worthy than anything is God. Augustine holds that every delight in human life is but a foretaste of God, and God is the only delight which will satisfy us completely.

And when we love something appropriately, be it a person or an object, we are loving God. Augustine insists that we have no choice about loving, just as we have no choice about wanting to be happy, but we do have choice about what we choose to love. We can direct our love towards love's true object, God. Or we can direct our love towards the things of the world, not relating them to God.

Before examining understanding, the third element in Augustine's trinity of mind, we need to examine how nature and person relate to will. In Augustine's account, our nature is equipped with wisdom which knows what is right for us, namely, God; and the person is equipped with knowledge about the world. In the world with which we are acquainted through knowledge, we constantly have to use our wisdom to choose between right and wrong, between what leads to God and what takes us away from God. Augustine holds that the person has a choice in life of two diverging paths – that of wisdom or that of power. Augustine's account of the paths of wisdom and power is effectively a developmental theory of personality. According to this account, we can seek with our wills the possession of God; this is the path of wisdom. Or we can seek with our wills those material things that can be obtained and enjoyed in this life; this is the path of power. The trouble with struggling along the path of wisdom, seeking God, is that there is no possession in this life. The trouble with travelling on the path of power, which does occasionally lead to possession, is that these material possessions do not fully satisfy us.

Augustine holds that the result of our choices is to restructure the person, because we are shaped by our aims and the habits formed in trying to achieve them. So we may choose the path of power and seek complete happiness in sex, money, personal relationships, prestige, knowledge or whatever. The result is that what we had sought as something to enjoy in possessing, such as money or prestige, in the end possesses us.

Augustine's path of power resembles the pleasure principle which Freud sees as governing human behaviour. In the Freudian account of development, we start life concerned only with obtaining pleasure by getting our instincts gratified. Freud holds that at first we regard other people only as a means to our own instinctual satisfaction. Freud passes no moral judgment but simply says that this is the way we are. He believes that what stops us using other people for what we can get out of them is that they equally want to use us for what they can get out of us. This is the reality principle; confronted by reality, we have to accommodate to other people's needs and the demands of the real world in order to obtain any satisfaction for our instincts. Freud believes that though we accommodate to what reality has to offer, maximum pleasure is still what we really want. For example, Freud holds that in sex, even as adults, beneath any apparent relationship or giving, our own gratification remains what we really want.

Though Augustine is very aware of the pleasure-seeking dimension to human personality, he differs from Freud in emphasizing the importance of relationships for human happiness. But Augustine also takes a moral stance: we should not use other people. Augustine holds that it is morally wrong to use other people for our own pleasure and satisfaction. For Augustine, other people are to be enjoyed but not to be used. He regards it as proper to enjoy others but wrong simply to make use of them.

Though Freud does not adopt a moral stance, he believes that there is a goal to human development; the goal is the genital personality. Freud holds that human beings need to become genital personalities. Such a development would normally be the result of experience over time with reality, particularly with the reality of other people and their needs, and that of the external world generally. If humans fail to develop in this way, society becomes a dangerous place to live in. For Freud, healthy development to the genital stage means that personality is capable of relationships, of giving as well as receiving, and is concerned with the needs and pleasures of others as well as with its own.

In Augustine's account of development, what we find on the path of power, such as the pleasures of the body, of society and the material world, are in themselves good. But these cannot fully satisfy ourselves, since only the possession of God can do that; this is why human existence is so restless. And travellers on the path of power do not always obtain wealth, pleasure and whatever else they want; or if they do obtain them, they find them not totally satisfying. Shaw comments in *Man and Superman*: 'There are two tragedies in life. One is not to get your heart's desire. The other is to get it.' Even the limited material satisfactions on the path of power are bedevilled by the passing of time and the thought of death.

In Augustine's view, for true human development to occur, the person should choose the path of wisdom. But to will to seek only God is not easy, and sometimes the best strategy is the negative one of refusing to seek happiness in the material goods of this world. Choosing the way of wisdom does not mean that other people or the material world are to be totally disregarded. On the path of wisdom we should value love, personal relationships, the natural world, the concerns of society. All these are to be appropiately used and enjoyed, as Augustine makes clear in *The Trinity*; they become wrong only to the extent that they take us from God.

But Augustine sees that for the most part, on the path of wisdom, there is no certainty about the future possession of God. Following the path of wisdom does not guarantee peace and happiness now, so in this respect it is no more preferable than the path of power. In Bernanos' novel, *Diary of a Country Priest*, the priest struggles from day to day strengthened only by the belief that what he is doing is right, and sometimes even this abandons him. For Augustine, even the path of wisdom leaves human life as a question which, as yet, has no final answer; the result is an anguished uncertainty. To seek happiness in God is not to possess that happiness but only to possess a hope; it is not to achieve beatitude but only to travel hopefully – Augustine is fond of journey as a metaphor for life. On the path of wisdom, one has to hold on, not denying the reality of one's longing for happiness. Nor should we scale down our desire for happiness and make do with what is obtainable here and now. That way lies cynicism and despair. The reality is that of Browning's 'Two in the Campagna', 'Infinite passion, and the pain/Of finite hearts that yearn.'

In Augustine's account, on both the paths of wisdom and power, humans are restless because their wills are incapable of finding satisfaction and happiness in the absence of God. Nothing finite will fully satisfy this desire for happiness, which is present in all the desires that motivate human behaviour; only an infinite God can do that. 'You made us for yourself and our hearts find no peace until they rest in you' (*Confessions* 1,1). Augustine holds that if human beings follow the path of wisdom, ultimately it leads to God who alone can make us happy. And in the Augustinian account of human development, the path of wisdom can be followed in two different ways: the way of faith, and that of the third capacity of mind, namely, understanding.

Faith, for Augustine, is an assent to what is not seen clearly. Faith requires an effort of will and calls for a choice or decision in the same way that atheism does. And Anselm's 'faith seeking understanding' is, in Augustine's account, one way along the path of wisdom. We do not seek to understand the things of God in order to have faith; rather, we make the effort of will to have faith, and afterwards we use understanding to help our faith. Understanding, by argument or by empirically exploring ourselves and the world, is the means by which we subsequently make sense of our faith and beliefs, and discover their meaning more deeply. This third capacity of mind, understanding, has a place on this way along the path of wisdom, but it comes after the first step, which is the commitment of faith. Intellectual analysis may help faith, but largely after the commitment has been made. And, according to Augustine, faith alone is enough to find God. As humans develop on this particular way along the path of wisdom, God is accepted first on the basis of faith, and an attempt at understanding may or may not follow.

The alternative way along the path of wisdom is provided directly by understanding, the third capacity of mind. Understanding alone, by itself, can lead us to God. Here, Augustine refers to the usual proofs for the existence of God. He also uses an argument characteristically his own. He points out that there is nothing about human beings which can guarantee the truth of things. We are transient; we change; we are contingent. And yet we do believe that there is a difference between truth and falsehood, right and wrong. So there must exist an absolute being who guarantees the truth and rightness of some things and the falsity and wrongness of others. There must be a God.

This argument of Augustine implies that great art, literature and music have significance. Modern deconstructionism denies this, arguing that in the arts, as everywhere else, no criteria exist against which values can be judged. The deconstructionist view is that since God does not exist, there is no real meaning in the arts, nor are there criteria for meaning anywhere; as a result, one view is as good or as valid as another. What follows from Augustine's argument for the existence of God is that if great works of art have meaning and significance – and many people feel that they do – there must exist something which gives them meaning and significance. This, of course, is God.

But Augustine regards this third capacity of mind, understanding, as only part of personality and a limited capacity of human mind. Augustine would agree with cognitive psychology's stress on mind, but he would also contend that the human person is much more than mind. Augustine would have regarded cognitive psychology's account of human beings as information-processing systems as limited and too cerebral. The search for God is cognitive only in part and involves love, will, passion, feeling, the search for delight – in fact, the whole human being. Augustine's emphasis on mind, in which he resembles cognitive psychologists, is placed within a view of personality as dynamically motivated, similar to Freud's. Augustine's famous account (*Confessions* 9,10) of his and his mother Monica's union with God at Ostia reveals that the movement to God involves will and the whole feeling person, not intellect alone. The understanding of the mind is limited, especially in the search for God.

Central on the journey to God is what Augustine confusingly calls reason. Reason helps us to God, whether on the way of faith seeking understanding, or on the way of understanding alone. There exists a grasping of God in a sort of direct perception by the mind; this is reason at work. Reason in Augustine has nothing to do with logic or rational thought, but refers to a 'gaze of the mind' which enables one to see something clearly. 'Under your guidance I entered into the depths of my soul, and this I was able to do because your aid befriended me. I entered, and with the eye of my soul, such as it was, I saw the Light that never changes casting its rays over the same eye of my soul, over my mind' (*Confessions* 7,10). Augustine here expresses a different account of human development.

This second account of development focusses on what Augustine regards as the core dimension of all human growth, the ascent to God. There are three steps – a withdrawal from the material world, a turning inwards to the soul, a rising above the soul to God. This can be expressed in terms of the three levels of nature – a turning away from the bottom rung of the hierarchy, bodies and the material world; a turning inwards to the soul and the things of the spirit; a turning upwards to God, the absolute Good. Very simply, there is a movement from what is outside the mind to what is inside the mind, to what is above the mind.

Human development can occur only over horizontal time; however, for Augustine, time has a second vertical dimension, concerned with the eternal. Though life is lived almost entirely on the horizontal, Augustine believed there to be moments when certain experiences move us on to the vertical. For most of us, these moments will not have the intensity of Augustine's ecstasy at Ostia; but there are experiences, such as great moments in art, music, literature and drama, which move us deeply. James Joyce, the novelist, spoke of epiphanies, by which are meant moments which take us out of the mundane, and which seem to hint at some revelation. Joyce's epiphanies refer to brief experiences, in art or everyday life, in which some important truth seems almost to be manifested. For Augustine these are foretastes of the divine, but he believed that the final movement from the horizontal vertically to God was made only in death.

Augustine stressed how God's grace is needed to choose and stay on the path of wisdom, and to help us ascend to God. It is difficult to seek and love God, because it is difficult to love and seek that of which we have no unambiguous experience. Augustine sees that this is why God's revelation in Christ is central for the Christian. In the New Testament, the Christian finds the eternal God made visible in a human being called Jesus. Augustine emphasizes that the Christian's attempts at faith and love are aided by the presence of Jesus Christ in the New Testament. But in spite of Christ in the Gospels, the pilgrimage remains guided by faith, by understanding and by the occasional direct grasping of what he calls 'reason'; only in eternity do these yield to vision. 'It will be ours to see him as he is, O Lord, but that time is not yet' (*Confessions* 13,15).

In Augustine's account, the purpose of personality is the possession of God, and only when we possess God will we become what we truly are. Since we will not possess God until after death, only then will we be fully ourselves. But even now we can recognize in ourselves and others traces of the divine, because our end and destiny is to become part of the divine. Until that time, according to Augustine, our lives remain a pilgrimage in a world which provides many satisfactions, but never lasting fulfilment. Human loves – of wife, husband, children, parents, friends – shelter the weary but restless traveller. And Augustine holds that such loves, and all human good, prove more satisfying if we treat them as refreshment stages on the way to God, rather than try to find complete fulfilment in them. But however refreshing they are, they are never enough, and the pilgrim travels on, searching for the complete and lasting fulfilment of God.

In *The City of God* Augustine writes of two cities, Babylon and Jerusalem, the earthly city and the heavenly city. The two cities have no visible form on earth but exist within human beings. The citizens of one are characterized by love of money, success, sex, power and prestige; the citizens of the other are characterized by love of God and the things of God. The path of power leads to the earthly city. The path of wisdom leads to the heavenly city, which it is already a part of here and now. But the joy of the city of God will only be revealed after death. Augustine believed that this joy in the possession of God will be a happiness both personal and collective, an enjoyment of God experienced individually in our resurrected bodies and as a community of the human species.

'Suffice it to say that this 'seventh day' will be our Sabbath and that it will end in no evening, but only in the Lord's day – that eighth and eternal day which dawned when Christ's resurrection heralded an eternal rest both for the spirit and for the body. On that day we shall rest and see, see and love, love and praise – for this is to be the end without the end of all our living, that Kingdom without end, the real goal of our present life' (*City of God* 22,30).

The Despairing Self:
Søren Kierkegaard's Christian
Existentialism

There was an emptiness about the heart of life . . . She pursed her lips when she looked in the glass. It was to give her face point. That was her self – pointed; dart-like; definite. That was her self when some effort, some call on her to be her self, drew the parts together . . .
(*Mrs Dalloway*, Virginia Woolf)

For the self is only healthy and free from despair when, precisely by having despaired, it is grounded transparently in God.
(*The Sickness unto Death*, Kierkegaard)

In Virginia Woolf's novel, Clarissa Dalloway looks into the mirror and sees herself. We know from our own experience that when we look in a mirror we see something more than just the body, face and clothes in front of us. Examining our reflection, we see an image projected to reveal or to hide ourselves. We are aware of feelings about the body and face in front of us. We recognize hopes and ambitions in the reflection. And – whether what confronts us is the face of an adolescent or of a mature adult – we see a past history and a hoped-for future. Like Mrs Dalloway, we see our self in the mirror.

The self is a central concept in both the existential and humanistic psychologies that have emerged during the second half of the twentieth century. Humanistic psychology contains important theorists such as Abraham Maslow, Carl Rogers and Sidney Jourard, and includes neo-Freudians like Erich Fromm. Both existential and humanistic psychology counsel us to look inwards. With God supposedly dead and nothing in the external world to give meaning to our lives, Clarissa Dalloway's feeling that 'there was an emptiness about the heart of life' seems common in Western society. Humanistic psychology, concerned with personal growth and realising human potential, says people can find meaning and value within their selfs.

In *The Transparent Self* (1971), Jourard relates psychological health to the self. He sees human beings as having a choice – between either masking their self and appearing different from what they really are, or allowing their real self to be open and transparent to others. Jourard reports that when he asked friends and colleagues what they knew about him, he hardly recognized himself in the answers they gave. Humanistic psychologies are often ambiguous about whether human beings are free. But Jourard sees humans as capable of deliberately disguising themselves and hiding themselves from others.

There are reasons why we might wish to pretend to be other than we are. As teenagers, we feel the need to disguise our real feelings, desires, anxieties from our parents. As adults, in various situations we regard it as unwise to let others know how we really feel. At work, especially in a competitive situation, we might think it politic or good taste to mask our true self.

Jourard and humanistic psychologists generally hold that self-knowledge, the Know Thyself of religious tradition, is essential for human development. Lacking self-knowledge, we are out of touch with a key area of reality, namely, our self. This can lead to anxiety, depression, phobias, poor personal relationships. Jourard's basic contention is that we can only know ourself if we are open to others. Disclosing ourself to another human being enables us to experience our true self and leads to psychological health.

According to Jourard, to achieve this transparent self it is not necessary to display ourself to all and sundry; just one other person will do. Whether we reveal ourself to one other person or to several others probably relates to temperamental differences, such as introversion-extraversion. The important thing is to have made ourself fully known and transparent to at least one person who is significant to us. After all, if no one else knows me, how can I know myself? If I do not know myself, how can I be myself?

But Jourard stresses that before one can disclose oneself to another, the assurance of confidentiality is needed, as in the Roman Catholic confessional. To become transparent requires that we convey how and what we feel. But what also needs to be disclosed to the 'other' is the cognitive contents of our self, our views, beliefs, ambitions, interests. Obvious 'others' to whom it might be appropriate to reveal oneself are mother, father, husband, wife, close friend of the same or opposite sex. Research reveals that the highest amount of self-disclosure is between husbands and wives. This confirms marriage as the most transparent human relationship, that is, the most mutually self-disclosing. Because of this, anyone reluctant to know or to be known by another is likely to find the prospect of marriage frightening! But Jourard points out that where love and trust exist, self-disclosure increases, and this self-disclosure in turn fosters more love and trust. He says, 'Self-disclosure begets self-disclosure.'

For Jourard, disclosing oneself – he refers to 'the courage to be known' – is an essential element in psychological development. He regards the refusal to be open and to disclose ourself to people significant to us as stunting personality growth and causing mental illness. Openness, self-disclosure and making the self transparent to another are partly what psychoanalysis, therapy, counselling are about. According to Jourard, we have become unwell by hiding ourselves from others, so we recover and maintain psychological health by revealing ourselves to appropriate others.

The self is central to Kierkegaard's account of personality, and much of humanistic psychology has been influenced by his ideas. But for the most part, humanistic psychology's exploration of the self is materialist and assumes that neither spirit nor God exist. The contribution of humanistic psychology has been considerable and is likely to continue. But humanistic psychologists have ignored the religious element in Kierkegaard's account; it is likely he would have disapproved of this secularization of his thought. For Kierkegaard, self is in part spirit, and a self without God is a crippled self, 'a king without a country'. In materialist humanistic psychology, the self is related to nature, the world, society, other people and itself, but not to God. For Kierkegaard, it is possible to understand personality, its anxiety and despair, only in the context of God's existence and of the self as spirit. Kierkegaard believed that materialism impoverishes our view of humans.

In a late work, *The Sickness unto Death*, Kierkegaard examines the self. He particularly explores the despair which he believes is a consequence of our failure to get the self in right relation to God. Despair, the 'sickness unto death', is a sickness of the spirit. Humans have little choice about physical illness, but despair is an illness which to some extent we choose – or at least we choose not to be cured of. The first few (very difficult) pages of *The Sickness unto Death* state: 'The human being is spirit . . . Spirit is the self.' This spirit-self is free. Kierkegaard sees a human being as a synthesis of spirit and body. He says: 'A human being is a synthesis of the infinite and the finite, of the temporal and the eternal, of freedom and necessity . . . Looked at in this way a human being is not yet a self.' (It would have been clearer had he reversed 'temporal and eternal' to be consistent with the other two polarities.)

That the human self is spirit means that human beings are not wholly natural and are not completely part of nature. In the humanistic psychology of Erich Fromm, humans are described as a freak of the universe, part of nature but apart from nature. Fromm sees humans as wholly material beings that are able to transcend the material world. The problem for a materialist, like Fromm, is to explain how a wholly material being can transcend matter. In Kierkegaard's account, human beings are free and able to transcend the natural world (for example, by thought and art) because self is in part spirit.

According to Kierkegaard, we are not born with a human nature, nor does an identity come ready-made with our biology. Kierkegaard's contention that human nature is not a 'given' remains a core notion of existentialist thought. His view, now basic to existentialist and humanistic psychology, is that human nature and personal identity are not innate but something which we have to achieve. How is this done? For Jourard, when our self is transparent before another human being we find our human nature and personal identity. For Kierkegaard, it is when our self is transparent before God that we become fully human and achieve our true identity. In Kierkegaard's account, the personality not open to God is alienated from its own true self and despairs.

Kierkegaard regards despair as a universal condition; everyone at some time in their lives – perhaps often – despairs. For Kierkegaard, apart from being painful, there is nothing wrong with despair; it is only through confronting despair that human beings develop. But facing up to despair is difficult, particularly when we realize that despair does not come from outside. Kierkegaard sees despair as inside us. When we realize that the despair is within, we know that a good holiday, a new job, a change of husband or wife, will not rid us of our despair. We would take the self that despairs with us on holiday, to the new job, into another marriage.

Kierkegaard describes two core despairs, and a third less important despair. The difficult opening of *The Sickness unto Death* reads: 'Despair is a sickness of the spirit, of the self, and so can have three forms: being unconscious in despair of having a self (inauthentic despair), not wanting in despair to be oneself, and wanting in despair to be oneself.' The first, the inauthentic despair of 'being unconscious in despair of having a self', is the less important and mildest despair; people do not even know they have it. The first of the two core despairs, that of 'not wanting in despair to be oneself', is the despair of weakness. The second is the despair of defiance; what Kierkegaard means by his paradoxical 'wanting in despair to be oneself' is that the self wants to be itself but on its own (and not God's) terms.

Kierkegaard sees personality as a synthesis – of the infinite and finite, of freedom and necessity, with a third polarity, the eternal and temporal, embracing the first two. (Kierkegaard sometimes uses the term 'possibility' instead of 'freedom'.) There is an eternal dimension in our personality which we experience as infinite potential and freedom; there is a temporal dimension in our personality which we experience as a restricting finite element and as the causal necessity in our lives. Both the eternal and temporal have to be involved if we are to achieve our true self. When there is a lack of balance between them, conscious (or unconscious) despair results. If we live only in terms of the temporal, we will live with the despairs of the finite and causal necessity. We need the temporal which is present in human existence. But in our lives we should reach after the eternal, through the possibilites that freedom and the infinite in us present.

For Jourard and other humanistic psychologists, human relationships with ourself and others are central to personality development. For Kierkegaard, also central to human development is a relationship with the infinite and eternal, namely, God. Humanistic and social psychologies are concerned with the self bestowed on us by others. Kierkegaard's existentialism is more concerned with the self bestowed on us by God. Kirkegaard holds that if humans live in a way that fails to acknowledge the reality of the self's dependence on God, despair is the result. Despair is caused by our rejecting a relationship with the divine.

Kierkegaard develops this analysis further. He sees specific despairs, those of finitude and infinitude, caused by an imbalance between the finite and the infinite. The despair of finitude occurs when the self does not grasp the infinite in itself. If we allow our personality to be dominated by the finite, we will live only in mundane reality. We exist engrossed in the everyday causal world, and though conscious of what our infinite potential makes possible, we make no attempt to convert it into reality. In Browning's poem, Andrea Del Sarto is aware of the infinite possibilities within him: 'Ah, but a man's reach should exceed his grasp/Or what's a heaven for?' But in the poem, Andrea complains that as a painter he never manages to go beyond a faultless depiction of the natural and capture something of the eternal.

The despair of finitude may manifest itself in our becoming a conforming personality. Such a person, like the marketing character or automaton conformist of Erich Fromm's analysis, tries to be like everyone else and lacks individuality. There is a deadness about personalities whose despair is of this kind. 'And I'm the weak-eyed bat no sun should tempt/Out of the grange whose four walls make his world', Andrea del Sarto complains in Browning's poem. Such personalities are often successful in material terms, probably because they are almost at home in the world, appearing only to want what the world has to offer. They may have everything that life can give – except a self.

Alternatively, the despair of infinitude occurs when the self does not sufficiently grasp its finitude and limitations. Here, people feel that infinitely extending will solve everything. If young, they may dream of utopias to come and, while planning the future, ignore the immediate needs of friends, neighbours, family. If they are intellectual, such personalities believe that by increasing their knowledge they will eventually find an answer. As young intellectuals they feel that the next book, the latest publication, something on the New Additions shelf as they enter the library, will have the answer. As such intellectuals age, after much disappointment at never finding the answer in print, they eventually conclude that nothing of any help can come out of a book.

The cause of this despair of infinitude is that, though we are infinite in our potential, we are limited too. If we allow our personality to be influenced only by the eternal dimension, we will end up out of touch with the finite world. The reality of the world brings us healthily down to earth, in the way Hamlet's nightmares did: 'O God! I could be bounded in a nutshell, and count myself a king of infinite space, were it not that I have bad dreams.' To deal with the despair of infinitude, we need to realize that we are finite as well as infinite.

There is another balance which can go wrong. The self may not get the right balance between the freedom and the causal necessity in life. On the one hand, we can have the despair of necessity where the self fails to grasp the reality of its freedom and possibilities. This may manifest itself in a certain fatalism, where we despairingly submit to 'the way things are'. Or we resign ourselves to a trivial level of existence, letting ourself be choked by the everyday and mundane, because we do not believe anything else to be possible. Despair of necessity occurs when humans let themselves be subject completely to what is determined in their lives.

Alternatively there is the despair of freedom, where the self lacks a grasp of the necessity that also attends existence. Here, one has become detached from the cause and effect in much of life. As a result, one fails to distinguish between what is attainable because freedom is real and what is unattainable because we are also limited, even in our freedom, by cause and effect. So one aspires to be an outstanding novelist or a great athlete, even though one lacks the talent.

Kierkegaard's distinction, between the two core despairs and the less important inauthentic despair, is based on the first two being conscious and the third being unconscious. Though he regards inauthentic unconscious despair as the mildest and least important, since one does not even realize that one is despairing, it remains 'the most common in the world'. A frantic pursuit of pleasure, or ensuring that one's job fills every moment of the day, may partly mask one's despair from oneself. I may be unhappy but manage to persuade myself – though perhaps not everyone else – that I am content. We remain unconscious largely because we are reluctant to admit to our despair; it is painful to do so, and it might even mean we feel obliged to do something about it.

But this is not true authentic despair, because it remains unconscious. The extent of despair relates to how conscious and aware we are of our despair. In *The Sickness unto Death*, Kierkegaard says, 'the more consciousness the more intense the despair'. There is a continuum. At one end of the continuum are people living in the everyday, scarcely self-aware, whose despair is slight because unconscious. At the other end is the considerable despair of people very aware of their situation and feelings. Modern literature is full of such self-consciously despairing characters. In Beckett's *Waiting for Godot*, though the despair of Estragon and Vladimir is rarely put into words, one has no doubts that the two tramps are aware of how they feel.

Kierkegaard regards the conscious despairs, 'not wanting in despair to be oneself, and wanting in despair to be oneself', as important and particularly revealing of human personality. The despair of weakness, 'not wanting in despair to be oneself', occurs when we are aware of what we must do to become ourselves but regard it as too demanding; so we do not try. We accept spiritual reality only in a notional way. We accept that we are spirit and have infinite potential, but do nothing about it. We accept the eternal in ourself and our free infinite dimension, but we do not relate them to the rest of our personality and fail to translate them into action. This despair of weakness, where one does not will to be one's real self, can take two directions; the despair can be over either the material or the eternal in one's personality.

Kierkegaard sees the despair (of weakness) over the material or earthly, a despair of finitude and necessity, as taking the form of enslavement to outward circumstances. People despairing in this way are engrossed in the world, completely dependent on circumstances, always fortune's fool. They are often very active, perhaps workaholics, inclined to run away from reflection and to avoid thinking about things. A despair of weakness over the earthly is characterized by submergence in the everyday and sense experience, by a preoccupation with the immediate and by a concern which has no appreciation of the eternal within one's self. Such personalities believe their despair to be the result of their supposedly unfortunate marriage, job, financial position. But the real cause is the absence of the eternal within themselves. They may put the blame for their despair on their situation in life, or on bad luck, and hope that their luck will change. But their despair may have to get worse before it gets better, because their despair will only end when the eternal in them breaks through.

According to Kierkegaard, the despair of weakness can also work in the opposite direction and cause despair over the eternal in oneself. This kind of despair is found in people who truly hunger for something eternal, but who eventually abandon all hope of finding any such absolute. These people eventually withdraw into themselves, become cynical and full of contempt, feel superior, despising what they regard as the unreflecting others. The introvert is more likely to suffer from this despair than the extravert. There is the danger that such a despair will end in nervous breakdown or suicide.

The despair of defiance, of 'wanting in despair to be oneself', is the other core conscious despair. Here we want to be ourself, but want to be a self of our own choosing and not the self which God wants us to be. Here we hold on to what is finite and temporal in our personality, and we defiantly reject our genuine spiritual possibilities because they involve accepting God. In this despair, we try by our own efforts to overcome the limitations of our time-bound existence with its finiteness and causal necessities. We try, Nietschze-like, to create ourselves according to our own specifications and pull ourselves up by our own bootstraps. Such despair can express its defiance when, with great pride, we destroy what we have achieved. Or the defiance may take a more passive form, where we do not want our unhappiness to be cured.

Kierkegaard gives as an example of the despair of defiance – he may have had himself in mind – introvert individuals 'of morbid reserve'. They are very conscious of the eternal element in their self. But they are prevented from breaking through to this eternal within them by pride and arrogance. They are determined that they themselves should stay in control. Such individuals will not let go;

they will not allow the eternal and temporal in their personality to join and form a self on God's terms.

In Kierkegaard's account, self is spirit, and though we can ignore or abuse spirit, it cannot be destroyed; we cannot annihilate our self. The writings of Samuel Beckett do not convey the sense that there will be peace when it is all over. It is never all over. Part of human despair lies in just that – there is no way out, since we cannot eliminate our indestructible spirit-self which is the source of our despair. But, according to Kierkegaard, all despair fortunately has within it the potentiality for faith and the movement to faith. All despair has the capacity to resolve itself by finding God. The experience of despair makes us aware of the nature of the problem and brings us closer to its solution, which is God and becoming our true self transparent before God.

For Kierkegaard, despair is unpleasant but unavoidable, something one has to pass through if the solution, a self established in God, is to be found. In Jung's analytical psychology, neurosis is seen as a positive, though painful, attempt by personality to achieve psychological health. Like neurosis in Jungian psychology, despair for Kierkegaard is a sign that something needs to be done and is the beginning of an attempt to do it. There is no escaping despair; and the cure often entails journeying to the point where implicit denial of our dependence on God becomes explicit defiance. With open defiance there comes the possibility of despair's only cure, admitting our self's dependence on God. Humans may move directly to finding their true self in God through acceptance. But Kierkegaard sees the indirect route via rebellion and despair as the more usual way. And, says Kierkegaard, 'the self is only healthy and free from despair when, precisely, by having despaired, it is grounded transparently in God' (*Either/Or*). Despair is only cured at the point where we become fully aware of our self's dependence on God.

Humanistic psychology helps people to discover meaning and values, to grow and to explore their potential, and to find their place and significance in a universe largely without God. Humanistic psychology helps humans to develop mainly by having them explore their social and psychological self. In contrast, Kierkegaard's existentialism emphasizes the religious element in the self. He sees human personality as existing in time but transcending time. For

Kierkegaard, human beings have to become aware that there exists within them an eternal as well as a temporal dimension. Personality develops when we correct any temporal-eternal imbalance within our self. The ultimate aim of human development is a self transparent before God, and this is achieved by a choice. According to Kierkegaard, human development – or at least the sort of development he is interested in – is the result of free choice and decision.

Most scientific materialist theories provide an account of personality development. Such theories differ on whether humans can affect their own development by choice and decision. Some accounts doubt or deny that humans can freely influence their own development. Freudian psychoanalytic theory sees the development of personality as triggered off and energized by the instincts which emerge as the biological body matures. According to Freud, these emerging instincts interact with social factors to determine personality development, and free human choice or decision involved is minimal or nil.

In the Freudian psychoanalytic account, at the first stage, the oral stage, the body's need for food constitutes the instinct element; mother or whoever is doing the feeding constitutes the social factor with which instinct interacts. The next stage of development, the anal, is triggered off when the infant's need to defecate is confronted by society in the shape of parents attempting to toilet-train the child. The next instinctual change occurs at the age of about four or five when, according to Freud, sexual feelings about parents emerge in the genital area. In psychoanalytic theory, the social factor here is the mother-father-child relationship, and the result is the oedipal conflict. Next, during a latency phase, from about five to puberty, no personality development occurs – because there are no new instinctual developments. Then with the arrival of sexuality comes the genital stage and the adult genital personality.

Freud sees the genital personality as capable of adult sexual relationships, and as much concerned with the needs and pleasures of others as with his or her own. But much may have gone wrong in the course of development; the individual may arrive at adulthood in part fixated at earlier stages, equipped with a variety of defence mechanisms, and possibly damaged by neurosis. What Freud emphasizes is that the personality that now emerges was already formed in the first five or so years. And what has happened in those first few years of childhood has largely been the product of the interaction of biology and social factors. The free choice involved is nil or minimal.

Freud's account of development has made us aware of the critical importance of childhood for adult personality. But Erikson, a neo-Freudian whose ideas relate also to humanistic psychology, stresses that significant change can and does occur after childhood. Erikson sees development continuing throughout life, even till death. And while accepting the importance of biological instincts, Erikson gives more emphasis than Freud to social factors. He takes the view that these social factors are not only those of the immediate family, stressed by Freud, but wider ones such as school and society. And according to Erikson, these social influences are different at different stages. Each stage has a specific problem to be solved: sorting out trust and mistrust in the early months of life, personal identity at adolescence, despair and integrity as death approaches in mature age. Erikson's perspective implies that human personality is potentially always developing.

Erikson also believed that ego factors were more important in human development than Freud realized. Erikson saw the ego as an autonomous structure of personality which thinks, plans, perceives, remembers, imagines. Erikson, like modern cognitive psychologists, held that such ego activities were central to human behaviour. He regarded the ego as actively involved in solving life's problems at different stages in development, often problems which relate to our relationships with others. As a result he believed that humans are more rational and more in control of their lives than Freud allowed. It is because Erikson sees not only instinct and social factors, but the autonomous ego also, as playing such an important part in human development, that he holds that change and development are possible right throughout life.

Erikson adopted from biology the epigenetic principle, which holds that everything which grows has a pre-existing ground-plan. For Erikson, personality too has a ground-plan and develops through a sequence of predetermined stages. Each stage differs significantly from the others. So it would be a mistake to regard a woman of forty-five as the same person that she was at twenty-five, only older; she is in many ways a different person. If at fifty-five I am psychologically the same person I was at thirty-five, then something has gone wrong – I have failed to develop. Personality is in a continuous process of development – or should be.

Erikson's use of the epigenetic principle calls attention to two issues central to theories of personality. The first is mind and the relationship of mind to body; the second is the connected issue of human freedom. Erikson regards personality development as the product of genetic pre-programming, interacting with social influences and the ego. But what is this ego with which biological and social factors interact? Is it mind? And since genes are located in the body, how can the genetic pre-programming of our biology cause developments in personality? Implicit in such issues is what philosophers call the body-mind problem, which asks how body and mind relate and, indeed, what mind is. Erikson attributes mind and the development of mind, which in traditional religious thought has partly been accounted for by soul and spirit and free choice, solely to biology, social influences and the ego, even though what ego is remains unclear.

The second issue is the puzzle of free choice. Kierkegaard's existentialism affirms that humans usually have choice about what they do. In contrast, Freud believes that real free choice does not exist for human beings. In Erikson's account of personality development, the position of free choice in relation to genetic pre-programming, social factors and the supposedly autonomous ego remains vague and unclear.

The cognitive-developmental is another tradition in which psychologists, such as Piaget and Kohlberg, have studied human development. Piaget's main concern has been with intellectual development. He holds that there exist structures of the mind which are innate and that mind itself is a pre-existing innate structure. But, according to Piaget, social and environmental experience is necessary for the development of intellectual structures which make human thought possible. In Piaget's view, an individual maturing in a situation without adequate intellectual stimulation might, for example, fail to develop a capacity for abstract thought.

In his account of moral development, Piaget regards the infant as pre-moral and he stresses the part played by intellect in moral growth. Piaget largely sees morality in terms of rules and moral development in terms of the acquisition of appropriate rules. So he regards the intellectual development of the child and adult as relevant to moral development, since he holds that intellectual development affects the capability of humans to acquire and understand moral rules. Can a child intellectually grasp the idea of intention, so that deliberately smashing a cup is seen as different from accidentally knocking it off a table? Does an individual regard moral rules as absolute and unchanging in the manner of physical laws such as gravity? – or merely as what is imposed by authority? – or simply as what is agreed between peers? For Piaget, the significant moral development is a move from a heteronomous to an autonomous stage. In the first, morality is seen by the individual as being subject to another's laws, which are externally imposed by an authority like parents, school, government. In the second, morality is seen by the individual as more democratic, and largely as accepting and abiding by rules agreed between equals.

Kohlberg, too, stressed the importance of intellect and intellectual development in moral behaviour; but he substitutes three stages for Piaget's two-stage account of moral development. In Kohlberg's account, at the first stage, the child – or young person, perhaps even adult – is a hedonist who operates at a pre-moral level. At this 'pre-conventional' stage, human beings operate in terms of pay-offs, are only interested in the externals of behaviour, and concerned with moral rules simply because they are rewarded for obeying them and punished for breaking them. In the later phase of this pre-conventional stage, individuals develop some slight awareness of the needs of others. At Kohlberg's second stage of morality, the 'conventional' stage, other people's expectations shape our moral behaviour. At this stage – though we may not be young – we are trying to be a good boy or girl, and conforming to society as a good citizen, neighbour, husband, wife, employee, dutifully filling our social roles. According to Kohlberg, such a level of moral development may well be as far as many of us go. And society would tick along very nicely if, in the later phase of the conventional stage, we all did our duty.

But the most obvious difference from Piaget comes at Kohlberg's third stage. At this 'post-conventional' stage, people live their lives by self-accepted moral principles, following Shakespeare's advice, 'To thine own self be true'. Here moral rules are viewed as independent of any validating authority. At this post-conventional stage, rather than self-interest or obvious social roles, it is a sense of authenticity or of a self to which one must be true that motivates us. If people advance in this post-conventional stage to its later phase, they move from rules which are obeyed because they have been contractually agreed with others to an idea of rules behind the rules, an abstract notion of universal justice. Both Piaget and Kohlberg hold that moral growth is influenced by normal intellectual development. But both seem vague as to the extent that the individual's free choice and decision are involved in moral development.

When it comes to Kierkegaard's theory of development, the situation is very different. He holds that human personality develops by acts of free choice. And in Kierkegaard's developmental account, it is not one dimension only of a human being which is involved, such as intelligence or instinct, but the whole self or personality. The free choice that moves the self from one stage to another involves a completely different orientation to life; and the freedom which makes such choice possible is the result of spirit. There are three stages in Kierkegaard's account of human development – the aesthetic, the ethical, the religious.

At the first stage, the aesthetic, a human being is preoccupied with pleasure, with seeking satisfaction and enjoyment and excitement, such as social or sexual, in leisure or work. At the aesthetic stage, the self is not necessarily crudely hedonistic. Sensuous enjoyment may be found in good literature, art or music; or, Wordsworth-like, one might discover it in nature: 'There was a time when meadow, grove, and stream,/The earth, and every common sight, to me did seem/Apparalled in celestial light.' There is often, to begin with, an innocence at the aesthetic stage. Children for the most part exist at the aesthetic stage, and Wordsworth's poem refers to early childhood.

Whatever the enjoyment sought at the aesthetic stage, whether in nature, food, sex, good music, wealth, health, good looks, good luck, it originates outside a human being. This makes personality passive at the aesthetic stage since it is dependent, as children are, on the external world. Personality at the aesthetic stage lacks inner resources. The aesthetic self has no plan or objective other than the pursuit of pleasure in the present and passing moment.

The trouble with the aesthetic stage is that the world and its contents are unreliable and not always easy to get hold of. They are also transient; this is particularly unfortunate, since the activities of the aesthetic personality are in part an attempt to escape from time. 'But at my back I always hear/Time's winged Chariot hurrying near.' Another shortcoming of the aesthetic is that the goods of the world fail to satisfy: 'The eye is not filled with seeing, nor the ear with hearing.' Good music, a lovely landscape, even human love, fail to fulfil completely, even while we enjoy them and try to forget that they will not last. Understandably, the self at the aesthetic stage is troubled by moods, like the melancholy of nineteenth-century Romantic poets – 'She dwells with Beauty – Beauty that must die.' In the twentieth century, writers like F. Scott Fitzgerald, in novels such as *Tender is the Night* and *The Great Gatsby*, capture the under-tug of sadness and despair in the aesthetic life, even while it is lived.

The aesthetic self is also troubled by boredom, which it tries to escape by rushing from one pleasure to another. Should we eventually give up on the present, there is always, if we are young, a utopian future to dream of, and if we are old, an idealized past to look back to. The word 'aesthete' means 'one who perceives', and at the aesthetic stage one observes but does not get involved. Kierkegaard points out that one method used not to get involved in life's problems and pains is the resort to irony, which laughs with despairing detachment at everything. We laugh because it is all absurd, and its absurdity means that we do not have to commit ourselves. But we are refusing to admit our underlying despair, partly because it is painful to do so, and the despair suggests that we want something better. Deep down, serious commitment is above all what we most want. 'It is impossible to exist without passion,' Kierkegaard declares in *Concluding Unscientific Postscript*.

Kierkegaard saw that another way out, similar to irony, and suitable for certain temperaments, is scepticism. A sceptic only plays with ideas and beliefs and, like everyone at the aesthetic stage, is one of life's spectators. But this is the very reason why the aesthetic stage ultimately fails to satisfy – human beings do not want to be just spectators. Human beings seek something in their lives to commit themselves to; they just do. In psychotherapy, some clients find they have to explore with the therapist why they are unable to commit themselves to something or someone in their lives.

Mozart's opera begins with Don Giovanni at the aesthetic stage, his manservant boasting of his master's 1003 sexual conquests. It ends with Don Giovanni's despairing defiance as he chooses not to repent. Despair is always present in the aesthetic stage. Growth in self-awareness merely makes the self more aware of its despair: 'My life has no meaning'. 'What have I done with my life?' 'What am I doing with my life?' Like Mozart's Don Giovanni, though perhaps not so noisily, we can be defiant and refuse to change. We can choose to continue to shun commitment, to stay at the aesthetic level, to luxuriate like Romantic poets in our unhappiness and melancholy. But in Kierkegaard's analysis, by doing this we are choosing not to develop our personality and to live without morality, because the aesthetic stage is prior to making moral choices. This is why it is only appropriate for young children.

Eventually we need to develop and become moral beings. This is not necessarily done, according to Kierkegaard, by finding something new to believe in. In William Golding's *Free Fall*, Sammy Mountjoy reports: 'I have hung all systems on the wall like a row of useless hats. They do not fit. They come in from outside.' Kierkegaard holds that we do not move from the aesthetic to the ethical by thinking, reflecting, intellectual analysis. He sees that the solution is to be found in the either/or of choice and decision, made possible by the freedom of the spirit-self. By exercising our freedom and making a commitment, we leave behind the aesthetic and move into the ethical.

But Kierkegaard reports that we learn a lot at the aesthetic stage. We learn from our lack of fulfilment that sensuous satisfaction is not enough. We realize despairingly that, regardless of whether the satisfaction is sex, playing tennis, listening to a Brahms symphony, we seek something more. It is the underlying despair at the aesthetic stage, especially if acknowledged, which prompts us to move on to the next stage by free choice. Kierkegaard is aware that free choice is complex and interacts with determinism within the human self. But he asserts that ultimately the human personality can freely choose to develop or not to. And if the human self at the aesthetic stage chooses to develop, the movement is into the ethical stage.

Counsellors have commented that young people, even if they first experiment with short-term sexual relationships, usually turn to seeking something more permanent. Abandoning casual short-term relationships for something committed would, in Kierkegaard's account, be moving from the aesthetic to the ethical. And Kierkegaard uses marriage as an example of the ethical. What we would normally regard as moral behaviour, such as concern for the underprivileged, tending the sick, the struggle for justice and, quite simply, love of one's neighbour are examples of the ethical stage.

Kierkegaard's view is that in making the act of choice that takes us from the aesthetic to the ethical, we become aware of the freedom involved in choice. Freedom expresses the deeper self of the human being. Free choice makes us aware of our true self, and we find that this true self is implicated in moral obligations. The self moving from the aesthetic to the ethical becomes aware of the existence of obligations and duties to others such as wife, husband, children, friends, neighbours, other human beings. Unlike the aesthetic, the ethical personality is not self-obsessed but genuinely concerned about others, whose needs it now regards as being as important as, or more important than, its own pleasures. Individuals who act ethically express, says Kierkegaard, the universal in their life. At the ethical stage, what is right for oneself is right for society; there is no conflict between one's personal needs and those of society. The ethical self accepts universal moral principles. In this and other ways, Kierkegaard's ethical stage resembles the later phases of moral development in the cognitive-developmental accounts of Piaget and Kohlberg.

For Kierkegaard, a certain moral self-sufficiency characterizes the ethical stage. This self-sufficiency enables human beings by their own efforts to choose between right and wrong and to act accordingly. Such moral self-sufficiency, of the 'I am the master of my fate' or Rudyard Kipling's poem 'If' sort, is approved of by humanistic psychology. Personality at Kierkegaard's ethical stage resembles what humanistic psychologists, such as Carl Rogers and Erich Fromm, advocate as the goal of personality development. For

Rogers, this is the 'fully functioning person'; and for Fromm, it is 'the productive character'.

Rogers reports that in psychotherapy he found that personality always developed in the same direction, regardless of the culture or background of clients. He says that clients emerge from successful therapy preferring to love rather than hate, showing concern for others rather than indifference, finding compassion for others more satisfying than contempt. According to Rogers, what clients invariably choose in therapy is to become morally concerned human beings, serving others, at the same time fulfilling their potential. This fully functioning person, Carl Rogers' model of mental health and his goal in therapy, is loving, caring, concerned, realistic, rational, open to others and their needs, and copes with the problem of time by living fully in the present.

Like Rogers' fully functioning person, the productive character is what Fromm believes we should strive to become. Fromm, like Freud, sees love and work as key areas for personality. In work, what matters for Fromm is not the content of the work, whether it be plumbing, accounting or teaching. What matters, and what shapes human personality for better or worse, is the individual's attitude to that work. According to Fromm, work done with the right productive attitude releases and realizes human potential. It is having the right productive attitude that makes what we do valuable and psychologically healthy. In humanistic psychology generally, the content of our actions – taking the children to the park, building a bridge, playing cards – is regarded as not always important. What is important is our attitude to what we do. This is clear from the sort of questions that clients are asked in therapy: 'How do you feel about it?' 'Does it feel good?' 'Is the relationship satisfying?'

Fromm's productive character and Rogers' fully functioning person are attempts to find, in a world where God is dead, a substitute for the standards and values traditionally derived from religious beliefs. Fromm says that 'the meaning of life is living', that 'there is no meaning to life except the meaning man gives his life by the unfolding of his powers'. What Fromm regards as important is the manner and style in which people do things. It seems that he stresses the importance of the way in which people do things because he has difficulty in concluding, from scientific psychology, what people should actually do. His conclusion is that if, as productive characters, we do what truly feels right, it will be morally right. He holds that this also works in the opposite direction, so that if we do what is morally and ethically good and benefits others, it will benefit us and be psychologically good for us. He says: 'Good in humanistic ethics is the affirmation of life, the unfolding of man's powers . . . Evil constitutes the crippling of man's powers.'

Kierkegaard's self at the ethical stage, Fromm's productive character and Rogers' fully functioning person know the right things to do and do them – caring about their neighbour, ensuring justice for others, loving their husband or wife, looking after children, being concerned about the oppressed, getting rid of discrimination, feeding the hungry. But Fromm and other humanistic psychologists are suggesting that people should do what is right and good because in this way they realize their potential and feel fulfilled. Kierkegaard sees people at the ethical stage doing what they do because they are moral; they are genuinely concerned about their neighbour, the hungry, the oppressed. If a woman does not leave her husband for a more glamorous and successful male colleague, it may be because she thinks it would be wrong to do so, not because the sacrifice realizes her potential and makes her feel fulfilled; sacrificing the other relationship might make her feel awful.

Kierkegaard regards the ethical self as a significant advance on the aesthetic. Certainly, at the ethical stage the self, like Fromm's productive character and Rogers' fully functioning person, may do what is moral partly because doing good is psychologically good for one, and because doing right makes one feel fulfilled. However, for Kierkegaard, at this ethical stage, the self does what is good and right largely because it is good and right and because it is what one should do. Kierkegaard holds that at the ethical stage the self becomes aware of the reality of the moral dimension – there is such a thing as right and wrong, good and bad. At this stage, we accept our obligations as human beings. At this stage, we realize that sometimes when we fulfil our duties we are fulfilling our own needs, but that sometimes we must subordinate our own needs to the good of others. A love and concern for others permeates the ethical. If we all lived at the ethical stage, regarding society as the ultimate good, subordinating when necessary our individual self to the needs of others, there would be little to complain of in society.

At the ethical stage, we become aware that our acts are not completely caused and inevitable. The ethical is admirable in the courage of its commitment, made in the face of the reality that whatever one commits oneself to will die. In marriage, Kierkegaard's favourite example of the ethical, partners know that one day one of them will have to face the loss of the other. Self-sacrifice involved in marriage and parenthood is made knowing it is done for a transient being. We know that the death of a partner or child, desertion, failure of the marriage, ends the relationship. Though this makes the concern and self-sacrifice and love of others at the ethical stage heroic, for Kierkegaard this is where the ethical fails. The ethical fails in part because of the excessive responsibility and guilt it places on human beings.

Kierkegaard sees the ethical as making us aware of life's problems but not enabling us to solve them. The ethical holds us responsible for what we cannot possibly be completely responsible for, leaving us trying to pull ourselves up by our shoe-strings. Kierkegaard would have regarded Jourard's disclosure of self to another, Fromm's productive character and Rogers' fully functioning person as not going far enough. He would have argued that developmental accounts in humanistic psychology, ending at the ethical, are incomplete. Humans are not self-sufficient, certainly not morally self-sufficient. None of us really can say 'I am the master of my fate' or 'I am in control of my life'. Responsibility for oneself and others is limited because we are not omnipotent. Whatever our courage and concern, human beings suffer, relationships fail and in the end people die. In every situation, what we are able to do is relative and limited. For Kierkegaard, this raises a question mark over the ethical.

For Kierkegaard, the ethical provides no real basis for moral life. At the ethical stage, we eventually come to realize that we cannot solve anything definitively, and we become aware of the significance of our failures. Specifically, at the ethical stage we come to appreciate the inadequacy of human reason, thought, intellect, to solve the old problems of: What am I? Does life have meaning? Suffering? Death? The failure of the ethical, and eventually our despair at its failure, makes us aware that the human is not enough. The ethical eventually brings us to the religious stage where we see that only faith and the transcendent is capable of taking us beyond despair.

A highly intelligent young woman with considerable scientific talent works for many years in medical research; then she decides to become a nun. She enters a convent of contemplative nuns who spend their lives in prayer. The nuns do not teach, care for the sick or do social work, and certainly do nothing in the way of scientific research. Now, there is no ethical justification for her life. Our reaction when we hear of such lives reveals how inevitably we adopt the ethical; our reaction – What a waste! – is ethically correct. But the young woman has taken a step that moves her from the ethical into Kierkegaard's religious stage.

What she has done does not invalidate the ethical. People enter convents and monasteries to become contemplative nuns and monks because of obligations that they personally experience as more imperative than a career and marriage. The usual reason for becoming a contemplative nun or monk is a response to some call. And for a particular woman or man, becoming a contemplative, suspends the ethical.

Kierkegaard holds that there are exceptional circumstances where one is justified in setting aside the usual ethical obligations; the religious stage originates in these exceptional circumstances. Human beings occasionally experience imperatives which make the social good and the ethical subordinate and relative before some absolute. The young scientist entering the enclosed convent will be making no use of her scientific training and talents for the good of others; she will be giving up the ethical possibilities of marriage and children. But perhaps while she was working as a scientist and living the ethical life, she felt a touch of despair and heard a call. She realized that her despair would be cured only if she answered that call and opened herself to God. For her, opening herself to God involved entering a convent. In the normal practices of convent life, the scientist-nun would be doing what Jourard advocates for human development, disclosing herself to another human, namely, her confessor. But for Kierkegaard, ultimately it is God to whom she needs to disclose herself, if her despair is to end.

In *Fear and Trembling*, Kierkegaard takes from the Old Testament the example of God's command to Abraham that he sacrifice his son. Abraham was aware of the ethical – he knew that killing Isaac would normally be murder. Abraham does not justify the breach of the ethical involved in killing his son by appealing to another ethic such as, 'It is right that one man should die to save the nation.' Quite the contrary; Abraham knows that God has promised that the nation will be saved by Isaac, whom he has now been commanded to kill. But Abraham, the knight of faith, will do what God asks, regardless of whether a justification will be provided in this life. Abraham's action, like the young scientist's in entering the convent, implies the existence of values that transcend the ethical. Their actions are justified only by an appeal to an unverifiable absolute called God. The existence of such exceptions, and the absolute which they imply, means that the ethical is not definitive – Kierkegaard refers to a 'teleological suspension of the ethical'.

According to society and the ethical, Abraham is about to commit murder; an alternative view is that he is about to do God's will. Unfortunately, there is no way of knowing before the event which view is correct. According to Kierkegaard, there are certain situations, such as Abraham's and the scientist's, where one simply has to make the leap of faith. Sometimes even after the event there is no way of knowing. Twenty years later the nun, aware of her ex-colleagues' scientific achievements and that her brothers and sisters now have wives and husbands and children, may occasionally wonder if she did the right thing. But, like Abraham, what she has demonstrated with her life is the existence of an absolute and transcendent source of morality that takes us beyond the ethical.

The woman entering the convent and Abraham called upon to sacrifice his son seem different from the rest of us. But they are different, says Kierkegaard, only in being obvious exceptions. Most of us are not called to give up our jobs, abandon the possibility of marriage and children, give up any work which we do to help others, and enter a monastery or convent. Nevertheless, we are all exceptions. Kierkegaard's insight is to see that at the ethical, beneath the satisfactions of job, marriage, children, good works and the concerns of everyday, despair continues as real and as troublesome as ever. He holds that it is despair which motivates us to find God.

According to Kierkegaard, it is only by moving from the ethical to the religious, like the scientist becoming a nun, that we will be cured of our despair. Even in the convent the young woman's despair will only end if her self becomes transparent before God. For Kierkegaard, that is the position of us all. It is only by the leap of faith that takes us from the ethical to the religious, and there, by becoming open and transparent before God, that the self moves beyond despair.

The religious stage involves dangers which the ethical with its obvious justifications does not have. I might blithely abandon my responsibilities without any qualms, and then justify my action by claiming my situation is exceptional and appealing to a higher authority such as God. But Kierkegaard stresses that a person can move to the religious only after the demands of the ethical have been recognized. Even at the religious stage, the ethical still stands; Abraham is aware of the universal which says 'Thou shalt not kill'. An individual claims to have heard not exactly voices but a call – to leave parents, forgo marriage, career and children, to enter a monastery or convent. In such a case it would be right to examine the behaviour of the individual in other areas of life. Outside this apparent call from God is he or she balanced and responsible or unbalanced and irresponsible? And it is legitimate to set aside the ethical and make the leap of faith only after the matter has been given a great deal of thought. Job eventually found the answer to his distress and despair in faith; but not before he had first thought and reasoned a great deal and tried to understand. And though there are safeguards, Kierkegaard's view that at the religious stage the individual is more important than the universal, and potentially an exception, will always cause difficulties.

However, we have no alternative but to become an exception and enter the religious stage if our despair is to end. Eventually Job – if he was going to get rid of his despair and develop as a human being – had to become an exception, make an act of faith and accept God's will. In Kierkegaard's view, we are all in the same position as Job and Abraham and the scientist-turned-nun. If we want to be rid of the despair that troubles us even in the ethical stage, we too have no alternative but to make the leap of faith which the freedom of the spirit-self makes possible. And by faith we commit ourself to a belief in an absolute moral authority whose existence justifies suspending the ethical. Only by arriving at such faith is it possible for Job and Abraham to act the way they do, and for men and women to enter contemplative convents and monasteries where their sole purpose is prayer to a silent God. Kierkegaard holds that for the rest of us, too, only faith will end our despair.

Faith is necessary because there are limits to the revelations of rational thought and objective enquiry. Perhaps in the domain of science we might eventually be able to arrive at definitive conclusions about the way things are. And when science and reason have said everything that they have to say, we will know much, possibly everything that there is to know, about the natural world. But we will still have no answers to the old despairing questions about the meaning of life, human love, good, evil, death, suffering, and whether God exists. Kierkegaard has made us realize that in this area, where science concludes with an agnostic 'don't know and cannot know', answers can only be found by faith. Arguments for the existence of God, such as Aquinas' five proofs, are fine and not to be ignored. For the Christian, research to find the historical Jesus is useful. But Kierkegaard sees that, in the end, believing Christians have to affirm in the knowledge that there remains agonizing uncertainty about what they affirm.

A computer programmer, weary of endless speculation about God, feeds into her computer all the data available on whether God exists, to let the computer decide. However much one might sympathize, we know the matter cannot be solved in this way. But Kierkegaard would contend that this is just what we are in danger of doing, less obviously, all the time. We attempt to deal with matters of whether life has any meaning, of whether God exists, of death and human love in this reasoning way. The same programmer, interested in two colleagues with a view to marriage, feeds data into the computer to help her decide who will suit her better as a husband. But here too this information-processing approach will not help much, even if she ignores the computer and processes the data in her head.

According to Kierkegaard, the solution to such problems is not to be found in reasoning and reflection. What matters in a choice of husband or wife, and subsequently in making the marriage work, is decision and commitment. Antoine St Exupery puts it more poetically: 'For the flower you single out is a rejection of all other flowers: nevertheless only on those terms is it beautiful' (*The Citadel*). Similarly, by reasoning alone, with or without the aid of a computer, we will not arrive at any definitive conclusion about the existence of God. A conclusion on God, whether for belief or non-belief, involves, as do all major life areas, a decision, a choice, a commitment, an act of faith.

And in the unlikely event of the computer coming to a conclusion about God's existence, or if we have reasoned in a cerebral way to a conclusion on God without using a computer, it would be almost irrelevant. If such a truth is to be of any value, it has to be felt, lived, experienced by the whole person. Kierkegaard rejects the idea that one can come to a solution on the deeper problems of life by disinterested research and objective speculation. Faith and what he calls subjective thinking and the existential self are necessary.

Kierkegaard's notions of subjective thinking and the existential self emphasize the personal nature of truth. A knowledge of mathematics and the laws of science, such as gravity, can be grasped completely in intellectual concepts and are valid regardless of who thinks them. But there are areas where this sort of knowledge has no relevance. There are areas where what can be arrived at is at best an uncertain truth, and this can be achieved only by subjective thinking of the existential self. There are areas where truth can be grasped and made one's own only by choice, decision, commitment. The computer programmer might sit ruminating indefinitely about whether God exists and which of her colleagues she loves enough to marry, but in the end it will get her nowhere. A certain amount of thought will certainly be useful, but whether this or that man is the one she should share her life with is resolved by making a decision and committing herself to the relationship. This is the existential self at work. When the programmer arrives at a meaningful conclusion about God, or which colleague to marry, it would mean that at some point she has stopped relying wholly on reason, or the computer, and made an existential choice.

According to Kierkegaard, there are areas of life where we mistakenly think that what we need in order to find a solution is more thought and knowledge. So we read another book or attend another lecture. But in such areas – and humanistic psychology would agree with Kierkegaard here – solutions are not to be found by more thought and knowledge but only by decision, choice, commitment. When it comes to God, love, death, the meaning of life and the rest, I have as an existential self to come to a decision, and my intellect and reason can help me only slightly. This puts all human beings, the clever, not-so-clever and the in-between, on an equal footing. Being clever is no advantage when it comes to the real issues of life, which is often difficult for clever people to accept.

Kierkegaard is not against reason; indeed, he uses reason to argue the limits of reason. He is also aware that there are problems where reason and intellectual analysis are wholly appropriate. Unfortunately, these never turn out to be in the important areas of life. What Kierkegaard rejects is the sole reliance on thought and reason in areas where their usefulness is limited. Does God exist? Human relationships. Suffering. Death. Who am I? What am I? In such areas, thought and reason are very useful as a preliminary exercise, to do some clearing away, to get rid of the nonsense. It will help the programmer a little bit to reflect rationally on whether God exists and which of her two colleagues is the right one to marry. But in the end there is only one solution – committing herself to God in an act of faith or to one of the men in a relationship. Having used reason and intellect for a preliminary weeding out, our existential self can decide on God's existence, or about our love for someone, only by commitment made in the face of uncertainty.

Kierkegaard would have rejected the artificial intelligence view of human beings as a kind of computer. He would not have been happy with cognitive psychology's more modest claim that human beings resemble computers in being information-processing systems. Even if, by processing the available information, humans could prove the existence of a creator and demonstrate that Christ was divine, it would be no substitute for personal commitment to God and for entering into a relationship with God become human in Christ. Similarly, it is unlikely that we would be moved by a detached consideration of Aquinas' five proofs into making God the centre of our lives. If, as cognitive psychology suggests, humans are information-processing systems, they are much else besides. And for Kierkegaard, they are also subjective thinkers and existential selfs operating in areas where doubts and uncertainties cannot be got rid of by an appeal to the data. There are areas where neither proof nor disproof is possible; the risk inherent in faith cannot be avoided. The existential self moves from the ethical to the religious in a leap of faith, motivated by hope and despair, and remains there by passionate commitment.

It is because of the passion, hope and despair involved that the believer has more in common with the convinced and committed atheist than with an agnostic. In the novels of Graham Greene and François Mauriac, atheists are usually nearer to God than lukewarm believers. In Mauriac's *The Knot of Vipers* the central character, professedly an atheist, eventually suspects – as does the reader – that he cares more about God's existence than do his property-obsessed Roman Catholic relatives. Belief and disbelief alike are motivated by hope and despair, because this is the way humans are. Our search for answers to the old questions is not the result of a disinterested pursuit of the truth which processes the data with serene detachment. We believe in God – or disbelieve – in part because we want to and choose to do so.

For Kierkegaard, faith is not the result of objective information processed by the intellect. The subjective thinking that achieves faith is motivated by a passionate despairing search for answers. And faith involves the whole personality; intellect and reason are involved, but the motivation is hope and despair. Only in faith do we find our own self and the answer to the old questions. Our despair is cured only by an openness which, beyond any disclosure of the self to other human beings, leaves the self transparent before God. The unease we experience with time at the aesthetic is resolved when, at the religious stage, we find divine and eternal significance in each passing moment. According to Kierkegaard, human personality ceases to despair when, transparent before God, the self finds in every moment the hope of eternal life.

Kierkegaard sees human life as beginning in despair. We have to acknowledge our despair and admit that life really is as awful as it seems. What Kierkegaard calls despair, and what we experience as despair, theologians call sin. Despair is sin; and sin pre-supposes human freedom. This despair-sin involves free choice and decision. And in Kierkegaard's psychological-theological analysis the opposite of sin is not, as in traditional religious thought, virtue or goodness; the opposite of despair-sin is faith. In

Kierkegaard's account, faith is also a description of life free from despair.

Kierkegaard regards this despair-sin as the result of our reluctance or refusal to find our self in God. Faith, for Kierkegaard, is its opposite, when like a confident swimmer, 'floating over 70,000 fathoms', we know that the water, or God, will hold us up. If we admit to our despair and, in the faith of the religious stage, acknowledge God as its only cure, we can open ourselves to God; then, according to Kierkegaard, the ethical and aesthetic return to be enjoyed. Now aware of right and wrong, good and bad, and aware that our human attempt to live according to the ethical leaves us despairing, we are nudged in the direction of an absolute God who alone can cure our despair. And Kierkegaard holds that the leap of faith having been made, the aesthetic awareness of life's finite pleasures returns, not obscured by the reality of death, but with the affirmation that death does not have the last word. The transient beauty of people, of music and a sunset hold the promise of a permanence beyond death in the vision of God.

3

A Seeker of Identity: Thomas Merton's Christian Self-Actualization

This tendency might be phrased as the desire . . . to become everything that one is capable of becoming . . . Self-actualization phrasings also stress the making real or actual of what the person already is, though in a potential form.

(Abraham Maslow, *Motivation and Personality*)

The secret of my full identity is hidden in Him. He alone can make me who I am, or rather who I will be when I at last fully begin to be.

(Thomas Merton, *Seeds of Contemplation*)

Contemporary philosophy and modern literature often question the reality of the self and human identity. But everyday experience and common sense suggest that our behaviour originates in part from a self; most of us believe that our self exists over time, has an independent identity, is an agent capable of making free choices. The self may be deconstructed in the plays and fiction of Pirandello, Beckett and other moderns. But the prince in Hamlet and the king in Lear, though they have identity problems, do not doubt that they have identities. Most plays and novels still have characters with selfs who think, feel and decide.

The self is also to be found in modern humanistic psychology. In common with common sense and human experience, with a central tradition in Western philosophy and with most literature, humanistic psychology assumes the reality of the human self. Humanistic psychologists go further and counsel us to be true to this self of ours. The advice, 'To thine own self be true', is not limited to the plays of

Shakespeare and the novels of Henry James but is central to humanistic psychology.

At the end of the nineteenth and the beginning of the twentieth century, when Henry James was writing fiction exploring this moral self, his psychologist brother William was analysing the self in psychology. While Henry was examining the reality and significance of human identity in his novels, William was attempting its scientific analysis. In *Principles of Psychology* (1890), William James provides the first important account of the self in modern psychology. His scientific analysis is perceptive, but the human self which he investigates does not differ much from the self of his brother's novels, the self of everyday experience and common sense. William James' self is real; it may change over time, but an identity remains, making free choices.

William James starts from the personal continuity of which we are aware in our lives. He writes of an empirical self or Me, divided into material, social and spiritual selfs. James' material self consists of our body, bodily instincts, dress, even possessions such as house, car and bank account. James' social self is the roles which we occupy in society, such as shop-keeper, parent, neighbour. The social self consists of the recognition that we receive from others, particularly from those close to us, and of aspects of ourselves such as ambition and envy. The third element in this empirical self is the spiritual self which, says James, is 'a man's inner or subjective being, his psychic faculties or dispositions, taken concretely . . . These psychic dispositions are the most enduring and intimate part of the self, that which we most verily seem to be.' Our intellectual and moral capacities, which his novelist brother was so interested in, are part of James' spiritual self. But James qualifies what he has to say about this spiritual self: '. . . the Spiritual Self, so far as it belongs to the Empirical Me'.

James's spiritual self overlaps with what he calls the pure ego. He sees this ego as the inner principle which constitutes the unity of personal identity, approximating to what we call consciousness. James regards the material, social and spiritual selfs which make up my empirical self or Me as based on empirical data; these selfs are part of my experience, and I experience them. But he is not happy with explaining in a similar empirical way this 'I' which does the experiencing. So, is this experiencing 'I' a special unknown immaterial substance of the sort that Descartes and others hold mind to be? Or is 'I' just a bundle of sensations, as Hume asserts? James in the end adopts an explanation in terms of a 'stream of consciousness.' We come to regard as our 'I' and very self the thoughts that pass through us, this 'stream of consciousness'. He sees personal identity and pure ego as an awareness of continuity, the perception of sameness among certain phenomena. Who or what is aware and does the perceiving remains problematic. But, says James, as far as psychology is concerned this will do; there is no need to come up with explanations in terms of something outside the realm of science such as a 'non-phenomenal Thinker' behind this stream of consciousness.

William James concedes that the suggestion that there is only this stream of passing thoughts runs counter to our experience; his novelist brother would have agreed. William James sees that a belief in a 'distinct principle of selfhood' seems commonsense. After all, introspection makes us aware of James' distinction between I and Me. I can know my Me almost in the way I can know my friend. The Me or empirical self seems in part an object of my experience. But the 'I' which does the knowing seems to defy explanation. The 'I' cannot be just another object of experience, since the 'I' itself does the experiencing. But, James points out, if we concede such a distinct principle – call it self, pure ego, 'I' or soul – we are left with something which science is neither able to describe nor explain.

James is trying to keep to what he sees as his brief as scientist. He believes that to regard the thinker as made up of passing thoughts is as far as psychology needs to go. He does not take this to mean that there is no further to go, since it remains possible that there does exist a knower independent of what is known. This possibility, he contends, moves the problem beyond the remit of psychology. If there does exist such an independent knower, who or what this knower is becomes a metaphysical problem. But James holds that any such spiritual and transcendental solution might be as valid here as any purely psychological solution, such as his own 'stream of consciousness'.

With the death of William James in 1910, and particularly while behaviourism remained dominant, the notion of the self became unpopular in psychology. In the middle of the twentieth century the self re-emerged as a key concept in various kinds of counselling and psychotherapy. Under the heading of humanistic psychology, the notion of the self has been developed by Abraham Maslow, Carl Rogers and others. In considering the ideas of Maslow and Rogers we are abandoning the self as a neutral philosophical concept; we are moving to a self related to ideas of psychological health, to a 'To thine own self be true' self. We are moving from self to self-actualization.

The self keeps recurring in psychology because the concept of self expresses something real in human experience. Self-actualization expresses what humanistic psychology regards as equally real, namely, that humans need to find meaning and fulfilment in life. As religion declined in the West, and evolutionary theory provided an explanation of human existence as a product of chance, it became difficult to discover meaning in the external world. So the question was asked: can meaning to our lives be found within ourselves, in our internal psychological world? To this question, modern literature in the form of writers such as Camus, Ionesco, Kafka, Pirandello and Beckett have answered 'No'. To the same question, modern psychology in the shape of humanistic psychology has answered 'Yes'.

Secular humanistic psychology maintains that individuals can find values which give meaning and significance to their lives by actualizing their true selfs. Techniques have been developed for helping people to self-actualize, such as psychotherapy, encounter groups, Gestalt therapy, psychodrama, counselling and co-counselling. All such approaches are based on the view that it is largely through human relationships that people grow psychologically and actualize their selfs.

Thomas Merton too is concerned with questions of self, of 'who I am and what I am', and of how to realize this identity. Merton, too, regards the answer to such questions as fundamental to human life and central to personality. However, for Merton, the universe in which such questions are asked is not empty and meaningless. Merton holds that the human self and identity have an absolute and ultimate reality, which is found in God. Our identity and self are literally God-given. Merton regards the search for the self as inseparable from the search for God.

For Abraham Maslow, the founding-father of humanistic psychology, the self refers to a human being's inner core or nature, part of which consists of ideals, values, goals, interests. Maslow held that a new psychology was needed, one not preoccupied with guilt, aggression, human unhappiness and mental illness, but based instead on joy, love, creativity and psychological health. Maslow's psychology is concerned with personal growth and achieving a fulfilled personality.

Maslow's holistic theory of personality holds that humans have a psychological structure of needs, capacities and tendencies which are genetically based. Just as humans have an innate biological structure, so too they have a core psychological structure. According to Maslow, there exists a genetic blueprint for everyone which lays down how their personality should develop for psychological health. Healthy and desirable development consists in actualizing this innate nature and potential. Learning and experience are important to the extent that they help, or hinder, personality to develop according to this genetic blueprint. When this 'essential nature' is frustrated, unhappiness, and even mental illness, result.

Maslow's account of personality is best known for its hierarchy of needs. The five needs are, first, physiological, followed by needs for safety, for belongingness and love, for esteem, and for self-actualization. The physiological needs are those such as hunger, thirst, sex. Safety needs refer to avoiding danger and obtaining security, varying from a baby's need for physical support in the mother's arms to an adult's concern for job security. Belongingness and love are social needs, and include both wanting to give and receive love and affection, and belonging to a social group such as the family. Esteem needs embrace a need for the appreciation and recognition which give humans a sense of worth and value. Lastly, but central to Maslow's account of personality, is self-actualization. Self-actualization, says Maslow, is the human need 'to become everything one is capable of becoming'. Self-actualization is about realising our true potential, becoming all that we have it in ourselves to be. In self-actualization, we become the self which we truly are. But such a need can never be completely satisfied.

Since needs are part of our innate psychological nature, healthy personality development is not the result of shaping by the environment. Personality development is a growing from within, is an unfolding of what is already there, is a fulfilling and actualizing of potentialities that already exist. Failure to self-actualize may be the product of ignorance, but more likely we fail because our environment and external social world have prevented us. According to Maslow, given the right circumstances we will always move in the direction of self-actualization.

Maslow holds that once our basic physiological, safety, social and esteem needs are satisfied, the need for self-actualization becomes insistent. His research confirms that having the four basic needs satisfied, though essential, is never enough to fulfil human beings; people still seek purpose and meaning in their lives. Humans are motivated not just to survive by satisfying their deficiences, but also by the need to achieve some kind of wholeness through psychological growth and self-actualizing.

On the basis of observations, reading, interviews and biographical data, Maslow has listed characteristics of self-actualizing people. It is particularly interesting that self-actualizers have what Maslow calls peak experiences. Such experiences are characterized by a variety of feelings – joy, ecstasy, awe, power, wonder, being outside time, a sense of closeness to something important like a valuable insight. In these moments, people become aware of the remarkable possibilities within them. The experience may be triggered off in a variety of ways, such as by the presence of a loved person or by hearing a favourite piece of music. The experiences are not long, but while they last they have an absorbed passivity about them and are a sort of inexpressible revelation. Whatever causes these peak experiences – the birth of a child, a moment of stillness in a forest, a creative moment at work, the awareness of other people in the street – they convey a sense of unity with oneself, with others and even with the universe. Maslow's peak experiences resemble Joyce's epiphanies and the 'timeless moments' of the poet T.S.Eliot.

Carl Rogers is another major contributor to our knowledge of the self and self-actualization. Working as a therapist, Rogers observed that people who came to him strove to achieve their potential and to live fulfilled lives. Though on the surface humans seem to have a variety of needs and motives, Rogers sees them all as serving one master motive, self-actualization. If we do not always act in a way that leads to self-actualization, it is because of inadequate knowledge and awareness. If we know what leads to self-actualization, this is what we will always choose. In Rogers' view, given the right experience we will always move in the direction of self-actualization and a healthy self.

For Rogers, the basic condition for a healthy self is the experience of unconditional love. If our parents loved and accepted us unconditionally as children, then as adults we can love and accept ourselves just as we are. If we have been loved without strings, we do not have to disown our self or any part of it. Unconditional love lays the foundations for healthy psychological development and self-actualization.

Unfortunately most of us do not receive unconditional love as children. Rogers sees children as usually being loved and valued only if they do what their parents want, or if they think and feel what their parents want them to think and feel. They are loved, for example, only if they stop bullying their younger brother or stop wanting to bully him. Rogers holds that this loving only conditionally is not an appropriate way of making children behave. But as a consequence of having been loved only conditionally, we grow up accepting our self only in part. The result is that our self becomes fragmented, full of guilt, not valuing itself, and unable to admit what it really feels and thinks. If the damage to the self is severe, neurosis is the result.

For Rogers, the opposite of a damaged self is the fully functioning person. Open to experience, alive in the present and trusting to their own reactions, fully functioning persons are Rogers' picture of how humans ought to be. Rogers claims that when people self-actualize and become fully functioning persons, they develop in the same direction, regardless of culture or background. As we have already seen, he reports that when people progress in psychotherapy the qualities which characterize them have 'a certain universality'. He found, for example, that people emerged from successful therapy wanting to love more, with more concern for others, with more acceptance and compassion both for others and themselves, trying to be more rational in their lives, seeking greater understanding of other people, seeking good relationships with others, and wanting to be able to trust others more.

Similarly, Rogers speaks of a 'valuing process', a wisdom of the whole human person, which knows what is morally good. This valuing process, though affected by our experience, particularly by our experience of unconditional love, is innate and resembles the conscience of traditional religion. Religious believers see conscience as in some sense the still small voice of God within, distinguishing between right and wrong in the interests of our soul's salvation. Rogers sees this valuing process as distinguishing between right and wrong in the interests of our living fulfilled lives and of achieving a true self.

For Rogers, becoming our true self does not involve becoming a new and different person. Quite the contrary. For Rogers and other humanistic psychologists, the change involved in self-actualization involves moving away from a false self, which one is not, to the real self, which one truly is. This brings us back to the novels of Henry James and forward to the ideas of Thomas Merton. In Maslow and Rogers, and the literary tradition of which James is part, the self may become stunted and twisted, but our true self remains always potentially there, regardless of any damage done by experience. And in our true self we discover values to live by and meaning in our lives. With this, as far as it goes, Thomas Merton would agree.

For Merton, God is central, not the self; the basic motivation of personality is the search for God. But Merton holds that the search for God is also the search for self, and the search for self and identity is inseparable from the search for God. Holiness is wholeness, and wholeness is holiness; finding God, we find our true self and other people. Merton, like humanistic psychologists, stresses that the discovery of other people is involved in the search. But according to Merton, only God possesses my true self or identity, and only God holds the secret of who I am. If I find God, I find my true self; if I find my true self, I find God.

The research of Maslow and Rogers confirms the commonsense observation that human beings are never satisfied. Both Maslow and Rogers relate human dissatisfaction to the absence of self-actualization and place the explanation in the natural order. However, for Merton, self-actualization is to be found largely outside the natural order of biology and society. Merton's account of personality differs critically from that of humanistic psychology in holding that one's true self is to be discovered only in God. The search for identity is in large part the search for God.

For Rogers, there is the fully functioning person and the damaged self. In Merton's account, too, there are two selfs. There is what Merton calls the true self; he also refers to this as the real, inmost, inner or hidden self, and as person or identity. In contrast is what Merton calls the false self. Merton uses a variety of terms for the false self – external self, superficial self, empirical self, outward self, outer self, shadow self, smoke self, contingent self, imaginary self, private self, illusory self, hedonistic and destructive ego, superficial ego. Human life involves a series of choices between our true and false self. Like many humanistic psychologists, Merton regards 'good and bad', 'right and wrong', as related to our true and false selfs. However, for Merton, the false self 'is not by nature evil . . . as long as it does not isolate itself in a lie, it is blessed by the mercy and love of Christ' (*Seeds of Contemplation*, 1972).

Like Freud's notion of life and death instincts, Merton talks of two forces at work in humans. One force is a tendency taking us away from God and our true self. As a result of this natural negative force, which works against finding God, we create a false self founded on illusion and fantasy. This first, negative force at work in us is what Christianity has traditionally expressed as 'original sin'. Merton sees original sin, and the Genesis account of the Fall and the ejection from Eden, as a statement about alienation. The human condition is one of alienation and exile from God and our true self. In our present state we are not united to God, ourself and other human beings in the way our nature longs to be. This is partly because of the work of this first, negative force within us.

Merton's second force is positive; it comes from God and moves us in the direction of God and of who we really are. Merton sees this force as the activity of the Holy Spirit. The incarnation, God becoming human, has made it possible for our condition of alienation to end. In the Christian account, God died on the cross to enable us to leave our condition of exile. The Christian life is a returning home to God, our true self and others.

Though Merton's account resembles that of humanistic psychology, he is also influenced by a much starker body of thought. Existentialism sees a terrible void at the core of human experience: we are permeated by and poised over nothingness; we live with a constant awareness of death, guilt, pain and the fragility of human life; we are haunted by anxiety and a sense of alienation; we are free, and terrified by the responsibility of freedom; we realize that life might be utterly meaningless. This is the existential perspective, and is where Merton starts from in human experience.

Existential psychology sees that life begins with human beings finding themselves, so to speak, thrown into existence. We wake up and find ourselves alive. And, to begin with, our lives have a very public quality: we occupy roles and in roles such as female, adult, wife, teacher, neighbour, 'one does this and one does that'. Martin Heidegger and other existentialist philosophers regard this everyday way of existing as below the truly human; Heidegger calls it inauthentic. In the inauthentic mode, we live as one of the crowd in the roles which society provides and we are in no sense a self. In the existentialist account, all of us start life at the inauthentic level and we are tempted to remain there.

But according to existentialism, we have a choice. I can choose to live inauthentically – at the level of my public mask, choosing to see myself as object rather than subjective self, avoiding the reality of suffering and change and guilt and freedom and responsibility, accepting the defences that society and culture provide. Such a choice relates ultimately to my attitude to death. To see death as just a boundary, the end of the road somewhere ahead, is to view it inauthentically. Alternatively I can attempt to achieve a true self and to be authentic. Authenticity and a true self involve confronting death as my own real possibility here and now, and my certain experience soon. Death so considered discloses that my being is permeated through and through with non-being.

But, in the existential account, I cannot win. If I choose to live inauthentically, I will have the guilt of my unrealized potential, of my failure to self-actualize. If I choose to live authentically by the exercise of my freedom, I achieve my real self, but at the price of constant anxiety. I will live with constant anxiety, because authenticity is achieved only by acknowledging that non-being permeates my being and death is always close.

Merton, too, sees that we have to acknowledge the void; there is no alternative, since it is within us. Merton holds that if we screen ourselves from the starker dimensions of reality by hiding our faces behind a mask, then the mask will hide our true self. We will find our true self only if we are naked and vulnerable before this terrifying dimension of life. Like existential psychologists, Merton holds that a solution to the void can only emerge through the exercise of freedom. We must use our freedom to renounce the false self and, for Merton, the self's freedom is rooted ultimately in God.

Merton differs from existential psychology in what he sees as the solution to the realities of the void, guilt, anxiety, pain, death, the negative force within us and life's apparent lack of meaning. He knows how true to our experience these disturbing existential realities are. He recognizes the apparent validity of a Camus-type absurdity and of Sartre's nausea at an alien, even hostile, world which asks questions but gives no answers. But Merton does not take such realities as the final word. The solution, for Merton, is to be found in the self's achieving an identity in God.

Merton sees that the transient natural world of biology and society contain nothing that will completely satisfy us – only God will do this. As human beings we are alienated from the ground of our being, which is the reality of God. The only solution to existential terror is another terror, that of discovering God. In finding God, we find our identity in God. Though the fragility of our lives remains, we know our selves to be real because they are rooted in the non-contingent reality of God, and loved by the One Who Is. Our reality comes from God, who is the only source of our reality; and this is more than enough.

In Christian tradition, the purpose of our lives cannot relate to anything created, such as pleasure, honour, power, material possessions. Our purpose and happiness are to be found only in the uncreated God. Merton sees that before we can come to God we must be detached from the natural world and from everything created. If we live according to the dictates of our false exterior self and solely in the passing world, we are immersed in fantasy and illusion; we are taking non-being as the basis for our existence. We need to take the reality of God, and of our true self in God, as the foundation for our existence.

For Merton, the Christian response to the condition that existentialism depicts goes further. Whatever guilt we feel, and however unlikeable we may think ourselves to be, God loves us. Christian belief proclaims that humans are loved by God and are loved irrespective of worth. The Christian revelation of God dying on the cross, for love of humanity, makes irrelevant any idea of worth, merit, deserts. According to Hamlet, 'Use every man after his desert, and who should 'scape whipping?' According to Carl Rogers, we need to be unconditionally loved by another human being. According to Merton, we need to be unconditionally loved by God and – more to the point – we are. Merton stresses how important it is for us actually to realize that we are unconditionally loved by God.

To discover this all-loving God, we can only start from where we are, at the inauthentic public level. To find our God-given self in God, we must begin from what we are, which – in Merton's terms – is a false self. At first, according to Merton, we have no alternative but to behave as if this false outer self is really what we are. But this exterior self which we tend to regard as real is a shell. We try to give pseudo-reality to this false superficial self, which at some level we already know to be an illusion, by stuffing it with pleasure, sex, power, honour, knowledge. For Merton, sin consists in holding on to this false identity; sin is a sort of mistake, a misguided attempt to be what we are not. No matter how much we bolster up this illusory identity with our egoism and pleasures, this fraudulent self remains an empty shell, destined to crumble into the nothingness it really is, leaving us aware how hollow we are. In *The New Man*, Merton quotes St Bernard: 'By enjoying perishable things as though they were its last end, the soul has put on mortality like a garment. The garment of immortality remains underneath, not cast off, but discoloured by the overcast garment of death.'

So the first step to discovering my true self and God is the realization that this surface self is sham. 'Everyone of us is shadowed by an illusory person: a false self. This is the man that I want myself to be but who cannot exist, because God does not know anything about him. And to be unknown of God is altogether too much privacy' (*Seeds of Contemplation*). If I try to live with this false self, to live the self that I am not, I am living a deception. Ibsen's Peer Gynt suggests a similar notion: if I live self-ishly, as the king of the trolls suggests, I end up, like the onion from which Peer peels skin after skin, with nothing at the centre. I have to realize that this false exterior self is a fiction of my own making, which I create by what I do, especially by actions and behaviour which are selfish. This may be the self which at one level I want to be; but such a self has no reality because it exists outside God's love – though the very reason why I cling to this false self is because it 'exists' outside God's love. In Graham Greene's *The Power and the Glory*, the whisky priest says, 'A man like me would run a mile to get away if he felt that love around.' But Merton says that, though the false superfical self is con-stituted of what is not God, such a self should not be regarded as wholly bad. Like the public inauthentic self of existential psychology, it is simply where we start from. I have no alternative but to start from where I am, which is the alienated condition of having a false self. But if I go on clinging to this external self it becomes an obstacle, keeping me from God and my true self. Merton sees that this false self is not so much false as external, what we are on the surface; beneath the surface exists an inner real self. Meanwhile this exterior self functions at the level of appearances and illusion; but ap-pearances and illusion can be seen through. Eventually by means such as prayer and contemplation we may see and recognize God beneath the appearances and illusion.

Merton believed that if we are to find our true self in God, it is also necessary to experience the void within us. Though painful, this should not be too difficult since, according to existential psychology and Merton, our experience is that nothing in the world fully satisfies. And death is always there to remind us of our transience and of the false self's fragility. Towards the end of the play, Hamlet achieves a sort of authenticity through an acceptance of death: '. . . there is special providence in the fall of a sparrow. If it be now, 'tis not to come: if it be not to come, it will be now: if it be not now, yet it will come; the readiness is all.' Death can make us aware that we are real only when we exist in God. We have to abandon, says Merton, any idea that the void can be filled by anything in immediate experience. In saying this, Merton moves away from any secular this-world solution provided by existentialist and humanistic psychology. Only by finding God, and in God finding our true self, can we fill the void within us.

Merton holds that many of life's problems are a product of our false self. This illusory self, not unreasonably, seeks to be happy, but happiness is not something that we can find by seeking. Our fantasies, phobias and neuroses are ultimately a product of this false self, and without God we have no way of overcoming them. According to Merton, without God humans have no way of transcending these desperate creations of the false self and are condemned to despair. These fantasies, phobias and neuroses possess a sort of sham immortality, since they endure as long as our false self exists. Without God, in this closed circle of the material world, there is no solution. Consequently, deep down we long (as Freud's death instinct suggests) for the only way out, namely, death.

But Merton's view is that we have a choice. The choice is between this false external mask and our genuine self, between the old man which St Paul invites us to put off and the new man he invites us to put on. The exterior self, when eventually recognized as a fiction of our own making, can be renounced. This is not the destruction of our true self, Merton stresses, but rather the abandonment of an illusion. By working hard, psychologically and spiritually, we come to recognize as an impostor this fraudulent self which we thought ourself to be. As our false self evaporates, the self that we really are begins to emerge.

Merton is at one with humanistic psychology in refusing to regard the true self as some ideal or desirable model we have to live up to. Merton, like Maslow and Rogers, sees this true self as something we already are and which needs only to be revealed. But Merton's account differs from that of secular psychology because he holds that the real self is what God calls us to, though God calls us to be nothing other than what we really are. Becoming a saint, says Merton, simply involves discovering my true self. The new self that we 'discover' has been there all the time, as a potential yet to be realized. This potential was always there because human beings are made in the image and likeness of God. The true self is God's call to us at the ground of our being to be one with God.

Merton holds that our true self, in some mysterious way, already exists in God. And the God who became human in Christ, died for us on the cross and rose again from the dead, is ever ready to give us our true self and identity. We do not have to steal our identity from God, like Prometheus stealing fire from the gods. Merton insists that God is prepared to hand us our true self as a gift. God is always calling us to our true self; but we fear this call, because we realize that our true self will involve the death of our false self. Just as faith is needed to discover God, so too faith is needed if I am to find my genuine self. Faith makes possible 'through a glass darkly' knowledge of our God-given self.

For Merton, faith involves risk, and eventually we have to risk allowing God's call to deliver us from the prison of our false self. This call invites us to a consciousness that is deeper than our exterior self. The call invites us to be reborn to the true self given by God, which was damaged by sin, but is restored by Jesus Christ. According to Merton, through such rebirth we come to an awareness that we are not just our own selves, but we are one with a God who transcends the limits of our individual humanity. This spiritual rebirth initiates in us the second, positive force that eventually transforms us within. If Merton's first force is like the Freudian death instinct, this second force within us resembles Freud's life instinct. The first force, a natural tendency taking us away from God and our true identity, has created a false self built on illusion and fantasy. The second force, coming from God, moves us to God and transforms us into who we really are. The transformation recovers that which is deepest in us, most uniquely our own, and most personal.

Merton uses the metaphor of a snake sloughing off its skin. Through a continuous process of rebirth, the false self with its superficial life becomes discarded like an old skin, and a true self is revealed. This rebirth moves us away from selfishness in the direction of greater love, away from the inauthentic self to Christ, away from a false self to where God's spirit acts through our true self. And Merton concludes that since our self is made in the image of God and God is love, we now realize that love is the reason for our existence.

Previously, as a false self, we were constantly on the defensive; now we experience no need to defend our self, because we know how real it is. The obvious Christian model for the real self is Christ. But Christ is more than our model; Christ is already deep within us, says Merton, united and identified with our true inner self. The answer for the Christian to the question of who and what I am is – I am one loved by Christ.

In the humanistic psychology of Maslow, Rogers and others, the discovery and actualizing of our self are a purely natural process. But

Merton, like many Christian writers, holds that we cannot find God and our true self by our own efforts. God has to act and intervene. Certainly of our own initiative we can use our mind to think about God. We can achieve an intellectual grasp of the reality of God, of our identity in God, and of the meaning these discoveries give to life. But these truths also need to come to us as felt experience.

Merton's guidelines for finding the true self are the same as those for finding God, since ultimately they are one and the same search. Find God and you find your self. And we find God, and our true self, through prayer and contemplation, through faith and love, through self-emptying in imitation of Christ. Prayer helps with this self-emptying and with revealing the falsity of the false self. Though no technique of prayer is going to sort everything out, Merton stresses that in prayer we become more open. We grow as human beings by opening ourselves to life's experiences; certainly we grow by opening ourselves to the experience of God, and here especially prayer is important. In prayer we deepen our faith and love, develop acceptance and trust, experience reverence and joy. In this way, prayer helps to liberate us from the inauthentic false self and to discover our true authentic self.

Merton holds that the conventional practices of religion play their part too, especially if we carry them out in a spirit of abandonment to God's will. Church-going, self-sacrifice, the service of others, listening to sermons, reading spiritual books. For Christians, there are the guidelines of the Ten Commandments, the Beatitudes, and the teachings of the church. For those living in the world, the duties of everyday life done for God, of family, of work, of social living, are part of the path. For those not called to contemplation, it is usually a large part of the path.

Merton takes the traditional view that for such ordinary Christians, living ordinary lives, the daily cross is central. Once Christ's cross has been accepted as part of our everyday life, we begin to be liberated from the world's illusions and to participate in everyday living in an appropriate way. Merton stresses that the love and service of others is central. Loving others is a manifestation of our love for God and involves the same love. 'A man cannot enter into the deepest centre of himself and pass through that centre into God, unless he is able to pass entirely out of himself and empty himself and give himself to other people in the purity of a selfless love' (*Seeds of Contemplation*). And if we are to find God and our identity in the world while we pray, love and serve others, we need silence and solitude. In society we tend to cling to false masks, but alone in silence before God a mask becomes pointless.

There are those who fulfil their vocation, of ordinary life in the world, by serving God in active ways, at the same time praying and attempting to live their lives in abandonment to God's will. Merton calls such people quasi- or hidden contemplatives. If these quasi- or hidden contemplatives live in the everyday world, praying, serving others and refusing to take as real the false self and its desires, something undramatic may happen. Merton declares that such people, aware of God's presence, may eventually enjoy moments of genuine contemplation. In their prayer life, church-going, service of others and everyday tasks, they may sometimes experience a unity with God.

But Merton is conscious that even at this quasi- or hidden-contemplative level there is the danger that the practices of religion may be used as an escape. He sees that Christians faithfully following their religion can still be dominated by an external false self. The danger is in using religious practices to evade a confrontation with the existential void within and to avoid acknowledging the possibility that life is meaningless.

There is always the danger of using religious practices to evade the experience of the void or to reduce its intensity. But Merton believes that we all have to enter the void sooner or later. Despair in the existential void, which resembles the mystic's 'dark night', makes us aware that the world is a desert and a place of exile. We are only at home in God, and we usually learn this in the void. The void, which existential atheists see as ultimate reality, is only part of the journey. Merton holds that if we are stripped in the void of all pretension and reliance on self, we will stop clinging desperately to the god of our false self, and the true God will enter. We discover that we have fallen out of the void into the liberating reality of God's love.

After much waiting, our true self and God emerge from this dark night. We discover that, though we had seemed alone in the void, God was always with us, as companion and (disturbingly) as adversary. It is God that we had been struggling with, as Gerard

Manley Hopkins, the poet, suggests: 'I wretch lay wrestling with (my God!) my God.' Eventually, and perhaps without even our knowing, we find God.

Quasi- or hidden contemplatives in the ordinary world, as well as contemplatives in monasteries and convents, have eventually to let go and trust God. At least we have started to develop and grow when, aware that our only hope is God, we stop clinging to our false illusory self. When this self has become empty, God can enter in. When God has entered in, we are transformed from a false to a true self. God reveals to us our true self and we discover our identity hidden with Christ in God. The self becomes what at its deepest level it always was, the image of God. For Merton, this discovery of God and the true self becomes at the same time a discovery of our responsibility and love for others.

In Merton's account, the only complete way – this side of death and eternal life – in which we discover God and actualize our true self is through the prayer called contemplation. Experience of God provides the real knowledge of who God is and who we are in God; the mystic has this experience, and so does the true contemplative. Merton makes an orthodox distinction between two kinds of contemplation, active and passive; he tends to use the term infused rather than passive. Merton suggests that mystical experience, and even the experience of infused contemplative prayer, is not for everyone. But he suggests that we can all prepare for such an experience; and the preparation takes us part of the way.

Everyday prayer, and participation in church liturgy and communal religious services, are examples of active contemplation. According to Merton, they affect our experience of reality since through them we can discover transcendent meaning within ordinary life. In revealing this meaning, they transfigure life. God's grace is present in this type of contemplation, but much depends on us and our active participation. This active contemplation of formal prayer and participation in liturgy is not only of value in itself but also prepares us for true infused contemplation. Merton believes that such active contemplation gives a foretaste of the real self experienced in infused contemplation.

Infused contemplative prayer is, in Merton's account, the most perfect self-actualization. But most Christians are not contemplatives in this elevated sense. Merton's view is that in such infused contemplation, the true self actualizes in a way that apparently loses itself and, by becoming identified with God, achieves its true absolute identity. This is not an alienation or loss of self, but rather a discovery of a true self in Christ and God. A human being is made one with divine Being. Merton sees such contemplation as a transforming experience in which the identity received is that of the self and of a Person other than the self. Merton takes St Paul's, 'It is now no longer I that live, but Christ lives in me,' as capturing the experience of infused contemplation.

For Merton, true contemplatives are existentialist in that they commit themselves to a choice and decision for which there is ultimately no proof. They do so in the hope that in the uncertainty on which they stake their lives, they will find a God beyond proofs. Merton holds that if genuine infused contemplation is achieved, contemplatives experience and know in a mysterious way a God beyond all knowledge, and will find their real selfs in God.

Merton regards the true self as beyond empirical and scientific observation, which is partly also the case with the self and self-actualization of Rogers and Maslow. For Merton, this true inner self is the image of God and, like God, cannot be defined and contained in concepts. Merton saw God as yet another victim of Descartes' preoccupation with the subject-object distinction. If I take myself as the subject and God as the object which I seek, then at one level the enterprise is doomed to failure. God cannot be experienced as an object; nor can my true self. This true self is subject, not object, and can be known only through an experience which is also the experience of God.

But such infused contemplation is mystical and out of the natural order. Merton sees this passive contemplation as taking human personality to a deeper level of experience than does the active contemplation of formal prayer, liturgical worship, and even human love. True infused contemplation, Merton says, goes beyond and transcends all objects, ideas, speculation, creativity, to rest in that which cannot be captured and expressed in concepts or words. But such contemplation is a gift of God and, apart from preparation through active contemplation, there is little the individual can do to obtain such a gift.

However, there are other more modest forms of contemplation. As might be expected of someone who has written much poetry, Merton has something to say about poetry and the arts, and their relation to the self. He regards an aesthetic response, to a Shakespeare play, a Beethoven symphony, a Rembrandt painting, as a valuable experience. Merton sees such experience as a form of active contemplation, like religious worship and human love. For Merton such experience, whether of aesthetic appreciation or of artistic creation, is like the mystical experience of the contemplative, but at a natural level. An aesthetic experience which is not mere hedonistic response goes beyond and transcends the order of the senses. 'In an aesthetic experience, in the creation or the contemplation of a work of art, the psychological conscience is able to attain some of its highest and most perfect fulfillments' (*No Man is an Island*, 1955).

Merton's account of such aesthetic moments resembles Maslow's peak experiences. 'Art enables us to find ourselves and lose ourselves at the same time. The mind that responds to the intellectual and spiritual values that lie hidden in a poem, a painting, or a piece of music, discovers a spiritual vitality that lifts it above itself, takes it out of itself, and makes it present to itself on a level of being that it did not know it could ever achieve' (*No Man is an Island*).

Merton's account of aesthetic experiences, resembling also James Joyce's epiphanies, T.S.Eliot's timeless moments and Virginia Woolf's moments of being, relates to his view of contemplative prayer. He says, of both artistic and religious contemplation, 'They belong to the much more mysterious realm of what one "is" – or rather "who" one is' (quoted in *A Thomas Merton Reader*, 1989). Merton believes that a consciousness of the true self is discovered in the experience of the arts. In such moments we discover in ourselves new potential, unexpected powers and a response that lifts us above the everyday level.

Merton believes that aesthetic experiences of the arts have a value for our prayer; but more importantly he regards such experiences as a form of prayer or contemplation in themselves. He speaks of the aesthetic experience as an intuition beyond reason 'of the latent perfection of things'. Merton is saying that in aesthetic experiences, whether creation or enjoyment of poetry, music, painting or other arts, the real self responds to a higher level of being in a way similar to true contemplation.

Research, particularly by anthropologists, confirms that all human societies have some form of the arts. Human arts range down time as well across cultures. From the earliest myths to contemporary graffiti they emerge with spontaneity and abundance. In cave paintings, simple sculptures, death masks, ancient pots, the human arts go back in time to our prehistoric ancestors. Confronted by the arts, we are not only aware of the presence of human beings, but we recognize a common humanity. When the Altimira cave paintings were discovered by a girl with her father in 1879, scholars at the time did not believe that they were the work of our ancestors of 10 to 20,000 years ago. Because the paintings were so fine, so obviously 'us', the scholars held that they could not be the work of prehistoric humans. Only years later were they accepted as just that. What had blinded the 1879 scholars was the recognition in the paintings of an artistic talent so obviously 'modern and contemporary'. Since then painters like Picasso, Klee, Leger and Miro have turned to such ancient work for ideas and inspiration, recognizing a common talent and humanity in this art of prehistoric humans. So what has psychology to say about the relation of the arts to human personality?

Plato proposed the presence of a 'divine spark' to explain the arts. He regarded artists as divinely inspired, declaring 'it is God himself who speaks and addresses us through them'. But modern psychology has proposed more scientific explanations. In Freud's psychoanalytic account, artistic creativity resembles neurosis in originating from conflicts within the unconscious. For example, confronted by the supposed age-old desire to kill his father, what is a son to do? He cannot kill his father because this is not acceptable to his super-ego, to society and his father. So, according to Freud, the desire will be repressed and the result could be a breakdown. Alternatively, a whole variety of defence mechanisms, such as projection, can come into play to reduce tension. With the artist, and with the rest of us, a particularly healthy defence mechanism is sublimation. So Dostoyevsky, instead of acting out the male fantasy of killing the father, writes *The Brothers Karamazov*, a book about killing the father. In the Freudian account, art is an expression of the unconscious, particularly of unconscious conflict, and is an escape from reality.

According to Freud, artists have personalities able to allow ideas and images generated by unconscious conflict to emerge in symbolic form. So Goya sublimates his unconscious aggression into the violent etchings of *The Disasters of War*. Freud's psychoanalytic account is scientific since it regards creative behaviour as caused and determined – by conflict within. His account is also reductionist and materialist, since creativity is seen as nothing but the sublimation of instinctual urges. Freud locates the origins of creativity in the conflicts which we all have, but which the creative individual is able to sublimate. So *Sons and Lovers* is the product of D.H.Lawrence's sublimation of unresolved oedipal feelings for his mother.

Humanistic psychologists, such as Carl Rogers, see artistic activity as related to self-actualization. What happens in a genuine aesthetic experience is that personality self-actualizes. Rogers holds that there exists in all living beings, but particularly in human beings, a spontaneous movement towards the fulfilment of potentiality. In a human being, creating art is part of this psychological growth and self-actualization. We are all capable of such activity, but it emerges in the lives of most of us not as something as grand as writing an opera or poetry; it emerges more modestly in our everyday work, in recreations such as gardening and home decorating, in appreciating opera or poetry.

The sociobiological explanation relates the arts and creativity to biology. Sociobiologists do not claim to have explained the arts fully as yet; but the claim is that one day sociobiology will do so and that the form such an explanation would take is already clear. Human artistic talent, say the sociobiologists, is the result of evolution: our capacity for the arts has developed because of their usefulness. Sociobiologists argue for the usefulness of the arts by relating them to religion and ritual and sympathetic magic. They regard the arts as having nothing to do with mind and free human agents who create, but as the product of our bodies, programmed by evolution. According to sociobiology, our artistic abilities developed for the good evolutionary reason that they increased our chances of survival.

Other psychological explanations of the arts are the behaviourist account and Winnicott's more recent transitional objects account.

Behaviourism holds that new artistic behaviours come to replace old behaviours as a result of trial and error, reward and punishment. Creativity is the process of substituting new behaviours for old. When new artistic behaviours are substituted for old or when new combinations of behaviours arise, as a result of conditioning, we have creativity and the arts. According to behaviourism, humans are born blank slates, and the arts are a product of environmental shaping, by reward and punishment, of trial and error behaviour. There is no active human agent producing art, and the supposedly free creative actions of artists are caused and determined.

D.W.Winnicott, working in the psychoanalytic tradition, suggests how childhood relates to the arts. Babies begin by sucking and enjoying mother's breasts; but they soon put thumbs, fingers and fists in their mouths instead. After a few months babies get attached to objects like a doll, teddy bear or other cuddly toy, which are not part of baby in the way that thumbs and fingers are. This attachment involves babies in a relationship with something other than themselves. In between these two stages is a third stage which, according to Winnicott, proves crucial for artistic creativity. In this 'transitional' stage babies, as any parent can confirm, take a corner of a sheet, blanket, handkerchief or a piece of string, and push this into or near their mouths. These corners of sheets and handkerchiefs are not the baby's own body like fingers and thumbs; nor are they distinct and separate like dolls and teddy bears. They are transitional objects, and Winnicott sees such transitional objects as the first 'not-me' possessions of a child. As a result, the infant ends up with three realities: the psychological world within; external reality, of which the child becomes increasingly aware; and the in-between world of transitional objects, such as corners of sheets and handkerchiefs which baby puts in the mouth. In this world of transitional not-me objects, human artistic creativity originates.

What Winnicott's account illustrates is that any materialist explanation, no matter how psychological, has to explain human artistic creativity in terms of biology or the environment. For the scientific materialist, there is nothing else. If only biology exists, and the learning which the environment provides, where else might creativity originate? This is the very question Winnicott asks of play: 'If play is neither inside nor outside, where is it?' Winnicott concludes that artistic creativity, and play, originate and exist in this in-between world of objects, transitional from inside to outside.

In suggesting a third area where play and creativity originate, Winnicott is stating in 'objects relations' terms the old body-mind problem. Winnicott's neo-Freudian account regards the arts as caused and determined; but the cause is not outside, as be-haviourism suggests, nor wholly inside within our biology, as sociobiology says. Since, according to materialism, nothing im-material like soul exists, Winnicott concludes that play and creativity originate somewhere between biology and psychology, in the space between body and mind.

In another explanation of creativity (1964), Arthur Koestler returns to mind. He argues that creativity in the arts and science, like humour, brings together previously unrelated frames of reference or experience. At any one time we normally work with one frame of reference or set of rules; we have to, or there would be chaos. When we work creatively, says Koestler, our minds free themselves from this constraint, and they concurrently operate with different frames of reference and sets of rules. In artistic creativity, different planes of experience are juxtaposed. In Keats' 'Ode on a Grecian Urn', one particular fragile urn is set against eternal beauty. The poetry moves us because beauty is described at the same time as its transience is evoked. Whatever the value of Koestler's explanation of the arts, it accords with modern cognitive psychology in returning mind to central place in human activity.

Mind seems always to be at work in the arts. When artistic products are unsigned, experts can usually identify painter, writer, sculptor from the style. Creativity and individuality manifest them-selves within the most precise rules and conventions. According to Alland (1977), the arts represent, and then they transform what they represent into something else. A dancer, conveying by her move-ments a dying swan, transforms the performance into something of wider significance. This is possible because in the creativity of the artist, as well as in the audience's response, mind is at work.

Art historians have demonstrated how throughout history artists have never just copied. Early artists constructed, for example, a face from a choice of forms and shapes. In a Cezanne painting, the order and form on the canvas are not out in the landscape; they exist in

Cezanne's mind, and he imposes them on the scene. Artists of ancient Egypt painted a face in complete profile with both eyes; they did this deliberately, because they took the view that everything important in a face should be included. In painting, and in all arts, there is always a process of selection, organization and active interpretation. This would suggests that the mind at work in the arts is free and active. The artist chooses what to put in and what to leave out, and to transform what is seen; this confirms the cognitive psychology account of humans as mind-ful agents.

Human artistic creativity needs to be explained. And though psychological accounts of creativity are useful and insightful, they do not seem to provide total explanations of the arts. In fact, the determinism of such accounts appears to make the arts impossible, since artistic creativity seems to require the free action of mind and the existence of choice.

Merton sees artistic experiences, whether of creativity or of appreciation, as moments of illumination and of value, like Maslow's peak moments. Merton holds that such aesthetic experiences are a form of contemplation and as such provide an intimation of God. Nevertheless, he sees them as remaining in the natural order. For Merton, their effect is not to be compared with that of infused contemplation which, he holds, takes human personality to a much deeper level than any artistic experience.

But Merton values highly the experience which the arts provide. Music, painting, films, plays, sculpture can lift us out of the mundane into something we experience as more worthwhile and satisfying. Better, they enable us to discover the transcendent within the mundane and so transfigure everyday life. Merton regards artistic experience as a form of active contemplation, like ordinary prayer, liturgical worship and human love. And like active contemplation, artistic experiences can change our view of reality.

Merton suggests that 'artistic contemplation' moves us in the direction of our true identity. The arts are valuable, Merton believes, because a genuine aesthetic experience provides a stepping-stone from the false to the true self. Aesthetic experiences, like active contemplation, anticipate the full actualization of the true self achieved in infused contemplation. In artistic appreciation we go beyond the experience of subject and object as separate. In this identification with what is contemplated, we have a foretaste of infused contemplation. In this sense, the experience of great art can be said to give us here and now an intimation of God and faintly anticipates the vision of God after death.

For Merton, by and large the natural world, of which the arts are part, is the medium in which we seek and find God. But in order not to attribute a false value to the material world, we need a certain detachment. There is a danger in becoming too attached to the world, taking it as an end in itself, and letting earthly things distract us from God who alone is our true end. An awareness of the transience and unfulfilling character of the world is a help to such detachment. However, for Merton there is nothing in the world that of itself is an obstacle to finding God. Quite the opposite. The world, the arts and all living being can lead us to a knowledge and love of God. What is required is that we recognize and react to the presence of God as manifest in the natural world and other people.

For humanistic psychology there is only the material world, and human relationships are part of this world. Humanistic psychology sees relationships, with other adults, with children, with parents, as crucial for the healthy development of the self and self-actualization. Merton, too, regards relationships with others as central to achieving our true self; we find our true self not only in God but in other people. There may be times when we need solitude to be alone with God, but if we isolate ourselves from others, we will never find our self. We find ourself only if we lose ourselves in a selfless love of others. But Merton sees that other humans, no matter how much we love them, are not enough by themselves; God is an essential element. For Merton, finding our true self, loving others, discovering and loving God, are part of the same equation.

And Merton has reservations about a certain kind of emphasis on self adopted in some psychological approaches to self-actualization. Humanistic psychology appears to take self-actualization as the criterion by which to evaluate our lives. For example, with regard to our relationships with others, the question humanistic psychologists usually ask is: do these relationships help us to fulfil ourselves and self-actualize? The danger in such an approach is that other human beings can become merely a means to self-actualization. If particular relationships appear to get in the way of self-actualization, do we end them? Do we walk out on wives, husbands, friends, even children, because we do not find our relationships with them totally fulfilling and self-actualizing?

Merton sees here the risk of becoming too self-regarding. If we cultivate 'being oneself' in the wrong way, there is the danger of placing the self, particularly the false self and its illusory world, at the centre of our lives. Merton holds that self-actualization requires an emptying out. Old-fashioned practices such as self-control may be needed for the transformation from a false to a true self. The search for pleasure, and particularly sexual pleasure, calls for traditional self-denial. Merton regards unrestrained appetites as no foundation for psychological and spiritual development.

With the concept of self-actualization, humanistic psychology possesses a psychological criterion by which to evaluate our lives. In adopting such a criterion, humanistic psychology is redressing an outdated and excessively ascetic approach to the development of personality, based on duty and a negative view of ourselves. Merton welcomes this new approach and the balance which the emphasis on self and self-actualization provides, but he retains God and the approach which the concept of God implies. For Merton, both approaches are needed; the point is that there is no conflict between them. Since the reason for my existence is to be found only in God, the fulfilment of my existence, my true self-actualization, is to be found only in God. And though 'God' at times seems as vague a criterion as self-actualization, and often fails to affect our behaviour, it should make some difference. For Merton, one difference is that the existence of God means that, though the material world is good, there are always questions to be asked of the societies which human beings create and inhabit. Eliot's *The Waste Land* is not a poem on the spiritual poverty of modern culture and the contemporary human self. *The Waste Land* is a statement that most societies, and the selfs which inhabit them, are spiritually impoverished.

Most societies are impoverished because humans always tend to exclude God. Merton certainly holds that the world is the place where we meet God, especially where we meet God in others. But human societies are continually generating accounts of the world which omit the divine. The veil which modern Western culture draws over death makes it possible even for death to be almost ignored. But we would never be naive enough to be deceived by such accounts if they did not have the support of society. We have to attempt to transcend the world where it culturally embodies the false self, and this the notion of God encourages us to do. And the attempt to transcend society where God is absent means that all Christians must at some level be contemplatives.

And what, according to Merton, do contemplatives do? His answer is that contemplatives, like artists and poets, call into question the world's truths and values; this makes contemplation a form of subversive activity. Whatever the society and culture, contemplatives – whether in monasteries and convents, whether artists or ordinary people in the world – proclaim that the truths and values which society attempts to impose on us are not definitive and final. Contemplation witnesses to realities that the world tends always to ignore, such as death and the transience of life. Merton sees that in a world of action – and all human worlds are worlds of action – the contemplative monk and nun, the artist, the kneeling and praying human being, is useless. Their uselessness asserts the irrelevance of human life, which death makes manifest. However, for Merton, this uselessness in the eyes of the world, this absence of doing, affirms being. The lives of contemplative monks and nuns, of artists, and of the rest of us to the extent that our lives possess a contemplative dimension, are an attempt to find something that makes death irrelevant. For Merton, contemplation is a statement on behalf of life, since it gives witness to the reality of God who alone gives life absolute relevance and meaning.

Merton holds that in contemplation we become what we truly are, what God has always called us to be. Finding who we really are is not a discovery but a rediscovery of an original identity that we never lost. We can never so damage ourselves that the divine image within our self stops calling us back to God and our true identity. The journey to God and our true self is a return journey. Though we seem to start in a far country in a condition of alienation, we are already at the goal of our journey, which is our true self in God. According to Merton, the false self disappears, and the real self emerges, as we discover or rediscover our reality in God. This is a reality where God is all in all, and the self, merged in God like a drop of water in the ocean, is unaware of itself apart from God. In moments of infused contemplation, which artistic or peak experiences and human love give intimations of, or permanently in the vision of God after death, the self is one with God. The true self or 'I' merges with God's 'I Am'. We find rest, happiness and fulfilment, because at last we are what we were made to be, partakers of divine being.

Christian tradition holds that we are both part of God and separate. And Merton does not see our eventual union with God as complete fusion. We will exist in a union of love with God, while retaining our identities. But we will not experience our self and God as separate; neither will we fuse in such a way that we cease to exist. But how we become identified with God and remain separate is a mystery. John of the Cross uses the example of a window flooded with light: the window continues to exist independently of the light shining through. Similarly, says John, the transformed soul becomes God by participation in God's being, yet retains a separate identity.

Merton believes that infused contemplation makes possible a participation in God's being during this life, for a fortunate few. For the rest of us, moments of human love, of ordinary prayer, of the experience of nature and the arts, are the closest we will come to partaking in God's being here and now. For most of us, full participation in God's being will only begin after death. With the discovery, through death, of God and our true self will come the full awareness of our oneness with God and all that God has created. Merton believes that this oneness will not be with God as object of our experience, nor with us as objects before God. In eternal life there will be no objects, only created subjects at one with the loving, knowing, rejoicing, uncreated, divine I AM. And for Merton, with the finding of God and our true self we discover our oneness not only with God but with all others in God.

And how we face death, says Merton, is important. 'If, at the moment of our death, death comes to us as an unwelcome stranger, it will be because Christ also has always been to us an unwelcome stranger. For when death comes, Christ comes also, bringing us the everlasting life which He has bought for us by His own death. Those who love true life, therefore, frequently think about their death . . . Every good death, every death that hands us over from the uncertainties of this world to the unfailing peace and silence of the love of Christ, is itself an utterance and a conclusion. It says, either in words or without them, that it is good for life to come to its appointed end, for the body to return to dust and for the spirit to ascend to the Father, through the mercy of Our Lord Jesus Christ . . . For the eloquence of death is the eloquence of human poverty coming face to face with the riches of divine mercy' (*No Man is an Island*, 1955).

4

A Distracted Searcher:
Blaise Pascal's Religion of the Heart

When I consider life, 'tis all a cheat;
Yet, fooled with hope, men favour the deceit;
Trust on, and think to-morrow will repay:
To-morrow's falser than the former days.
    (John Dryden, 'Aureng-Zebe')

Imagine a number of men in chains, all under sentence of death, some of whom are each day butchered in the sight of the others; those remaining see their own condition in that of their fellows, and looking at each other with grief and despair await their turn. This is an image of the human condition.
    (Pascal, *Pensées* 434)

Knowing God without knowing our own wretchedness makes for pride. Knowing our own wretchedness without knowing God makes for despair. Knowing Jesus Christ strikes the balance because he shows us both God and our own wretchedness.
    (Pascal, *Pensées* 192)

According to one twentieth century writer, the only really serious problem for philosophy is that of suicide. The view that 'To be or not to be' is the question epitomizes existentialism at its most bleak. Much of modern existentialism's tragic analysis of human life was anticipated three centuries ago by Pascal. His *Pensées* give an account of humans searching for a happiness which eludes them; and happiness eludes them not because of circumstances that can be changed, but because human life is inherently wretched. Pascal sees human personality as a contradiction of wretchedness and greatness.

But his answer to the 'Is life worth living?', implied in the question about suicide, is 'Yes'. For Pascal, what makes life worth living is God: human beings are wretched only because they are without God. In the *Pensées*, Pascal moves from the contradictions in personality which make being human so painful to their resolution in God and specifically in Christ. To find happiness – if not in this life, then in the next – we must go beyond the natural order of experience to the divine.

Modern secular existentialism's account of personality remains in the natural world. Existentialism emphasizes freedom and stresses our responsibility for making something of our lives, in spite of their tragic dimension and their contingency. Contingent means dependent; a contingent event, dependent on something else happening, might not have happened. What existentialism sees as especially contingent about a human life is that it might never have happened. A man and a woman come together sexually, and subsequently we are born; but it seems that we might so easily have not existed. Existentialism regards this chance element about existence as puzzling and as raising certain questions. Does my existence signify anything? What does it mean to exist, to be? What are the implications of my being?

These are the questions which religion traditionally asks in some form. But for existentialists who are atheist or agnostic, there is no God or divine revelation to answer such questions. According to secular existentialism, humans just . . . exist; and there is no God to give meaning to this existence. For Dostoevsky, in the nineteenth century, this had implications: 'If God does not exist, everything is permitted.' Similarly, twentieth-century existentialism holds that if God does not exist or is irrelevant, then there are no God-given values or rules of conduct. Human beings have to decide their own values and rules to live by.

Having emphasized how strange existing is, existentialism calls attention to particularly odd contingent features of everyone's existence. We might, for example, have been born the opposite sex. We might have been born into a different family, class or country. A man and a woman, realizing that each might easily have married someone else, wonder in what way their lives would have been different. Contingency means that our lives and personalities are what they are because of . . . chance? That the circumstances of our lives are seemingly so contingent and fortuitous gives a disconcerting and frightening feel to life.

In the *Pensées*, Pascal anticipates existentialism by emphasizing this contingent and seemingly chance element in life. He suggests that the course of history was altered by the length of Cleopatra's nose (413) – presumably because of Caesar and Mark Antony's infatuation. Pascal is aware of the more radical contingency: 'I feel that it is possible that I might never have existed' (135). But he comes to a different conclusion from that of secular existentialism: aware that he is not a necessary being, he concludes that he 'can see that there is in nature a being who is necessary, eternal, and infinite' (135).

Pascal and existentialism see that if we manage to look at human life and personality as if for the first time, our 'being here' in the world does appear strange. We are simply . . . here. In Tom Stoppard's very existential play, *Rosencrantz and Guildenstern are Dead*, the two characters have little idea how they came to be in the royal palace, other than that they were summoned. And being in the palace, they have little idea of the reason for their being there. And what are they supposed to do now that they are there? The human situation is no different; it is one of bewilderment about how we got here and what we are supposed to do now. Unlike Stoppard's two characters, we are not even aware of having been summoned. Our situation is like that of a child presented with a high-tec toy for Christmas, who finds the manufacturer has not included instructions. Without the instructions the child has no idea of how the toy works or even its purpose. But it is only a toy, and the child can always write off for instructions. What we as human beings are bewildered about is nothing less than our lives, and there is no one we can write off to. According to Pascal and existentialism, the position we first find ourselves in is that we are simply here, on Earth, existing, without knowing why.

This experience of finding ourself in existence without any explanation finds constant expression in twentieth-century literature; Kafka is one example among many. Pascal's three-hundred-years-old description is modern in feel. 'When I see the blind and wretched state of man, when I survey the whole universe in its dumbness and man left to himself with no light, as though lost in this corner of the universe, without knowing who put him there, what he has come to do, what will become of him when he dies, incapable of knowing anything, I am moved to terror, like a man transported in his sleep to some terrifying desert island, who wakes up quite lost and with no means of escape' (198). Pascal goes on to report that when he asks those around him for an explanation – the next best thing to do in the absence of manufacturer's instructions – he finds that they too have no idea why they are here. Like Rosencrantz and Guildenstern in Stoppard's play, Pascal then looks about for clues. And though the vast universe does not have much to say as to why we are here, Pascal holds that there are a few clues to be found.

Pascal holds that this frightening bewilderment, caused by the situation in which we find ourselves, is increased by the nature of the material world. He was aware that the universe in which we exist is immense. 'The eternal silence of these infinite spaces fills me with dread' (201). And against the immensities of time and space, Pascal sees how short human life is and how small a space it occupies. He was also aware that nature extended from the vast down to the microscopic. Isolated between the very large and the very small, human life appears insignificant; and the individual personality seems an irrelevance in a seemingly indifferent universe. For Pascal, this disturbing intermediate position of humans, between the very large and the very small, is expressive of the contradictions in the human condition. We are feeble, insignificant and wretched; but we possess a greatness, grandeur and majesty. And though we know now that geographically we are not the centre of the universe, humans beings remain psychologically at the centre; as Pascal was aware, it is human beings who observe, understand and attempt to make sense of the cosmos about them. 'Man is only a reed, the weakest in nature, but he is a thinking reed. There is no need for the whole universe to take up arms to crush him: a vapour, a drop of water is enough to kill him. But even if the universe were to crush him, man would still be nobler than his slayer, because he knows that he is dying . . .' (200).

In contrast to Pascal, modern secular existentialism takes the view that there are no clues as to the reason why we are here; this is because there is no reason. According to such existentialism, finding ourselves here we have no alternative but to make up our own reasons. But before we do this we should examine the situation in which we find ourselves. And one thing that eventually becomes obvious is that we will not always be here; one day we will die. Like Rosencrantz and Guildenstern in Stoppard's play, we have little idea of what the future holds and where we are going; but we do eventually realize that we are being taken to our death. Pascal held that an awareness of our own unique death – 'we shall die alone' (151) – is central to any understanding of the situation.

In both Pascal and the modern existential account, we gradually become aware of other features of the situation besides death. We also have mixed feelings about some of these features, or simply do not like them. Among them are sickness, suffering, anxiety, guilt, despair, fear of the future, loneliness, boredom, growing old, and life's apparent lack of meaning. Secular existentialism recognizes these tragic features as inherent in human life, and inescapable. In the existential account, we grow and become fully human only by coming to terms with this tragic dimension to our lives.

Existentialism is not saying that since death, sickness, guilt, despair and other existential realities reflect the way things really are, we should make ourselves realize this. Existentialism is saying that we already realize that this is the way things are. Death, anxiety, suffering, life's lack of meaning and other tragic existential realities have already – if we did but admit it – driven us almost to distraction; as a result, psychologically we are on a knife edge. But society shields us from the full terror of the realization. Society does not lessen life's horrors – nothing can do that. The influence of society is in mitigating the situation by providing customs and rituals and social habits and cultural practices, and these help to prevent us going over the edge. They enable us to evade having to face up fully to death, suffering, the uncertain future, guilt and anxiety. Ceremonies at a funeral exist to enable the bereaved to mourn a dead loved person. But, according to anthropologists, such ceremonies are also there to help the living close ranks and fill up the breach that the death has caused in the ranks of the living. Existentialism has mixed feelings about these defences which society provides. In the existentialist account, if we allow ourselves to be shielded and distracted by society from life's tragedies, we will exist only at the public level and never become fully human.

Pascal, too, is aware that human beings are shielded from life's disturbing realities. But Pascal sees the defence in terms of human psychology; humans fill their lives with distracting diversions, like Rosencrantz and Guildenstern in Stoppard's play, joking and tossing coins. A full social life, sports, study, pursuit of power, reading (or writing) a book distract us and make it possible to avoid thinking about the tragic conditions of our life. Their job might do this for some people, like the character in a Scott Fitzgerald novel who says that he is going to work so hard that he will forget that really nothing is worth doing. Pascal comments: 'I have often said that the sole cause of man's unhappiness is that he does not know how to stay quietly in his room' (136). His point is that if we sat quietly and started to think about things, the awareness of our wretchedness would become intolerable; we would have to leave the room and find something to distract ourselves. 'If our condition were truly happy we should not need to divert ourselves from thinking about it' (70).

So, for Pascal, the motivation of much of our activity is to avoid having to consider the awfulness of our human situation; this means that the real reason for such activity is often different from what we think. We say that we are playing sport for pleasure or to keep fit, that we are studying out of interest or to get a better job. The reality, according to Pascal, is that we are doing whatever it is largely to distract ourselves from the way we really feel, like drinking 'to forget'. In Pascal's account of personality, the emphasis is less on the evil which humans do and more on the absurdity of what they do. He sees the human condition as one of tragi-comedy, like Horace Walpole's 'This world is a comedy to those that think, a tragedy to those that feel.'

But Pascal makes a further point: it is not the satisfaction of our activities and antics that motivates us. When we achieve whatever it is we are pursuing, whether it be fitness, a qualification, promotion, money, power or whatever, we soon realize that they do not satisfy us in the way which we had expected. So, disappointed, what do we do? We start chasing after something else. Having got the promotion, we want to go even higher . . . having made our sexual conquest, we attempt another . . . having bought our first house or car, we want a better one or a second one. Pascal's point is that what really motivates us cannot be life's goods and pleasures, since eventually we invariably find them unfulfilling. 'That is why,' he says, 'we prefer the hunt to the capture' (136). It is chasing after whatever is next on our list that distracts us from the present, and from our lack of fulfilment and the pain of our emptiness. But because the distraction of the chase diverts our attention from this emptiness and meaninglessness, we are not forced to confront them and do something about them. In Pascal's account, what we want to forget and be distracted from – whether or not we realize it – is the absence of God. The only thing that we could usefully do in the situation is turn to God.

In modern secular existentialism, God is dead. In the modern secular account the solution – though 'solution' would be regarded as too optimistic a word – is found in the exercise of human freedom. We are free to choose to face up to these realities. We are free to turn away from the diversions and distractions that society and our personality provides. With our freedom, we can choose to achieve individual identity and values to live by. But all this has to be done – it is part of the process – in the full knowledge of our own death as a real personal possibility here and now. Death in the existentialist account is not 'We've all got to go sometime'. Finiteness and contingency do not surround human personality like a set of boundaries, with death as the end of the road; death is at the very core of human being. The grave-digger scene in Hamlet – 'Alas poor Yorick' – is powerful because it evokes just this. Existentialism holds that our 'To be' is permeated through and through with 'not to be'.

This is one reason, according to existentialism, why anxiety is a permanent condition of personality. Certain psychological theories attribute anxiety to bad toilet training or repressed sexual fantasies or poor mothering; this may be part of the explanation with some personalities. But in the existential account, our real anxiety is inevitable, existential, not a product of past experience and individual history, but a result simply of being human. We are anxious because we hover over nothingness; non-being is at the centre of our being.

Some modern approaches to psychotherapy have been influenced by existentialist thought. Since despair, anxiety about death and non-being, guilt and other existential realities are at the centre of our personality, it is only within us that they can be dealt with.

Existentialism is not denying the influence on personality of social, sexual and economic factors such as poverty and unemployment. What existentialist psychotherapy is saying is that even when such influences have been dealt with, the existential factors remain. And these will always be there, because they are not problems of a particular situation but are part of what it is to be human, and inevitable. Psychotherapy influenced by existentialism is not concerned with helping personality to develop by getting rid of despair, fear of non-being, guilt and the rest, but by working through them, even by accepting them and what they signify.

Central to such existential psychotherapy is the idea that personality is something each of us has to create. We are each responsible for achieving our identity. This involves free choice and a psychological journey through the anxiety-producing awareness of death. In the same way – since according to existentialism there are no absolute truths to guide us – we have to find for ourselves values to live by. In such psychotherapy, humans have to discover for themselves, in an objectively meaningless world, a meaning to give to their lives. This can only come when they find in their lives something to which they can give a commitment, a commitment which makes guilt, suffering, death and the other tragic realities of life, if not irrelevant, at least endurable. For the modern existentialist, life involves a project. The project is to create – since these do not already exist – one's own personality, one's own identity, one's own values and meaning. A symptom of clinical depression, and sometimes of being just plain low, is feeling like doing nothing, even feeling that nothing is worth doing. For personality to develop and become healthy, according to existentialist therapy, individuals have to find something that they can regard as worth doing and worth living for.

Freedom is central to the solution. According to existential psychotherapy, such freedom may be limited by contingencies such as having had a bullying father, an unfeeling mother, a childhood scarred by economic deprivation. But freedom with the possibility of choice and decision is central, because a valid solution will not just be cerebral. Thought, knowledge and reason are useful, but by themselves they provide no answer. The answer to the question of who and what I am does not require further study. The puzzle of what values to live by does not need me to think harder. What I am to do with my life is not to be solved by reading another book. Intellectual insight and analysis by itself is not enough for human psychological growth. For personality to develop, and for progress to be made towards a solution in such therapy, decision and resolve, will and commitment are needed.

In such therapy, the therapist might get clients to consider why they have not found something in their lives which they could fully affirm. The therapist might ask clients to reflect on why they have failed or refused to find someone in their lives to whom they could commit themselves. These aspects of their lives, and of therapy, relate not merely to mind, though intellect and reason play their part. Such matters are related to the whole person and to a person's free will. Another way of expressing this notion of existentialism, and of the psychotherapy which it has influenced, is to say that truth is related to the whole person – to what Pascal calls heart. Secular existentialism, most psychotherapy and Pascal would hold that human personality is not just the thinking machine of modern artificial intelligence, nor even the information processing system of cognitive psychology. Modern existentialism, most psycho-therapeutic theory and Pascal agree that a whole human being has to be seen as . . . a whole human being.

In other ways, Pascal's *Pensées* anticipate much in modern existentialist analysis of the human situation and suggest similar answers. But ultimately Pascal would have regarded the modern existentialist solution as inadequate. He would have seen such a solution as an attempt to pull oneself up by one's shoe-strings, and Pascal held that any such attempt at self-sufficiency is useless. He saw God as central to genuine human development. We are unhappy because we are without God; a real solution involves placing God at the centre of our lives. The attenuated figures of the twentieth-century sculptor Giacometti, sunk in on themselves in despair, express in part the spirit of modern existentialism and Pascal's view of human beings without God. El Greco's figures, also attenuated, but by their longing as they stretch upwards to God, is the spirit of Pascal alone.

In Pascal's account, the problems of personality and the human situation are in large part a result of the Fall in the Garden of Eden,

recorded at the beginning of the Old Testament. Though Pascal
regarded the Bible as divinely inspired, he stressed that it should
not always be understood literally. But when it comes to the Fall,
while acknowledging its essential mystery, he does take the story as
the record of a historical event in the way that many modern
Christians would not. Whatever the historical truth about any such
Fall, human life does seem alienated, as if we have been deprived
of our true nature. Prior to any Christian notion of a Fall, Aristotle
expressed a similar idea in the *Nichomachaean Ethics*: 'Life seems
like a punishment for a crime committed in a previous existence.'
Both modern Christians and secular existentialists agree that the
contradictions and conflicts of human personality are a puzzle that
has no simple and obvious explanation. Pascal, in seeing human
wretchedness as like that 'of a dispossessed king' (116), is expressing this notion of our seeming to have fallen from a better
state.

Pascal develops this image of royalty fallen on hard times. He sees
a contradiction between majesty and wretchedness as characteristic
of the structure of human personality. Our restlessness is evidence
that we seek happiness without finding it; and our pursuit of
diversions and distractions seems to confirm this. His comment that
'we never actually live, but hope to live' (47) echoes his near-
contemporary, the English poet, Alexander Pope: 'Hope springs
eternal in the human breast;/Man never is, but always to be blessed.'
And in Pascal's view, in this present moment while we wait for what
the supposedly wonderful future will bring, we are all – when not
preoccupied with diversions – so bored. The neo-Freudian, Erich
Fromm, says that humans are the only animal that can be bored. In
Pascal's account, humans vacillate between boredom and distracting
diversions.

Pascal sees the contradictions within the structure of personality
as present not only in the conflict between our greatness and
wretchedness. Human personality is characterized by pride, vanity,
self-love, self-interest, a capacity for self-deception; but personality
also possesses altruism, a capacity for self-criticism, a passion for
truth, together with an extraordinary self-awareness. 'Man's
greatness comes from knowing he is wretched: a tree does not know
it is wretched' (114). The contradictions extend further, and Pascal

recognized long before Freud a 'civil war in man between reason and passions' (621).

Pascal sees these contradictions of human wretchedness and greatness as significant. That we are wretched is evidence of our greatness, since it shows that we are equipped for something better. We are back to Pascal's 'wretchedness of a dispossessed king' (116). But even this image fails to capture what Pascal and poets like Baudelaire are aware of: that in our distractions, whether they are vices or everyday pleasures, it is the infinite which we seek. We are indifferent to and ultimately bored with anything less than the infinite. A saint, heir to a wealthy aristocratic family, said when others called attention to his worldly inheritance, 'I was born for better things.' All of us are; because what all of us are born and equipped for, as the saint was suggesting, is nothing less than God. For Pascal, what specifically motivates us in our pleasures and our distractions is the happiness that only an infinite God can give. In Pascal's account, what we want to forget and be distracted from – whether or not we realize it – is the absence of God. And in the absence of God, or of diverting activities that enable us to forget God for a moment, we are bored.

What is the answer? Pascal bases his answer on a certain view of reason. He recognized that reason was part of human greatness: 'Man is only a reed, the weakest in nature, but he is a thinking reed . . . Thus all our dignity consists in thought' (200). But at the same time Pascal saw – and this is yet another contradiction – that, in certain areas, thought and intellect are of limited usefulness. 'Reason's last step is the recognition that there are an infinite number of things which are beyond it. It is merely feeble if it does not go as far as to realize that' (188). For Pascal, the starting point for any solution is the recognition of the limitations of intellect and reason. And Pascal, like Freud, was aware of how prone to self-deception humans are, even in their use of intellect. Freud's defence mechanisms are examples how part of personality can attempt to deceive intellect.

Related to the limits of reason, Pascal makes a distinction between the mathematical mind (*l'esprit de géométrie*) and the intuitive mind (*l'esprit de finesse*) (512). Different types of personality have different types of mind; so one person might have more of a mathematical mind and another more of an intuitive mind. The person with the more mathematical mind would be better at coping with one type of knowledge, and the person with the more intuitive mind would be better at coping with another type of knowledge. And this is the point: there are two different types of knowledge with which human personality has to deal. In the area of 'mathematical' knowledge, reason holds sway. The mathematical mind is master, or should be, in the area of clear ideas and concepts, and the deduction of their logical consequences. The mathematical part of mind works well where knowledge can be reduced to laws and axioms. But Pascal maintains that reason has only a subordinate role to play in the area of 'intuitive' knowledge. In the area of data and knowledge which are not amenable to logic, the intuitive part of the mind is – or should be – master. The arts are an example; in an area such as the arts, where knowledge and experience are concrete, specific, but possibly also complex, logic can prove a handicap and even obstruct a solution.

Pascal's distinction between the mathematical and intuitive underlines the constraints of reason. Personalities with more mathematical minds will cope better with science. But his point is that all of us, whether mathematically or intuitively inclined, should use reason and the mathematical part of our mind for science and areas of knowledge where clear ideas and concepts, logic and deduction, are of primary importance. Similarly, in areas such as the arts and religion, it is personalities with more intuitive minds that work best. But again Pascal's point is that all of us, whether mathematically or intuitively inclined, should use the intuitive area of our mind to handle such knowledge. Reason and intellect, appropriate for scientific knowledge, are not wholly appropriate in areas such as religion, which calls for a different sort of analysis. Religion requires arguments that appeal to intuitive understanding.

Pascal is saying that there are areas where we should rely mainly on intellect and reason, and that there are areas where reason is too confining; here we should rely on intuition. Not only religion and the arts, but real life also seems often to be one such area. Perhaps real life is too concrete and specific, and not abstract enough for its problems to be solved, like a game of draughts, wholly by reason and logic. Much of the time human affairs are the stuff of confusion and not amenable to laws and axioms. In real life, human beings constantly face situations and problems which might best be solved, not by the information-processing of Pascal's mathematical mind, but by the operations of Pascal's intuitive mind. Many decisions deeply affecting one's life, such as choice of a marriage partner, require more than the use of reason and intelligence, if the right decision is to be made. Pascal regards the mathematical mind, with its reason and intelligence, as only part of the structure of human personality and mind.

We should pause before dismissing this qualification of the value of reason as seventeenth-century obscurantism. As we have seen, such an idea is also central to twentieth-century secular existentialism. And, like Kierkegaard 200 years later, Pascal is not rejecting reason but suggesting that there are limits to its usefulness. Pascal is rejecting scientism, the view that only the methods of the natural sciences, such as physics, are appropriate and correct for studying human beings. Pascal, like Dostoevsky in *Notes from the Underground*, held that human beings cannot be captured in 'two plus two equals four' formulations. However brilliant are the accounts of the world that science and mathematics provide, they do not appear adequate when it comes to human beings. In Pascal's view, life and human beings are bigger than all abstractions and theories. And his assertion of the limitations of reason, rather than being out-of-date seventeenth-century thought, is found not only in existentialism, in contemporary psychotherapy practice, but in modern literature from Dostoevsky onwards. William Golding's novels seem to say that reason alone is inadequate to explain human beings. And Tom Stoppard's plays often contrast, in a Pascalian way, the objective deterministic scientific view of the world against the human experience of freedom and values such as right and wrong.

Pascal's essential point has relevance to modern cognitive psychology. Modern cognitive psychology takes the computer as providing an account of the way the human mind works, namely, as an information-processing system. Perhaps, when what Pascal calls the mathematical mind is at work, the human mind does operate like an information-processing system. If humans did always operate as mathematical minds, cognitive psychology's information-processing model might prove adequate. But Pascal's idea of the intuitive mind suggests that this is an incomplete account of the workings of mind.

'We know truth not by the reason only, but by the heart' (110). The existence also of intuitive mind means that if the human mind works by information-processing, it does not work only by processing information, nor does it do so all the time. If Pascal is correct, then human beings are not just information-processing systems because they also operate much of the time as intuitive minds – or have the capacity to do so.

Related to the intuitive mind is what Pascal calls the heart. Pascal sometimes uses heart to refer merely to our emotional side, but this is only a part of what is involved. Heart in Pascal's sense – which we shall refer to as supernatural heart – is not just feeling as opposed to reason. For Pascal, supernatural heart refers to the core of personality structure, which emerges when feeling and will and intelligence combine. This happy combination, which happens in certain moments and situations in life, is the intuitive mind at its best. And what this supernatural heart or intuitive mind at work makes possible is a direct apprehension and knowledge of the sort which reason by itself cannot obtain. In 'the heart has its reasons of which reason knows nothing' (423), 'reason' is deliberately being used in two senses. Here, and elsewhere, 'heart' and 'reasons of the heart' are making the point that intellect is only part of personality structure.

Pascal's notion of heart refers to some centre of personality where the true self is to be found and where in our most genuine moments the whole person exists. For Pascal, heart refers to a total human self which, at its most profound, has an intuitive apprehension of the truth. Certain existential truths are intuited, experienced, felt, lived, grasped by a direct apprehension of the supernatural heart. When it comes to religious faith, it is this supernatural heart, and specifically the intuitive mind, that is at work. 'It is the heart which feels God, not the reason. This then is faith: God felt by the heart, not by the reason' (424). Belief in God and religious faith are not arrived at by reasoning alone. Faith is an intuition of the supernatural heart, of the core human person. This is illustrated by La Bruyère's affirmation: 'I feel that there is a God, and I do not feel that there is none: that is enough for me.' It is this supernatural heart, this intuitive mind, which Pascal regards as involved in genuine and significant faith.

Pascal's view that God's existence cannot be proved one way or the other illustrates his position on the limits of reason (809). In his view, there are no arguments for the existence of God that can completely convince the mathematical mind. But Pascal's point is that even if there were, they would be irrelevant; they would be irrelevant because such arguments lead only to cerebral belief, to a God of the philosophers. Pascal could see no point in a mathematical type of knowledge with regard to God; it might lead to intellectual assent, but not actually to doing anything about one's life in relation to God. This is why the supernatural heart and the intuitive mind are relevant. Pascal believed that, experiencing the contradiction of misery and grandeur in our personality and situation, the supernatural heart or intuitive mind is able to move to an appropriate knowledge of God. If God becomes known to the heart or intuitive mind, then the faith that results is of a sort that leads to action. Cerebral detached belief is not important; what matters is belief of the heart or the intuitive mind that gets one to do something about God, oneself and other people.

For Pascal, it is absurd to postpone a decision about God until we are convinced, one way or the other, by arguments that appeal only to intellect. Such arguments are never completely convincing; those who want to believe will find mathematical mind proofs convincing, but they will not convince those who do not want to believe. This itself says something about personality. Pascal's more central point – it also says something about personality – is that a God that one believes in as a result of mathematical-type proofs would not satisfy personality. Such a God would be too cerebral to fulfil the infinite longing of human beings. Mathematical-type proofs are relevant in mathematics and the natural sciences, but their relevance in areas such as religion is restricted; when it comes to God, what matters is choice and decision and commitment. Reason has some part to play here, clearing away intellectual confusion. Similarly in psychotherapy, intellectual analysis and insight have a role; but the client grows and develops when some shift occurs within personality. When it comes to God, Pascal holds that in the end intellect has to submit as the individual waits and prays for the gift of faith. When it comes to God and faith, what matters more is the intuitive mind and the supernatural heart; this is the way human personality works.

Many contemporary psychotherapists and personality theorists, uninterested in religion, would agree that in certain areas the appeal must be to what Pascal terms supernatural heart and intuitive mind. There are questions to which answers – if they are to be of any value – have to be given, not by the intellect alone but by the whole person. Do I love him/her? Do I feel that she/he loves me? Am I lovable? Who am I? Am I responsible for this? How do I feel about this? And for Pascal, with questions of faith, any helpful answers that emerge will do so largely from the supernatural heart and the intuitive mind. Only if such answers emerge from the supernatural heart, the intuitive mind and the whole person, will they change our lives. And a positive answer to the question of God, like a 'Yes' to 'Do I love him/her?', is irrelevant unless it changes our lives.

The involvement of decision and commitment in religious faith and belief, if they are to be worth anything, is illustrated by Pascal's Wager (418). For Pascal, the Wager is a meaningful exercise in itself. But the Wager also demonstrates Pascal's view that, when it comes to God, only what we would now call an existential type of knowledge will do, because only such knowledge motivates. Only existential knowledge leads to action.

Pascal's Wager suggests that when it comes to God we have no alternative but to make a decision between the existence and non-existence of God, and risk is involved. This is the gamble which the Wager invites us to take; and Pascal concludes, on the basis of the following argument, that self-interest dictates that we should gamble on God existing. If we are wrong and God does not exist, we have lost nothing. If we are right and God exists, then we win now and after death, and our winnings are immense. The only alternative, because – he points out – we do have to gamble, is to gamble on God not existing. If God does not exist, then again we do not lose much. But this time, Pascal suggests, if we are wrong and God exists, then we stand to lose a great deal. But the Wager is also intended to motivate, which is why it illustrates the existential dimension to Pascal's account of personality. The Wager is attempting to force commitment one way or the other. For Pascal, when it comes to God and religion, only knowledge which leads to commitment and subsequently to action is relevant.

But the Wager is also saying, as are the *Pensées* as a whole, that there are areas of life where we cannot stand on the side-lines and stay neutral. With regard to the God-question, Pascal contends, we have no choice but to make a choice and to take the risk involved. The sceptical bishop in Browning's poem, 'Bishop Bloughram's Apology', reflects that what is gained by unbelief 'Is a life of doubt diversified by faith/For one of faith diversified by doubt'.

The Wager is no proof; however, for Pascal there is no proof one way or the other about God. The Wager is an attempt – and this is the point – to stir us into action. In life's important areas, we have to take a decisive step. In human relationships, love is more a product of a decision and commitment than of knowledge and reasoning. On key issues, like love and belief, we cannot afford to sit on the fence; lack of involvement solves nothing. Most modern psychotherapies, not just those influenced by existentialism, support such a view.

Implicit in Pascal's notion of heart, and explicit generally in modern existential thinking, is the idea of the human will. Many of us, intellectuals especially, would prefer to be able to settle our problems by reason and academic study. But there are certain problems that cannot be solved by intellect alone, and where our will has to be involved. With such problems, and the Wager proposes the existence of God as one of them, we have no choice but to resolve our problem by choice, decision and act of will. Central to Pascal's thought, and to that of modern existentialism, is the view that growth and development in human personality sometimes involves intellect but always involves free will and choice and decision and commitment. This is illustrated by Pascal's theory of the three orders of experience.

Pascal distinguishes three types of human being; the distinction he makes is according to what they value in life (308,933). First, there is the personality that values the material and bodily side of human experience; secondly, there is the personality that values the activities of mind; and thirdly, there is the personality that values the spiritual. Pascal sees a hierarchy with those occupied with the body at the bottom, those interested in the the mind next, and those who primarily value the spirit at the top. But more importantly, Pascal sees these three orders of experience as present in every human personality – as the physical, the intellectual and the spiritual (131,821). The first two are the natural orders of body and mind; the third is the supernatural order of spirit or (to use Pascal's other terms) heart and intuitive mind. All are necessary: the habits of the body, the workings of mind, the actions of the supernatural heart. But personality development consists in moving from body to mind to spirit.

First, as physical body we are unthinking automatons, consisting of habits and conditioned reflexes. Secondly, as mind, we have reason and intellect. Thirdly, human personality has a supernatural order of experience, that of spirit and heart. If we embrace this third order and incline our hearts to God, all is reconciled within us. With the love of God at the centre of our lives, our bodily desires have their proper place, and mind recognizing its limitation functions for our happiness and well-being. In this ordering of experience, it is crucial that spirit and the supernatural heart come first. The two other orders of experience have value in their appropriate place. There is value in our bodies and in the human mind, but only if they are ordered according to the guidance and promptings of the supernatural heart. In the truly developed personality, supernatural heart and spirit are in charge and guide mind as well as body.

This view of Pascal is Jungian in its assertion that human beings need to know and embrace all levels of themselves. 'Man is neither angel nor beast, and it is unfortunately the case that anyone trying to act the angel acts the beast' (678). All three orders of experience need to be accepted into our personality. But personality development according to the three orders of experience is not a smooth process. Significant shifts are involved as personality discards an exaggerated valuing of body and mind to move on to the true ordering of the supernatural heart.

But we cannot live at the pitch of constantly converting ourselves: '. . . we must resort to habit once the mind has seen where the truth lies, in order to steep and stain ourselves in that belief which constantly eludes us, for it is too much trouble to have the proofs always before us. We must acquire an easier belief, which is that of habit' (821). Having achieved belief and faith, and having arrived at the life of the supernatural heart and spirit, we keep ourselves there by means of the first order of experience, by acquiring good habits and customs. Habits help to subdue unruly passions; and good practices, such as morning and evening prayers, keep us in the divine life of faith. 'Habit is a second nature that destroys the first' (126).

The habit-inclined automaton part of our nature needs to be put at the service of our life, lived according to belief in God and our religious faith.

The same is true of mind. But though Pascal stresses that a human being is a 'thinking reed' and that 'thought constitutes man's greatness' (759), he sees human development as also involving a less obvious use of intellect. This is using intellect both to accept the constraints of intellect and the mathematical mind, and to take reason's last step of submitting to supernatural heart, intuitive mind and faith. But before we can inculcate good practices of body and mind, we need to have first arrived at the life of faith and the supernatural heart. The conversion of the heart has to come first.

For Pascal, only conversion to God makes possible the fulfilment of human personality. It is only in the individual's relation to God, seen by Pascal in the Christian perspective, that a human being can be fully human. However great human personality is, it remains shot through with wretched conflicts and contradictions; however fine and ennobling are human relationships, they never fulfil us completely, and inevitably end with death; however impressive is the grandeur of our human condition, it remains a tragic one. The solution and true happiness are to be found only in God. And for the Christian the solution is specific – it is belief in Jesus Christ. For Pascal, it is through Christ that we come to know both God (189) and ourselves (417).

Pascal holds that a solution to the wretchedness of the human condition requires a belief in our immortality and in a life of joy with God after death. 'It affects our whole life to know whether the soul is mortal or immortal' (164). Pascal is not saying that faith in God will make our life a happy one – there is a sadness and wretchedness in all human existence. But Pascal declares that, with God and Christ, this sadness and wretchedness lead eventually to true life, to eternal life, to God's own life. What emerges from this tragic view of human beings is hope.

Pascal is very modern; in some respects he is post-modern. He realized that relying solely on what he called the mathematical mind ends in what he would have called 'scepticism'. He foresaw what post-modernism has discovered, that relying on reason and intellect alone ends in the deconstruction of all values and beliefs, and leaves no vantage point from which to obtain a perspective on truth. This is the conclusion of contemporary deconstructionism. For Pascal, the mistake is in starting from the view that reason, intellect and the mathematical mind will by themselves solve everything. Starting from such a beginning, we will inevitably be disappointed when reason and intelligence fail to provide definitive and comprehensive answers. Pascal holds that there is no need for us to end up stranded in a relativist universe, in the manner of deconstructionism, with no toe-hold on truth. For Pascal – and here he is existentialist rather than post-modern – the answer is to provide oneself with some sort of foundation by making an act of faith. Certainly a human being needs to examine all sides of the question using the mathematical mind, but in the end personality has to enlist the help of the supernatural heart, the intuitive mind.

We should not give up the search and, in the manner of post-modernism, abandon ourselves to complete relativism, simply because we find that the whole truth is beyond us. Nor, alternatively, should we resort to unreflecting dogmatism. We simply do our best with what we have. And since reason by itself takes us into a dead-end, it is up to reason to recognize that it is a dead-end that we are in. It is then up to reason to realize that we need to turn to something other than reason to get us out of the dead-end. Though the truth which we eventually obtain will be only part of the truth, mixed with error and, perhaps, half-truth at the best, it will be something to have even a glimpse of the truth. And such a glimpse will to some extent be achieved through the action of the supernatural heart. When the heart opens itself to God, it is like discovering the key that fits, which one has been looking for all one's life.

Pascal's solution, like that of modern existentialism, is to be found in the exercise of human freedom. Human beings can turn away from all the distractions to repossess their inheritance by freely choosing God. Such an achievement is made through faith and is the result of an existential decision. In the end one has to make a choice for God, who is the only solution. But Pascal holds that even the supernatural heart and intuitive mind, aided by reason and the mathematical mind, are not enough. We need a revelation from God. Pascal partly bases his case for God and religious faith also on the revelation of the Bible and on the arguments of influential thinkers within the Christian tradition. He values what he sees as significant sources of authority: divine revelation in the Bible, the teaching of the Christian church, the tradition of important thinkers within the church. Pascal does not regard the opening of the heart to God, and for the Christian to God's revelation in Christ, as an obscurantist closing of the mind's search for truth. For Pascal, it is in opening the mind to revelation that personality is fulfilled.

The incompleteness of the *Pensées*, a historical accident, is a sort of metaphor for Pascal's thought, since Pascal saw human beings as incomplete. For Pascal, no system will ever contain and express the whole of personality, because a human being is unfinished. But this incomplete unfinished quality is not that of something static, like a house without a roof, but of something dynamically motivated, straining beyond itself. Human beings are incomplete, unfinished, since they strive towards the infinity of God, at some level aware that in God they will find completion. Pascal saw that only in the acceptance of this unsatisfied incompleteness and in the painful life-long search for wholeness is a modicum of fulfilment to be found. Complete fulfilment is to be found only in experience of God after death.

There is an emptiness in things, above all in ourselves. For Pascal, nothingness, a void, non-being, are real; they are around us and within us; they are the absence of God. Each of us has to choose between the void and God; for the Christian, the choice is specifically between the void and God become human in Christ. For Pascal, the existence of God and the Christian account make sense of the conflicts and contradictions of human personality. The analysis of personality by reason alone takes us so far and no further; but the dead-end we arrive at is also the beginning of the solution since it reveals the confinements of reason. One has to go beyond reason for a solution. Pascal holds that, to find a way out of the dead-end, humans have to commit themselves in an act of faith to God; and for Christians such a commitment is to Christ as revealed in the Gospels (449).

We drift through life in a dream, only half-awake. 'Sleep, you say, is the image of death; for my part I say that it is rather the image of life.' Life eventually ends. 'The last act is bloody, however fine the rest of the play. They throw earth over your head and it is finished for ever.' Though there are fine moments, life is also wretched, with 'the wretchedness of a great lord, the wretchedness of a dispossessed king'. And in the end what does it all signify? 'What else does this craving, and this helplessness, proclaim but that there was once in man a true happiness, of which all that now remains is the empty print and trace? This he tries in vain to fill with everything around him . . . though none can help, since this infinite abyss can be filled only with an infinite and immutable object; in other words by God himself.' But 'after this life we shall be restored by a promised Messiah'. This makes it bearable, even worthwhile. 'Everlasting joy in return for one's day effort on earth' (5, *Additional Pensées*; 165; 116; 148; 281; The Memorial).

5

The Resolute Traveller:
Teresa of Avila's Inward Journey

Let nothing disturb you,
Nothing frighten you,
All things pass,
God never changes,
Patience
Gains all;
Whoever has God
Wants for nothing;
God alone suffices.
　　　(Teresa of Avila)

Among all my patients in the second half of life . . . there has not been one
whose problem in the last resort was not that of finding a religious outlook
on life. It is safe to say that every one of them fell ill because he had lost
what the living religions of every age have given to their followers, and
none of them has really been healed who did not regain his religious
outlook.
　　　(Carl Jung, *Psychology and Religion*)

We only have to pass a single night in this inferior inn, says Teresa.
But life, besides being a rather poor inn, a prison, an unendurable
absence from God, is also a journey. In *The Interior Castle*, using the
castle as an image of the soul, Teresa describes this journey through
seven rooms to the centre where God is. Life soon ends – perhaps,
she suggests, sooner than we expect – and our reward is great;
meanwhile there is much to be done for God and our neighbour. In
her description of this inward journey to the centre of the castle,
Teresa provides a developmental account of personality.

For Teresa, there are really two journeys: the first is through the beginning three rooms, and the second is through the last three, with the fourth room transitional and the start of the second journey. In the first three rooms, we move from being a novice Christian through spiritual adolescence to Christian maturity. These early rooms are characterized by active prayer and concern for our neighbour; and we can manage them by our own efforts and with the help of God's everyday grace. But from then on, progress is possible only with God's special help. In the last three rooms the concern for other people increases, but what is obviously new in this second journey is true contemplative prayer and abandonment to God. In the final room there is union with God. With most of us, Teresa says, this complete union is likely to be achieved only after death.

Carl Jung speaks of every psychological theory, his own included, as having the character of a subjective confession. *The Interior Castle* is based on Teresa's own experience but, like Jungian psychology, has a wider application. Jung, in his extensive writings, never strays far from the quest for wholeness or (the original title of a collection of essays) from *Modern Man In Search of a Soul*. Jung calls this quest for wholeness and meaning, often expressed in the arts, in religious beliefs and practices, in philosophy and personality psychology, individuation. For Jung, individuation is the process of becoming one's true self. In Jung's outline of individuation he provides, like Teresa, an account of personality development. In his book *Spiritual Pilgrims: Carl Jung and Teresa of Avila* (1982), Welch points out resemblances between Teresa's journey and Jung's individuation process. Many of Welch's ideas on these similarities are used in the account which I give here of *The Interior Castle*.

Like Teresa in *The Interior Castle*, Jung sees life as dividing into two stages, each requiring a different kind of individuation. The first half of life is concerned with healthy integration into the external world. This involves education, adjustment to culture, good personal relations, usually including sexual relations, and work. The hero myth of St George and the Dragon expresses this initiation into outward reality. The ego (St George) emerges from parental domination (the dragon), establishes itself in the world (wins the throne), and achieves sexual maturity (marriage to the princess). Mozart's *The Magic Flute* describes a similar hero myth. In Jungian terms, what is required to enable us to journey successfully to mid-life is to develop and strengthen our social mask, which Jung calls the *persona*, and the ego.

But Jung is more interested in the different kind of individuation required for the second half of life. When men and women are in their late thirties, sometimes earlier, sometimes later, they realize in a way which they have not realized before that one day they will die. Teresa speaks of the importance of keeping in mind the speed with which all things pass. One day, perhaps tomorrow, or the day after, this afternoon even, I will die. This realization tends to make all achievements and all preoccupation with the external world seem rather pointless. At this period in our lives we usually start asking again the 'What's it all about?' questions which we originally asked in late adolescence. The sight of our final horizon triggers off what nowadays we would call a mid-life crisis. Jung sees this early middle age as a sort of second adolescence and a period of hazardous transition; he believes that if it is not dealt with successfully, the result may be personality damage which lasts for the rest of life. The *persona* or social mask, which we have carefully built up over the first half of life, cracks or collapses.

The *persona* is that part of personality, its outward face, which in the first half of life the individual develops to present to the external world. It enables the young person to cope with outer reality and to relate to other people in a healthy way. In middle age, the *persona* begins to disintegrate, or the individual clings to this mask and feels empty within. Jung saw that another sort of individuation is required for the second half of life, one concerned with inner reality. Hero myths, like St George and the Dragon, often continue beyond the winning of the throne and the princess to the death of the hero and rebirth in another world.

For Jung, second-half-of-life concerns are about ethical and spiritual values, and the meaning of life. The solution in Jungian second-half-of-life individuation is achieved by enabling the individual to become a whole personality and a unique self. Jung regards individuation as a process triggered off naturally in cultures with a dimension which gives meaning to life – what Jung called a religious dimension. A culture's religious dimension provides beliefs and rites. Such rites, like the mass in Roman Catholicism, operate at the boundary of the known and the unknown; with the religious beliefs which they express, together they strengthen consciousness. Until the advent of secular Western society, according to Jung, all cultures had a religious dimension expressed in beliefs and rites and symbols, and this helped humans with their second-half-of-life individuation. But Jung saw this as no longer happening in contemporary Western society, because its scientific materialist culture was so cerebral and rational. He held that in modern technological societies this second individuation now had to be achieved individually, and usually with the aid of an analyst or therapist. This, he felt, was where his own psychological theory was helpful.

The journey through Teresa's first three rooms corresponds to Jung's first-half-of-life individuation in the external world. Like Jung, Teresa holds that what happens after the first three rooms is a different sort of journey, and she stresses that an experienced confessor becomes necessary. These later rooms of the castle correspond to Jungian second-half-of-life individuation, and Jung too emphasizes the importance of a therapist's help at this stage.

Before examining resemblances in the accounts which Teresa and Jung give, there is a difference to consider. The different perspectives can be expressed by saying that Teresa is concerned with the soul and Jung with personality. Soul, in Teresa's use, explicitly has reference to God. Soul goes beyond what can be empirically observed and is therefore not a scientific term. For Jung, personality is a scientific concept, concerned with what is empirical and observable. Personality – Jung more commonly speaks of 'psyche' – is intended to exclude any explicit reference to a transcendent and unobservable God. For Jung, personality refers to the individual and to the individual's relationships with others, which can be observed. When Jung brings God into the account, he carefully speaks of a God-image or a God-archetypal symbol; images and symbols are observable and empirical.

Jung believed that in modern Western society some people still achieved wholeness by means of beliefs and practices with a religious dimension. Such people still found 'what the living religions of every age have given to their followers' through the traditional way of personal and communal religious belief and practice. Jung would have regarded the journey which Teresa describes in *The Interior*

Castle as an account of such individuation, achieved by living according to religious beliefs. Jung held an approach such as Teresa's to be psychologically valid. But he regarded the truth of its underlying religious beliefs as being beyond the competence of science and as certainly requiring faith. Jung felt that this was not the case with his own scientific second-half-of-life individuation.

In his therapeutic work Jung discovered that humans had a need to find meaning in life, and that this need was so strong that it generated a considerable amount of psychological energy. This need had not been met in the people who came to consult him. He found people seeking 'what the living religions of every age have given to their followers', but for them a solution in explicit religious terms, with beliefs and rites, was not possible or not acceptable. He saw such people as seeking a meaning and personal wholeness which at its best religion had traditionally provided. In *Psychology and Religion* Jung says, 'The place of the deity seems to be taken by the wholeness of man.' It was to help these people that Jung developed individuation. Eventually Jung concluded that this wholeness came from accepting and reconciling the various parts of conscious and unconscious personality.

Jungian individuation involves making conscious large areas of personality which are unconscious. To the extent that areas of personality are unconscious they determine, or at least shape, the individual's behaviour. When what is unconscious becomes revealed to the light of consciousness, it can be integrated into personality, and wholeness results. To the extent that unconscious elements are integrated, they no longer control the individual, but the individual controls them; then they become valuable sources of energy and motivation. The more unconscious contents are reclaimed by consciousness, the more humans are able to choose what they do. For Jung there is purpose, as well as cause, in human behaviour.

Jung uses the term personality or psyche to embrace both the conscious and unconscious. Jung sees consciousness as only part of personality, only the thoughts, memories, feelings of which we are directly aware. Ego is the term Jung uses to refer to the centre of this consciousness. Like Freud, Jung held that our behaviour is affected by our individual personal past, such as our childhood. But Jung believed also that the past of the human species affected the individual; just as our bodies embody evolutionary history, so our personalities embody the collective experience of the whole human species.

Jungian individuation describes in scientific and psychological terms, without religious concepts, a developmental process which seems to resemble the journey to God outlined by Teresa in *The Interior Castle*. Whether Jung and Teresa differ only in the terms they use, or whether what they describe are really different journeys, is difficult to know. We can pose this as a question: is Jungian individuation an account, in scientific and psychological language, of the finding of the God of religion, or is it an alternative to finding God?

As a scientist, Jung felt that he could not comment on the truth or otherwise of the beliefs which religions proposed as an account of the external world. But he felt that as a scientific psychologist he could suggest what truths these beliefs, and their expression in religious symbols, were stating about the internal reality of personality. When in *The Interior Castle* Teresa speaks of serpents, devils and water, Jungian psychology asks – what do such symbols mean? Symbols are central to Jungian psychology.

Much of human activity is directed towards the ordinary business of living, such as the satisfaction of bodily needs. Jung refers to the energy involved in this as libido; libido is psychic energy. But Jung found, in the people who consulted him, needs other than the material needs involved in day-to-day living. These were needs for – we can use many different words – meaning, wholeness, God. The psychic energy involved in satisfying such needs is, according to Jung, libido redirected and channelled from our everyday bodily needs. Symbols do the redirecting.

A symbol expresses something rather intangible in an effective and concrete way. We could use words to announce that we support such-and-such a football team; but wearing a scarf with the team's colours expresses our feelings more powerfully. Jung's account of symbols and libido is complex, but implicitly confronting us here is the problem of the body-mind relationship.

Jung sees symbols as having two functions for personality, the expressive and the impressive. First, symbols express something. A woman dreams that, like Red Riding Hood, she is walking through a forest in danger of being attacked by wolves. In Jungian terms, the dream might be expressing symbolically that the woman has yet to come to terms with her instinctual bodily desires, what Jung calls the shadow. But secondly, a symbol does something: it makes an impression, it is instrumental in causing something to happen. Symbols stimulate the flow of psychic energy and influence the direction of that flow, causing the energy to move in a certain channel. For Jung, the Red Riding Hood dream of being in danger from animals is likely to trigger off energy which enables the woman to relate to her instinctual bodily desires. The scarves of the football supporters not only express what they feel about their team but make them feel it more strongly. Symbols, for Jung, are transformers, activators and energizers in the psychic process.

In a Jungian account, the castle and other symbols in *The Interior Castle* not only express personality development but also trigger off and energize that development. Teresa often refers to water. Jung sees water, usually found in valleys and other low places, as a common symbol of the unconscious. It is from unconscious psychological life, symbolized by water, that human consciousness emerged, the waters in the mother's womb as well as the oceans from which our evolutionary antecedents crawled. In *The Interior Castle*, Teresa, obviously attracted by water, takes water as an image of God's work deep within us. In Jungian terms, the water is a symbol both expressing and activating psychological activity.

Jung was particularly interested in symbols which he regarded as universal; he called these archetypes. Perhaps Leonardo's 'Mona Lisa' moves because it symbolizes some mysterious power of nature in us all. Perhaps the effect of Beatrice on Dante, since after all he hardly knew her, lay in her symbolizing something that he felt was lacking in himself. Jung refers to these Beatrice-type images as *anima* symbols, and he regarded the Virgin Mary in Christianity as a powerful *anima* symbol.

Jung saw archetypal symbols as innate images, rather like negatives in photography waiting to be developed. Archetypal symbols resemble the idea of an innate capacity for language which, according to Noam Chomsky, all humans have. We acquire a specific language such as English or Russian because this is what we have been exposed to. But that we learn a language at all is because as humans we have a genetic predisposition for language; so with archetypal symbols.

Jung regarded archetypal symbols of the self as particularly important. He saw that religions used images which focussed on a centre, such as circle, square, sphere and cross. He believed that such symbols had the effect of orientating human personality on wholeness. To describe these symbols, Jung adopted the Sanskrit word 'mandala'. Teresa's castle seems to be a mandala symbol. From the beginning of *The Interior Castle*, Teresa focuses on the central seventh room where God is, and this emphasis on a centre is typical of a self-symbol. In a Jungian account, Teresa's castle would, as an effective symbol, both express the whole self which we seek and energize us to achieve the wholeness. Similarly, Jung takes God and Christ as symbols for the wholeness of the self. This further illustrates the difference between Jung's psychological and Teresa's religious account; for Teresa, Christ is not a symbol but the reality of God become a human. As we look at the seven rooms in Teresa's castle, we examine her account of the inward journey in terms of Jungian individuation. In doing so, we use ideas on their re-semblances from John Welch's *Spiritual Pilgrims*, referred to above.

In Teresa's account in *The Interior Castle*, life begins for most of us on the plains outside the castle or in the outer courtyard. Outside the castle we have largely been absorbed in the pleasures, material concerns and everyday affairs of the world. Eventually, with God's help, we tentatively decide to turn to God – or at least, to turn away from our unsatisfying absorption in the everyday world. What has probably facilitated this decision, and made possible a start on the journey to God, is that even in the plains outside, while involved with the affairs of the world, we reflected on our life, turned to God occasionally, cared about and helped others, perhaps sometimes prayed. At the core of human personality is a relationship with God; but that relationship needs to be activated. While it remains dormant, we stay outside the castle. What really triggers off the relationship is mysterious, and Jung would see archetypal symbols in the unconscious at work here. Whatever the cause, we have a sense that all is not well with us and enter the castle.

The first room is that of the novice Christian. But at least we are inside, and our having entered means that we want to find God. We have probably begun to pray and to listen for God's voice, but there are distractions. In the first room we are so close to the perimeter wall that much of what is happening in the world outside can be heard; and human pleasures retain a powerful hold. But Teresa says that valuable self-knowledge and humility can come to us in the first room, though she advises that the best and least discouraging way to obtain them is by regarding the majesty of God. There is more benefit to be gained in attending to God than to ourselves. In the first room, perhaps for the first time in our lives, we reflect on the grandeur of God. Jung too regards the humility and acceptance of ourselves which arrive with self-knowledge as central to psychological development.

But when we enter the castle, according to Teresa, snakes and vipers and other poisonous creatures slip in with us. Teresa uses these creatures to suggest the distracting things of the world which hinder our journey to God. They range from everyday preoccupations, such as food and clothing and work, to natural desires, bad habits, and an interest in status and possessions. For Teresa, such natural concerns are not invariably to be shunned, only when they are sinful. And they should be avoided when they impede self-knowledge and distract us on our journey to God. Even more troubling are the devils who distract us with the natural pleasures of the body.

The first room is only a start and there is a long way to go. Teresa says that the light coming from the centre of the castle, where God dwells, hardly reaches these outer apartments. At least we are in the first room; according to Teresa, this signifies that we are no longer totally preoccupied with ourselves, that we have turned to God, that we have the humility which comes from realizing what it means to be a created being, that we have the beginnings of repentance, that we occasionally pray vocal prayer with words on our lips and sometimes with God in our thoughts. This turning of the individual to God is done by an effort of the will; it is conscious and deliberate and active. All this corresponds with Jung's emphasis on the active and effortful nature of first-half-of-life individuation.

Teresa says that if progress is normal in the first room, we will inevitably move on to the second. If we have made this initial turn to God, God will respond. As a result, we realize even more that the real purpose of our life is to find God. There are fewer distractions in this second room, and we hear God's voice more clearly, addressing us personally. But Teresa holds that God's voice comes to us in everyday ways, like good moments in prayer, in helpful books, through the words of other people, perhaps even when we feel depressed. In the second room we become receptive and responsive to the call of God and Christ. Attending to God more, we grow in humility, insight into ourselves, awareness of our sinfulness, perhaps in awareness of how little we really know about ourselves. By now we have begun to make prayer a habit, and we pray to bring our will into conformity with God's will.

In this second room, according to Teresa, we begin to realize the need to conform to God's will. As a result, there is an increase in the struggle in our lives and its accompanying tension. The choice of continuing on our journey or of returning to the world becomes starker. We have to remind ourselves that there is nothing so wonderful about the world and that in life outside we have often found what the poet Virgil described as 'the tears in things'. We have to call on faith to help us realize that this world, though for the most part good, is not where we find fulfilment. But the things of the world remain appealing, and we may have to struggle to persevere with our journey. In the second room, says Teresa, the possibility of a new direction in our life opens up, and this may throw us off balance.

Teresa writes that as early as the second room we hear God calling from the centre of the castle. We should never be wholly occupied with external activities, she says, no matter how worthwhile they may be; we always need an interior life, even when we are young. Jung too holds that we hear the call to be our true self even in the first half of life. Like Teresa, he sees that conflict will occur if we respond to this call, because in the first half of life the conscious ego rightly has taken control; and we have developed a *persona* which enables us to cope. The dimly heard call means that one day we will have to relinquish control and respond: to the voice of God, according to Teresa; to the voice of the unconscious and the as yet undiscovered self, according to Jung.

By the time we have arrived in the third room, says Teresa, we are decent Christians and living Christian lives. We have developed the practice of prayer, religious observance, devout reading and penance, of turning to God; we care about and are concerned for others and our neighbours' needs; we wish to avoid offending God. But our charity is limited, we do not suffer fools gladly, and though no longer obsessed with worldly matters we remain attached to success, status, money, power.

To have got this far is an achievement, and Teresa says that those who arrive in the third room are blessed. She suggests that for many the third room is as far as they are likely to go. God may expect no more of us than a safe but limited Christian life, caring for our families, concerned about our neighbour, doing what practical good we are able. Partly because Teresa's writings are largely addressed to nuns, there is some uncertainty about how far Teresa thought most Christians are likely to travel through the castle. At one point she suggests that Christ will help those who so desire to enter the seventh and final room; but she also seems to be saying that God may expect from many of us no more than reaching the third room. So the third room, a decent and Christian enough habitation, may be our journey's end this side of death, where we will live out faithfully the rest of our lives.

For others, though by the third room they have come to the end of Teresa's first journey (and completed Jung's first-half-of-life individuation), the travelling continues. They feel that what they are doing with their lives is not enough and that their experience of God does not sufficiently fulfil them. For these, according to Teresa, the Christian life in the third room lacks depth; they do not abandon themselves to God there but hold back from completely trusting themselves to God. In the third room they come to feel anxiety, timidity, staleness, discontent. These people are capable of something more, says Teresa, of turning inward and away from the external world, of responding to God's invitation to enter the more interior rooms of the castle.

Teresa believed that there were risks in such people staying too long in the third room. She lists the dangers – what once was believed with confidence seems less certain and doubts of faith arise; aridity in prayer; touchiness; resentment when decisions and opinions are challenged; good works being done partly for the wrong reasons. For such people there now comes God's call to risk moving on into the fourth room, a place even more concerned with transition.

Jung too holds that first-half-of-life individuation may be all that our personality requires of us. But for others there comes the call from the unconscious to develop their personality further; like Teresa, Jung sees danger for such people in staying too long at this stage. His description of the mid-life crisis resembles Teresa's account of delaying in the third room and of the difficulties at the fourth stage when the traveller moves on. For Jung, the mid-life crisis is also characterized by feelings of meaninglessness, of what seemed real and important no longer doing so, of depression and anxiety, of strains in personal relationships. Jung sees this as the consequence of the ego staying in control too long and refusing to let go. The individual is no longer happy identifying with the *persona* adopted by the ego to fulfill society's roles, and personality ossifies. For Jung, second-half-of-life individuation involves a letting-go, with the ego's control diminishing as the demands of the self become insistent. Jung stresses that from now on a more inward and recollected orientation is required for personality development. For Teresa, in the fourth room the traveller turns inward and begins a more interior journey to God.

The first three rooms are really concerned with integration into the world, like Jung's first-half-of-life individuation; they can be managed, says Teresa, by our own efforts and the everyday help of God's grace. The last three rooms are more concerned with integration into inner reality, like Jung's second-half-of-life individuation; we can manage them, says Teresa, only with God's special help. The fourth room is transitional and is also the start of the second journey, particularly with regard to prayer.

At the beginning of her account of the fourth room Teresa says: 'supernatural experiences begin here'. The most obvious transition in the fourth room relates to two kinds of prayer. The traveller begins to move from the active prayer of the first three rooms to a more passive prayer, which eventually characterizes the remainder of the journey. Teresa uses an image of two troughs filling with water to illustrate the different kinds of prayer. The first trough is filled by water brought from a distance by canals and aqueducts. This is active prayer, initiated by the individual, calling for work on our part;

the water fills the trough as a result of our own efforts. In the first journey, it is through the use of our mind – memory, understanding, will – that we move by active prayer to God. The second trough is filled without human effort from an adjacent spring; this is passive God-initiated prayer of the second journey, where the individual is no longer in control. For some of us, this more passive supernatural prayer may never happen.

Teresa makes clear the difference between the first and second journeys, and both kinds of prayer, by distinguishing between two kinds of experience, what she calls consolations (*contentos*) and spiritual delights (*gustos*). Consolations, says Teresa, occur in active prayer. Our own efforts are the source of consolations, like the water in the trough brought by means of canals and aqueducts. By contrast, spiritual delights involve no human effort; they occur in the passive prayer of quiet, like the trough filled from a nearby spring. In spiritual delights the water wells up from within, coming directly from God. Consolations begin in the personality and end in God. Spiritual delights begin in God and end in personality.

Consolations are experiences of peace, of joy, of satisfaction in prayer, and they may happen during meditation and good everyday acts. We have to work at it and be active, sometimes intellectually, to have such experiences. We may experience consolations at any time on our way through the castle, but they are associated chiefly with the first three rooms. In contrast, spiritual delights are experienced only in the fourth to the seventh rooms. They are supernatural, and no effort is required on our part to obtain them. Such delights are infused by God, passively received by the soul, and Teresa regards spiritual delights as supernatural and God-given.

Consolations, though God is involved in them, have a natural dimension. According to Teresa, we partly earn consolations by our own efforts, and though they end in God, consolations begin from us. Consolations resemble certain natural experiences, such as joy or happiness at seeing someone we love. Teresa's emphasis on the natural element makes consolations rather resemble James Joyce's epiphanies, Eliot's timeless moments, Virginia Woolf's moments of being.

In *A Sketch of the Past*, Virginia Woolf talks of a cotton-wool quality to everyday experience, a sort of non-being which cuts us off from reality. She suggests that we occasionally experience moments which seem 'a token of some real thing behind appearances'. She believed that they can happen in everyday life or may be evoked in the arts. In her novel *To the Lighthouse*, the description of Mrs Ramsay alone when the children are in bed, of Lily Briscoe finishing her painting, can evoke this experience of some reality behind the surface of things. Virginia Woolf suggests that such a moment of being, which may be happy, sad, frightening, even painful, 'is or will become a revelation of some order'. As with Teresa's consolations, the limiting boundaries of the individual seem for an instant to be breached, and the self becomes part of some totality.

Between consolations and spiritual delights there is a divide. Teresa regards it as legitimate to want such spiritual delights, since they are wonderful and evidence of being close to God; at the same time, she says, the traveller should not struggle to acquire them. But if any human effort can move the individual from consolations to spiritual delights, and from the third room across to the fourth, Teresa says it would be recollection.

In prayer it is possible to quieten down the activity of the mind and induce tranquillity; this is recollection. In recollection, individuals praying concentrate on God, perhaps attempting to hold their attention by means of short prayerful phrases. Teresa's account of recollection is reminiscent of what Jung calls active imagination, a practice he proposes for the individual to raise contents out of the unconscious mind. Teresa regards recollection as transitional between consolations and spiritual delights, though it may not succeed in moving the individual from one to the other. Recollection is a borderline activity between active prayer that starts in personality and ends in God, and passive prayer that starts in God and ends in personality. This makes recollection typical of the transition from the third to the fourth room.

By and large Teresa holds that if God does not give the traveller the experience of spiritual delights, no amount of recollection, going passive and suspending mental activity, will make a difference. And in daily prayer, intellect should not be put on 'hold' in an attempt to obtain spiritual delights. The mind usually needs to be active in turning to God. And Teresa asserts that even in the second journey, from the fourth room onwards, it is possible for travellers to make progress by their own efforts, thinking, reading and reflecting on God and the life of Christ. Ordinary Christian practices of penance, good works, concern for our neighbour and prayer always remain available. If God intervenes and gives special experiences to certain people, that is God's business. God gives or does not give spiritual delights and there is little, perhaps nothing, that can be done to obtain them. In holding this view, Teresa differs from a number of other spiritual writers.

The fourth room, according to Teresa, is not a comfortable one to be in, since it contains much discouragement, distraction in prayer and depression. Teresa says that people should not allow themselves to be troubled by this, which is not the result of anything they have done but is usually because of the situation they are in. By the fourth room, says Teresa, travellers have arrived at a stage in the journey where they need to stop clinging to the safe and secure, and where they should be ready for the new and risky. In her autobiographical *Life*, Teresa describes how she eventually determined to open herself to God. She was reluctant, since allowing God to enter her more fully meant that she would lose control over her life and she could not know where this might lead. At the same time, she was aware that she wished to give herself wholly to God, though uncertain how to do so. She wanted both to continue living in a way over which she had control and to abandon herself to God. The situation resembles a marriage where a husband or wife, aware of their partner's love but terrified of involvement, hesitates and draws back from the passion and commitment they really desire. In his novel *The Woman of the Pharisees*, François Mauriac comments: 'God is very often the good temptation to which many human beings in the long run yield.'

In leaving the first three rooms for the fourth, travellers move from where progress is achieved by their own efforts to where progress is largely out of their hands and in God's. This change in the transitional fourth room illustrates a key difference between the first and the second journeys. Teresa describes the change in terms of a movement from the individual doing things for God to God doing things to the individual. And when God intervenes and does things, a process is begun in which initiative and control, especially in prayer, gradually moves from the person to God. But travellers' attempts to relinquish the control which they exert over their lives involves them in a paradox. How can someone try to let go? How do travellers on the inward journey move from active control of their lives to a more passive acceptance? By an active attempt to become more passive?

This difference which Teresa stresses between the first and second journeys resembles a change between Jungian first- and second-half-of-life individuation. In Jungian psychology, moving from the first to the second individuation also involves a move from controlling to letting-go and presents the individual with the same problem. How is it possible to arrive at a passive letting-go in Jungian individuation? By an active decision? – 'I've decided; at ten o'clock tomorrow, I am going to let go.'

Central to Jungian psychology is Jung's notion of a collective or universal unconscious. Such an idea was hinted at by Freud in *An Outline of Psycho-Analysis*, where he refers to material which is 'part of the archaic heritage which a child brings with him into the world before any experience of his own'. Jung sees such a universal unconscious as a storehouse of memories from our common ancestral past. Stressing what all humans have in common, Jung regards as central to personality this universal psychological inheritance of all human beings. He holds that this collective experience of the human species is contained in archetypal symbols within every personality's collective unconscious. Such symbols are expressed in myths, in rituals and ceremonies, in the arts, in our dreams. As we have seen, Jung regarded such symbols as initiators, energizers and directors of individuation. And Teresa's castle appears to be a self-archetype, expressing the wholeness which we seek, and energizing us to move in the direction of that wholeness.

According to Jung, second-half-of-life individuation is achieved by the integration of what is contained within the personal and collective unconscious. Second-half-of-life individuation is partly the process of bringing the light of consciousness to the personal and collective unconscious. In Jungian psychology, what is dangerous and damaging when unconscious becomes a source of useful and creative energy when conscious. Two steps are involved: first, we attend to what our unconscious contains by methods such as dream analysis; secondly, we then integrate the unconscious into our conscious personality. For Jung, an important step in this process is a coming-to-terms with what he calls the shadow archetype within the unconscious.

Standing in the sun, humans cast a shadow. We cast shadows because we are material beings. Whatever psychological or spiritual dimensions we might have, we certainly have bodies. For Jung, the solid flesh-and-blood bodies which all humans have, as evidenced by their cutting out the light of the sun, is expressed by the shadow archetypal symbol. The shadow symbolizes that we have bodies with instincts, needs, desires, emotions.

The shadow archetype, says Jung, is eighty per cent gold: these instincts, needs, desires and emotions are the source of creative energy and of much that is best in us. But Jung holds that what is useful and creative when conscious is dangerous when unconscious. Unconscious, the shadow is potentially explosive, a threat to ourselves and others. In Christianity, Original Sin can be seen as the shadow archetype projected inwards. Devils, such as those in *The Interior Castle*, can be seen as the shadow archetype projected outwards. But the shadow is not only something so dangerous that it must be tamed, but something so powerful that it should be harnessed. Without what is symbolized by the shadow, we are not fully human and scarcely human beings at all. In horror films, Dracula is detected by the fact of his not casting a shadow, which shows him not to be human. Jung says that a human being without a shadow is unreal. When we say of people that they are too good to be true, in Jungian terms this suggests that they are out of touch with their shadow.

According to Jung, if we are unaware of our shadow we will incline to self-righteousness, since we project this unconscious part of our personality on to others. People project on to others, Jung says, unconscious parts of themselves which they do not like, such as their aggression or envy. They then intensely dislike these features (of themselves) in other people. But it is psychologically much healthier, Jung suggests, to withdraw the projection and acknowledge that these features are parts of one's own personality; this gives rise to a certain humbleness.

Teresa, too, stresses the importance of humility, particularly in the later rooms of the castle. She suggests that many trials and problems at this stage occur through lack of insight into ourselves, which suggests an awareness of the unconscious. In *The Interior Castle* (1,2,17), Teresa warns against preoccupation with other people's faults with the advice: 'Let each one look to herself.' She points out how readily those who live well-ordered lives are shocked; perhaps, she comments, with a hint of awareness of projection, 'we could truly learn from the one who shocks us what is most important' (*The Interior Castle* 3,2,13). It is in ourselves that the devils have to be faced up to, confronted and come to terms with, says Teresa. And she adds that if people could understand themselves better, they would realize that often what they take to be faults in themselves were good.

In Jungian psychology, what needs to happen with the shadow, as with all contents of the unconscious, is to become conscious. When the shadow is recognized as part of ourselves and integrated into conscious personality, then the powerful instinctual elements which the shadow symbolizes become a source of energy for commitment, creativity and appropriate self-assertion. Jung holds that if we have embraced the shadow in ourselves we have done well. He suggests that for many of us this may be the extent of our psychological development. In saying this, Jung resembles Teresa's view that for many of us, arriving at the third room is a considerable achievement, and as far we are likely to go.

For Jung, as for Teresa, moving from the first to the second journey, from first-half-of-life to second-half-of-life individuation, involves the individual in a movement from an active to a more passive mode. In Teresa's later rooms and Jungian second-half-of-life individuation, an openness, a letting-go and a new receptivity is needed. How can God, or the unconscious, do anything if people keep themselves tightly controlled? Teresa held that new life and healing come at this stage from the relationship with God. Since at this point the soul can do nothing, she believed that God may directly intervene here in the individual's spiritual development. Jung's notion of 'letting the unconscious do its work' resembles Teresa's view. For Jung, too, healing and psychological health may now emerge in some mysterious way. He held that they emerged from the unconscious. Jung in his research discovered that such a transformation in personality is often symbolized by the metamorphosis of the butterfly. In *The Interior Castle*, Teresa uses the butterfly image.

She speaks of preparation work that can be done to foster development in the later rooms, such as prayer, penance, getting rid of self-will and becoming less attached to worldly things. Teresa likens this to weaving the butterfly's cocoon (which she has confused with the chrysalis). Within this cocoon-chrysalis, Teresa sees the start of the liberation of the soul; the process ends with the emergence of the transformed soul, expressed by the butterfly image. For Teresa, the butterfly is an image of dying to oneself, being reborn in Christ, and emerging to a new life with Christ. Teresa's butterfly is the soul transformed by union with God, particularly in the prayer of union which may occur in the later rooms. 'When the soul is, in this prayer, truly dead to the world, a little butterfly comes forth' (*The Interior Castle* 5,2,7). Teresa's butterfly is an image of the soul's potential for change and transformation, its capacity to develop new life, specifically to die and rise again in union with Christ. And the chrysalis-cocoon image seems a symbol of a sort of Jungian unconscious from which the butterfly will emerge. 'The truth is that the treasure lies within our very selves' (*The Interior Castle* 5,1,2). For Jung, a butterfly symbolizes the human capacity for change and also the transformation of personality which happens in second-half-of-life individuation. As with all such symbols, for Jung the butterfly both expresses and causes the process of individuation.

Considering Teresa's images as Jungian symbols raises again the question of the resemblances between Teresa's religious and Jung's scientific-psychological accounts of human development. Are Teresa's images really symbols in the Jungian sense? Perhaps Teresa, intuitively, really has chosen images that are expressive symbols. Perhaps her images are also impressive and instrumental in triggering off and energizing psychological processes of growth, in the way in which Jung suggests that true symbols are. Alternatively, Teresa's images may simply be poetic illustrations and imaginative descriptions of what is hard to put into more objective language.

Jung sees personality growth, especially when the unconscious is involved, as a development through crises, collapses, blockages, loss of direction and of life no longer under control. Teresa's butterfly of the fifth, sixth and seventh rooms is a complex image which also contains the notion of growth through difficulties. The butterfly emerging transformed from the cocoon-chrysalis expresses what Teresa emphasizes, and what Jung and much of modern psychology confirm, namely that personality growth involves change, even a sort of psychological death. The Christian Teresa holds that there are invariably crosses and trials on the journey, and that these are especially to be found in the later rooms. But though the carrying of the cross is a sort of a death, within such deaths there are the seeds of new beginnings, of transformation and life. After all, the central Christian miracle is Christ risen from the dead.

By the fifth room the soul, with the will beginning to be united to God, is well into the second journey. If a soul was fortunate enough to have experienced being held by God in the fourth room, such spiritual delights, according to Teresa, are likely to increase here. Teresa declares that in these later rooms what usually happens to those who receive spiritual delights is a more permanent and total prayer of union. She says that this union, in which there seems no awareness of anything outside, is above all earthly joys and while it lasts gives a certainty of God's presence. 'God so places Himself in the interior of that soul that when it returns to itself it can in no way doubt that it was in God and God was in it' (*The Interior Castle* 5,1,8).

Teresa again stresses that this prayer of union cannot be achieved by human effort and depends on God. She also emphasizes that, though these experiences given by God are wonderful, those who do not receive them can still achieve union by surrendering to God and doing God's will. By now the human will should have been surrendered to God. And she insists that what really matters, and makes spiritual delights mere icing on the cake, is the actual union of the will with God. Teresa seems to hold that though only a few experience spiritual delights, all those seriously engaged in a life of prayer – and she is writing for contemplative nuns – can arrive at the fifth room. And to have reached this far she regards as a considerable achievement.

The fifth room, too, has its tensions, confusion, unhappiness and restlessness, and in such times the traveller can only wait for God's consolation. Everything is wearisome to the soul which has experienced God, and the butterfly 'fails to find true repose' (*The Interior Castle* 5,4,2). A soul which has glimpsed God, no matter how briefly, knows that no creature, nothing created, nothing less than God, will satisfy. This causes a conflict in the fifth and subsequent rooms. Those who have glimpsed or experienced something of God want to leave the world and go to God; but now, filled with love of God, they also want to remain on earth to serve God. The more travellers progress in the castle, the more they withdraw into a relationship with God. But that journey to God also takes the individual back to service of others in the external world. Time and again, Teresa returns to love and care of others as the infallible criterion.

For both Teresa and Jung, human relationships are central. For Teresa, religious worship celebrated with others in community is necessary for the individual. She stresses the need all people have for human love, friendship and the support of others. She sees everyone's journey to God as involving other people. But in the end, according to Teresa, only God's love is enough, and only the promise of eternal life makes meaningful the love of others. Jung, too, is aware that individuation, though an inner journey, can only happen in the human community. Individuation involves relationships.

According to Teresa, the sixth room is characterized by an increase in mystical experiences, and she describes three main types. First, there are what she calls visions. She states that in 'intellectual' visions nothing is seen, but there is usually a sense of someone such as Christ present. In 'imaginative' visions there are usually images, though Teresa comments that these are seen with an inner eye. Sometimes in such visions, says Teresa, God reveals something important. The second type of mystical experience is what she calls ecstasies (or raptures). These may be brief experiences, perhaps triggered off by some word or thought, which hold the soul absorbed in God; or they may be experiences which affect the body in a stronger and more dramatic way; or they can be what Teresa calls a 'flight of the spirit', when another kind of consciousness replaces everyday awareness. The third type of mystical experience, called locutions, is hearing a voice which may not communicate information but which makes the hearer feel loved by God.

These experiences which Teresa describes, both in her autobiographical *Life* and in *The Interior Castle*, have a parallel in Jung's own life. In *Memories, Dreams, Reflections*, also a kind of autobiography, in the chapter 'Confrontation with the Unconscious', Jung describes a range of unusual personal experiences. He speaks of voices, of inner voices and those heard as if by the ears, which usually said something helpful to him. He reports dreams which, after he had studied them, revealed something important for his own personal development. Even awake, he had vivid visions and fantasies; in them people spoke and said much that was to prove useful, both for his own psychological growth, and for his work and ideas.

Are these experiences which Teresa and Jung describe visions or hallucinations? Are they 'a revelation of some order' or psychotic disturbance? Are they merely the result of self-induced hysteria? Jung does not account for his experiences in religious or mystical terms, as Teresa does. But he held that such experiences are evidence that certain psychological processes have a reality independent of the person. There were, he decided, contents in the psyche which have a life of their own. Such contents, he concluded, exist as a reality not only at a personal level but also, since other people have them, at the collective and universal level.

It was to explain such experiences that Jung proposed the concepts of the collective unconscious and archetypal symbols. According to Jung, archetypes manifest themselves not only publicly in the images of culture, the arts and religion, but also personally in dreams, waking images and voices. They exist and operate independently of the individual and independent of conscious control and activity. For Jung this meant that the ego at the centre of consciousness is not the only important force in human personality. In the second half of life, though the ego is reluctant to relinquish control, archetypal symbols and the collective unconscious are, or should be, significant forces.

Jung said that in second-half-of-life individuation an analyst may be necessary because of the dangers of self-deception. Similarly, Teresa stressed the importance of a good spiritual director, especially at such a time of unusual experiences. And Teresa was aware that these experiences could have a variety of causes and that an over-active or misguided imagination might be one of them. So she gives guidelines for distinguishing between the genuine and the spurious. Teresa is clear that even when such visions are genuine and of divine origin, the human personality is involved in co-operating with God in producing them. But she suggests that if the experience is genuine and from God, it will give peace and not anxiety. Another of Teresa's criteria for distinguishing the genuine from the false is how health-giving it is for personality. Genuine experiences foster spiritual and psychological development. And again, the ultimate criterion remains whether they result in the individual turning to others and loving and caring for them.

Teresa lists a number of other outcomes of a genuine experience. They are self-knowledge and humility, a knowledge of God's grandeur, little esteem for the things of this world apart from those that can be put to God's service, and a joyful desire to praise God. A further outcome is the desire that this life of exile end so that the soul can be with God. After such an experience, she comments, life feels painful, little on earth satisfies and the soul is full of such longing that it desires to die and be with God. 'O poor little butterfly, bound with so many chains that do not let you fly where you would like!' (*The Interior Castle* 6,6,4). Religious writers state that what humans seek is not concepts and words about God but the experience of God. Similarly, in the *Life* Teresa comments: '. . . it is extraordinary what a difference there is between understanding a thing and knowing it by experience' (79).

But perhaps visions of the intensity of Teresa's are not necessary for human beings to realize that only God will do. A sense of a paradise seen and lost, leaving the individual bereft and full of longing, is common in the arts. Pasternak's novel, *Dr Zhivago*, conveys the sense of a great happiness just missed. What we tend to interpret as nostalgia in the arts, Proust's recollection of childhood, the longing for an irretrievable past in Elgar and Richard Strauss, is perhaps not about the past at all. Perhaps the nostalgia is for a half-glimpsed possession of God. What such deeply felt moments in the arts may express is not the experience of a lost paradise but the partial vision of a future beatitude.

Teresa says that, regardless of remarkable experiences, the traveller who has reached the sixth room should not ignore the human figure of Christ. She stresses the need to be aware of Christ, God become human, of his love, and of how he suffered and died on the cross for humanity. She emphasizes the individual's in-debtedness to him. But Teresa adds that Christ, the God whom humans need, as a suffering human being, also needs humans. In

Teresa's view, there is no firmer foundation for a sense of personal worth than being needed by Christ. As the centre of the castle comes nearer, Teresa speaks more and more of Christ, and she reports in the sixth and seventh rooms an increase in visions of Christ.

For the Christian Teresa, Christ is a historical reality, God become a human being. Teresa's religious faith moves her on from her experience to what she sees as the source of that experience, namely, God. For Jung, as a psychologist concerned primarily with the experience itself, Christ – whatever else he may be – is an archetype of human wholeness. And Jung regarded the image of Christ crucified, central to Teresa and Christian tradition, as a particularly satisfactory symbol of the self.

Christ crucified on the cross symbolizes the psychological crucifixion of a human being during the second journey. In second-half-of-life individuation, the ego is forced to abandon the illusion of its own autonomy. In Jungian terms, in the interests of the wider self the ego has to give up its domination of personality which characterized the first half of life. The ego, terrified by the threat of losing control, fights back, and the result is internal conflict. For the ego, anything is preferable to relinquishing the control which humans imagine that they have over their lives. In religious terms, the individual's resistance is a refusal to accept the reality of its status as a contingent creature dependent on God. In the journey through the castle, as the centre approaches and the ego lets go of its control, the personality learns by relinquishing everything and abandoning itself to the will of God that the ground of being, God, can be trusted.

By the sixth room of the interior castle, travellers have resolved the paradox which characterizes much of the second part of the journey – how by striving to stop striving and how actively to become passive. Similarly, in Jungian second-half-of-life individuation, the ego eventually enters into a new and enlarged relationship with the self. Problems and obstacles begin to resolve themselves, and further progress becomes possible. Conscious ego adjustments were no longer adequate, according to Jung, so something new had to emerge from the unconscious to enable personality to achieve a more balanced relationship centred on the self. Jung sees such a solution as coming from the collective unconscious; for Teresa, the solution comes from God.

Teresa holds that in the sixth room the individual should be aware of the Blessed Virgin. According to Teresa, Mary should be valued not only as the mother of God-become-human but for herself, since she is what all Christians should seek to be, holy spirit fused with body. For Jung, Mary is an obvious *anima* symbol.

Teresa says of the sixth room that for some there are now not merely words and concepts but the experience of union with God. However, she constantly stresses that mystical experience should not be sought; what really matters, she says, is progress in love, and for this love to reveal itself in the service of God and others. It is union with God's will that matters in this life, and this does not necessarily involve visions and voices. But Teresa reports that for those who have spiritual delights, there is now an explosion of such experiences, as if some barrier has been broken through.

In these last rooms, with words unable to convey what is happening, Teresa uses images to express the closeness of this union with God. The union resembles rain falling into a river; it is like a stream entering the sea; it is like two beams of light entering a room by different windows and becoming one. She is especially fond of the metaphor of marriage. In the seventh and final room a spiritual marriage takes place in which complete union with God is achieved, or as complete a union as is possible in this life. And in finding God in this spiritual marriage, the travellers find themselves. *The Interior Castle* is a journey not only to God but to a true self.

Jung regarded marriage as a powerful symbol. He saw the opposite gender as symbolizing for many human beings the otherness which all need to make themselves complete. He regarded 'male' and 'female' as often functioning for the other sex as symbols of what is required for psychological wholeness. The terms *anima* and *animus* were used by Jung to refer to archetypal female and male symbols in different cultures. For Jung, coming to terms in the second half of life with the psychological otherness symbolized by *anima* and *animus* was an essential part of the development of a whole self.

Both Teresa and Jung are concerned with human development. But while Jung sees and describes such development scientifically and psychologically, Teresa does so in spiritual terms. For Jung, individuation is essentially a discovery of the integrated self. For

Teresa, while the journey to the centre leads to the self and self-knowledge, its purpose is primarily to discover God. And though the travelling ends within personality, at the self or the centre of the castle, for both Jung and Teresa the journey returns the individual to the external world. For Teresa, the journey which ends in God, in this life or after death, results in greater love and work for other human beings now. With Jung, too, individuation which produces an integrated self also leads to a greater concern for other people and human responsibilites.

But examining Teresa's spiritual marriage, and Jung's *anima* and *animus* process, suggests an important difference between them. For Jung, such *anima* and *animus* symbolism relates to a wholeness to be discovered within the human self. For Teresa, too, personal wholeness matters, but such wholeness involves God; and for the Christian Teresa, union with God also involves Christ. As we have seen, Christ is God-become-human for Teresa; for Jung, Christ is a symbol of the individuated human self.

Teresa and Jung may be describing the identical journey from two different perspectives or levels, one religious and the other psychological. In this view, Teresa provides a religious spiritual account of a journey, while Jung gives a scientific psychological account of the same journey. Alternatively, they may be describing different journeys which have much in common. That God is central to Teresa's account but not much referred to explicitly in Jung's would suggest that they are describing different journeys. However, Jung sometimes seems to suggest that God is to be found in the collective unconscious and is to be experienced in the integrated human self. So if Jung's wholeness and Teresa's union with God are similar, perhaps identical, then the two journeys which they describe may be the same.

According to Teresa, the union with God in the seventh room differs in one respect from the ways in which the soul is united in previous rooms. Since the exercise of the mind has in some way been suspended in previous experiences, there was an absence of awareness about what was going on. In the seventh room, says Teresa, the soul has some knowledge of what is happening. And in the seventh room, she says, the individual may experience at a deep level an intellectual vision of the Trinity. Perhaps this is not surprising, since the Trinity is a central Christian mystery.

Teresa stresses that the pains and tribulations of life are still felt in the seventh room, but that the transient joys and sorrows of human existence affect the traveller less. There is tranquillity at the centre of personality in spite of what is felt and suffered at the surface. Human beings remain frail, still capable of sin. She writes about the delight of the union with God in the seventh room; there is now no fear of death, only a desire for exile to end and to go to God. But the soul wishes to continue serving God as long as God wants. The purpose of the spiritual marriage is clear: 'the birth always of good works, good works . . . Martha and Mary must join together in order to show hospitality to the Lord'. Prayer and good works. And these good works may be externally important or very ordinary. 'The Lord doesn't look so much at the greatness of our works as at the love with which they were done' (*Interior Castle* 7,4,15).

Teresa says that this spiritual marriage does not come to perfect fullness now. Those who reach the seventh room in this life experience union with God only intermittently and for short periods. And Teresa sees that most travellers do not enter the seventh room this side of death. But in *The Interior Castle*, Teresa, constantly affirming the value of all human beings, stresses that we are all invited to an intimate relationship with God. Teresa sees this as a relationship between equals; in doing so she is again affirming our value to God who became a human being and died for us on the cross. This relationship with God develops the way any relationship does, but is different since God's love for us was there from the beginning. God was always already present at the centre of personality.

Teresa knows that only few have mystical experiences. For most of us, there are at best only occasional moments of what she calls consolations. She is aware that for many of us such moments are as near as we come to a foretaste of eternal happiness. But such intimations convey that God is there behind the cotton wool, and they make us aware that only union with God and with other human beings in God will satisfy us. Teresa reports how in a vision she thought that she was being taken to Heaven, and the first persons she saw there were her mother and father.

Teresa reassures us that we will soon be at our journey's end and that nothing suffered now compares with the reward prepared. The few hours which we spend in this unendurable prison go by; the single night in this poor inn ends. We have to pass through death first, but Teresa assures us that if we have tried to put aside the things of this world, and to love God and serve others, death will come gently. 'It comforts me to hear a clock strike,' says Teresa in her *Life*, 'for when I find another hour of life has passed away, I seem to be getting a little nearer to the vision of God.'

6

A Questioning Theologian: Karl Rahner's Transcendental Christianity

Nature as we know it, with its order and with its laws, is thus largely a product of the assimilating and ordering activities of our mind . . . Our cosmos bears the imprint of our minds . . . our theoretical creations can be controlled and tempered by self-criticism . . .

(Karl Popper, *Conjectures and Refutations*)

This ultimate mystery at the root of reality and of our lives is nameless, impenetrable, something we cannot dominate with our concepts and life calculations, something that gives itself only when we yield to it in worship. We call it God.

(Karl Rahner, *Christian at the Crossroads*)

Isaac Newton, the great physicist and mathematician, said that he seemed 'to have been only a boy playing on the seashore, and diverting myself in now and then finding a smoother pebble or a prettier shell than ordinary, whilst the great ocean of truth lay all undiscovered before me'. Newton's view of himself serves as a metaphor for Rahner's account of personality. If the pebbles and shells on the seashore are the objects of our everyday and scientific experience, then the undiscovered ocean beyond is God.

Rahner calls the world of experience, of pebbles and shells and sand, categorial reality. This is the world we are in and never out of. Rahner, influenced by existentialism, sees that we have no alternative but to start from where we are, which is this world we are in. Whatever the inventiveness of science fiction writers, the fictional worlds they create are always an extension of our present world.

But Rahner sees that though we exist in the world of experience, we attempt to reach out beyond. One way we do this is by asking questions, and Rahner regards this questioning as characteristically human. Humans ask questions about the material world which they inhabit of pebbles, shells, sand; science is one result. Science owes its origin and development partly to the human preoccupation with questions. In science, these questions usually take the form of questions and criticisms about existing views.

But there are questions that humans ask about the material world which science cannot answer, such as why the world exists at all. Why is there something rather than nothing? What does the existence of the material world signify? What does anything mean? Death? What are we? In these questions we are stretching out across the shore to the mysterious ocean beyond. If asking certain kinds of questions about the pebbles, shells and sand ends in science, so asking these other sorts of questions about the mysterious ocean beyond leads to philosophy and theology.

Science probably began with tool-use and tool-making. Thinking is always involved in tool-making, and this thinking is characterized by inventiveness. Humans go beyond trial and error in tool-making, and subsequently in the technology and science to which tool-making has led. For it to be possible to go beyond trial and error, humans need to be able to classify and think in categories. Because humans can classify and categorize, they are able to plan and to give order in their thought to the material world about them. When our remote ancestors wanted something to cut with, they picked up a flint with a sharp edge or broke a flint along the grain to get an edge. They did this because they already knew that sharp edges were best to cut with, and also they knew that breaking along the grain was likely to produce a sharp edge. They knew all this because they had thought out for themselves the advantages of a sharp edge and of working along the grain to get an edge. There is first an idea, and then one tries out the idea to see if it works; the idea comes first. This is the way of human tool-makers past and present and, according to philosophers of science, it is also the way of modern scientists. Before Copernicus, the earth under our feet appeared stationary and it was the sun which seemed to move. In spite of this being the way it looked – and still looks – Copernicus could assert that this was not the way it is. Human ideas in some strange way are in advance of facts, and scientific hypotheses in part precede the data.

Rahner has always emphasized this creative freedom which humans have. The world provides a material reality for our senses; but Rahner sees that the thinking of human mind, such as is involved in science, presumes the existence of free creativity. Because of this freedom of mind, human thinking is not completely determined by the appearance of the material data; humans can liberate themselves from total immersion in the world of the senses. In holding this view, Rahner is at one with modern philosophy of science.

The improved cutting tool and Copernicus' perception that the earth went round the sun illustrate this creativity of the human mind in technology and science. The creativity is manifest in an ability to classify and categorize, in a capacity to plan and impose order on the material world, in criticism of one's own ideas and in testing by trial and error. These all suggest that the human mind is innately equipped with certain structures that make technology and science possible. Rahner would agree: the human mind consists in part of innate pre-existing structures.

Rahner adopts Thomas Aquinas' view of how the mind acquires knowledge. Aquinas held that there are two powers of intellect, a receptive agent and an active agent. Immanuel Kant later made a similar distinction between a passive and active element in human knowledge. Aquinas and Kant are saying that there is both a passive acceptance of the world by the senses, and an active interpretation of sense data by the human mind. Through our senses we receive our experience of the world. But the mind also constructs the reality we see and experience; the knowledge we arrive at is in part the product of mind using its pre-existing structures. This view of the relation between human mind and material reality is the basis of much of Rahner's thought. This is illustrated by a certain similarity between Rahner's approach to personality and that of George Kelly's personal construct theory.

Kelly's cognitive approach to personality, now very influential in psychology, takes as a starting point the human capacity for science. Kelly regards all human beings, not just the few working in laboratories, as scientists. He suggests that human beings, because of the structure of their minds, always function as scientists, even in their everyday lives. According to construct theory, humans try to make sense of their lives and the world they inhabit; and they do this just like scientists in laboratories. Humans adopt viewpoints – professional scientists would call them theories – to help them understand the world. These viewpoints are essentially ways of categorizing the world; Kelly calls them 'constructs'. Because of these categories or constructs, humans perceive the world and other people in certain ways. Someone might see other people in terms of whether they are tall or short, intellectual or down-to-earth, aggressive or easy-going. Such categories or constructs are adopted to impose a meaningful order on our experience.

According to Kelly, our personal categories or constructs partly determine how we view the world. The world offers material reality to our senses, but we see the world only through the preconceptions of our pre-existing constructs. We see the world through our preconceptions in the way that scientists see data in terms of their theories. The idea that scientists start with the raw data and go on from there is now regarded as incorrect. There are no 'data' out there in the world; there is only confusion of impressions which scientists order and make sense of. Like a scientist making sense of the world by means of theories, so the everyday human uses constructs and categories to impose meaningful order on the raw data of everyday experience. Once this is done the world no longer exists as a chaotic confusion of impressions but becomes a place which we can make sense of. Then we know what to think, feel and do.

For Kelly, scientists are what all human beings are all the time. Similarly, for Rahner, it is not just a few people who are theologians, but all humans are. Partly because of the kinds of questions we often ask, we are all theologians. In Rahner's account of personality, human beings are frequently informal theologians in their everyday lives and their reflections on everyday life, as well as in special moments.

The categories or constructs which humans use to view the world differ from one individual to another. A personal construct system is unique to a particular person, and Kelly's main point is that a person's constructs say something about that person. A particular individual may categorize others in terms of constructs such as tall/

short, intellectual/down-to-earth, assertive/easy to get on with, generous/mean. According to Kelly, the constructs and categories adopted reveal something about the person using them.

In contrast to Kelly's interest in exploring the unique personality of every 'human scientist', Rahner is interested in what is universal and common to all 'human theologians'. Kelly is concerned with the particular concepts and constructs and categories that a particular person uses to make sense of his or her world. Rahner is concerned with the way in which all humans use their minds to understand the world. If in Kelly's account the constructs or categories that an individual uses reveal something about him or her, so in Rahner's account how all humans view the world reveals something about all humans. Expressed in Kelly's terms, Rahner is suggesting that there is a construct system which is common to all human beings. Rahner goes on to say that if we study this structure of mind which we all have and the way in which we use this common structure, we will discover something about ourselves as human beings. One obvious way in which we can study this common structure is by examining how the human mind works with the categorial reality of the pebbles, shells and sand on the shore. We might also study how the mind occasionally thinks about the ocean beyond. First, how does this mind work with the categorial reality of pebbles, shells and sand?

I look up at the sky and think 'That's a plane up there'. My recognition of a plane is partly the result of the visual data that registers on my passive and receptive senses; this is *a posteriori*, 'from what comes after', experience. But I could not recognize a plane unless I already knew beforehand what a plane looks like. This pre-existing knowledge, which enables me actively to recognize a plane, exists prior to the event, is *a priori*. This 'from what comes before', *a priori*, category of thought existed before I saw this particular plane. Of course, this knowledge of what a plane looks like is also the result of experience, the experience of seeing what are called 'planes'.

For Kant, as for Rahner, there is *a priori* knowledge in the human mind which goes back much further than knowing what a plane is. For both Kant and Rahner, this *a priori* refers to what is even more prior; it refers to pre-existing structures of the human mind which we bring with us into the world. Kant is concerned here not with our everyday or even scientific knowledge of the world, but with structures of mind which make such knowledge possible in the first place. Kant uses the term 'transcendental' to describe such structures. Contemporary cognitive psychologists would regard such structures as innate. Kant uses the term 'trancendental knowledge' to refer to knowing about these mental structures of ours which make it possible to know anything at all about the world. Our knowledge of such knowledge is arrived at by what Kant calls 'transcendental deduction'. Transcendental deduction works by asking: what are the *a priori* conditions for, say, seeing and recognizing an object in the sky as a plane? And the answer to such a question tells us something about the *a priori* transcendental structures of the knowing human person. Rahner adopts this position as a starting point for an exploration of human personality.

Like Kant, Rahner holds that human knowledge comes partly from what is experienced by the senses. Though human personality is characterized by pre-existing structures of mind, what the mind contains is the product of *a posteriori* experience; it is 'from what comes after' knowledge and experience. This is the categorial reality of the pebbles, shells, sand and seashore. Categorial reality relates to a being or a manner of being which is historical, limited, particular, concrete. Rahner uses categorial particularly to refer to the specific definite content of everyday knowing and choosing. Categorial knowledge is *a posteriori* knowledge. Categorial refers to what humans obtain from the world of objects and other human beings – that is, from the experience of quite simply living, thinking and behaving. Categorial reality is the world of everyday experience. Categorial reality is the stuff of science.

Rahner agrees with modern existential psychology in holding that humans can only find answers by addressing the world they inhabit, the seashore-world of categorial reality. But he also holds that by means of exploring the categorial world of everyday experience we can get to know something about ourselves, particularly about the permanent *a priori* structures of our mind. In this way we will more obviously become what we already are, theologians as well as scientists. It happens in the following way.

In our everyday activities like going around a supermarket we ask questions. Are the tomatoes ripe? Which cereal is good for the children's health? Is there a cheaper product? When humans ask questions about this material world of Rahner's categorial reality, they are Kelly's informal scientists of everyday life. If they go further and ask questions more formally about, say, the chemical make-up of a tomato, they become professional scientists, and we have science. But whether as informal or professional scientists, whether studying planes, tomatoes or the nutritional content of cereal, what we are concerned with here are the pebbles, shells and sand on the shore, the material world of objects and beings.

But human beings also ask questions about the being of these objects and beings, about reality as such. Why am I here in the world at all? As everyday theologians we ask questions about existence, and we even end up asking questions about the source of these questions, namely, ourselves, human beings who ask these questions. What is the point of my existence, here in the supermarket or anywhere? When humans ask questions about being as such, including questions about themselves asking the questions, they become informal theologians. When humans do this, the direction of their questions would seem to move from the horizontal to the vertical, from scientific to philosophical and theological enquiry. But in Rahner's account – and this is important – we often do both at the same time. After all, even in our philosophical and theological questioning we can never escape from the physical world. Whatever the nature of our enquiry, we remain contained in the empirical world of our senses and of everyday experience and science.

We examine the pebbles, shells and the sand on the shore. We study these material objects and arrive at some everyday or scientific knowledge of them. But Rahner maintains that this is possible only because our minds in part consist of *a priori* transcendental structures that make such knowledge possible. These transcendental structures are not directly observable and their existence has to be inferred. So we look at human thinking, and we reason out what structures must be present in the human mind for this thinking to be possible. So we study human choosing, and reason out what mental structures must be present in a human being for such choosing to be possible. So we examine human experiences, and reason out what structures must be present in human personality for us to have such experiences. If we examine our thinking, choosing, experiencing of the material world of pebbles, shells and sand, we might discover something about our *a priori* pre-existing structures which make the thinking, choosing, experiencing the way they are. In other words, we might get to know something about personality. Rahner illustrates with the example of light. Because of light we can see the world; but it is only by reflecting on our being able to see the world that we become conscious that there is such a thing as light. Rahner further suggests that if we find out something about our own nature by means of this transcendental questioning, we might even discover the meaning of our existence.

The transcendental method asks questions about what it is in human personality that makes human knowledge and human activity possible. We have seen that if we look at human behaviour in general, and science in particular, we find that humans ask questions. Everything we know presupposes that we have asked a question in the first place and, in science, usually that we have made a criticism. This tells us something about human personality: humans ask questions; it is part of their *a priori* human nature to do so. It is what made tool-making possible in the first place and eventually led to technology and science.

In Rahner's account, human personality stands at a point where a horizontal and vertical line intersect. The horizontal line represents the human being's relation to the world, which is primary since human experience begins in the world; this is the domain of ordinary experience and science. It is our starting point, and there is nowhere else we can start from or start our questioning from. And though, in Rahner's view, we never really manage to leave this material world behind and go beyond it, the vertical line represents our attempt to do so. The vertical line portrays our attempt to move beyond the boundaries of the material world, if only conceptually. The vertical expresses how we try to obtain access to what – if anything – is beyond the material world, by studying the material world of sense and experience. Human personality is the point at which biology and mind, matter and spirit, the temporal and the timeless, interact. For Rahner this vertical attempt to move beyond the physical world, and our awareness of almost doing so, characterizes human personality. Secular existentialism also holds that humans are capable of some sort of going beyond, but rejects the view that humans are anything other than biology.

Unlike Kant and Kelly, Rahner is not primarily concerned with these *a priori* transcendental structures operating in the horizontal direction of pebbles, shells and sand. Rahner wishes to move from the study of such horizontal structures into a vertical direction or – to return to our earlier image – to the ocean stretching out beyond the shore. He holds that implicit in our horizontal *a priori* knowing is a vertical dimension; this vertical dimension is a knowing beyond categorial experience and not open to direct inspection. We are not scientists and then theologians; we are both at the same time.

Rahner holds that in every human being there is an *a priori* structure that makes it possible for humans to know and behave at all. This innate structure provides the condition of the very possibility of human knowledge and behaviour, and therefore of being human. For Rahner there are two fundamental distinguishing characteristics which mark out humans as humans and not as something else: knowing and freedom. These two key features of human personality, knowing and freedom, are possible because of innate *a priori* structures. A human being is a union of being and knowing, and transcendental knowledge can come from an examination of these activities. But transcendental knowledge can result from exploring a variety of other areas of human life, such as loving and making decisions. Using the transcendental method, Rahner explores the *a priori* structure of personality, asking the questions 'What must we presuppose to be necessary in the human mind for certain experiences to be possible?' 'From the experiences which we have, can we work out what is present in human personality?'

Shopping in the supermarket, I am occupied by a consideration of the goods in front of me. Do I need one of those? Where are the onions? What are the prices? This is categorial reality and this is categorial thinking. While this categorial activity goes smoothly I will probably stay at this categorial level. But there are certain moments when the everyday does not seem enough. I might, for example, feel depressed in the supermarket and find myself asking why so much of life is taken up with shopping. The depressed reflection in the supermarket is an example of an important moment of self-awareness. According to Rahner, in such moments humans move from a down-to-earth preoccupation with the objects and reality in front of them and seem to go beyond the everyday categorial world.

In an art gallery, standing before a Rembrandt painting, I react to the colours, to the lines, to what it represents. But at the same time I go further to an awareness of how deeply I am moved by the painting. I stand there realizing, perhaps only slightly, that the painting has made me sad and elated, and has aroused in me wonder at the human condition, its beauty, its transience and tragedy.

Humanistic psychology's account of personality also emphasizes such moments, when we are moved by the beauty of the universe, the joy in a relationship, the wonder of great art. Humanistic psychology, as we have seen, terms these 'peak moments'. In literature Eliot's poetry is often an exploration of such 'timeless moments'; Virginia Woolf speaks of 'moments of being' and James Joyce refers to 'epiphanies'.

When such moments are experienced in the everyday they do not last, and we know this. In 'Two in The Campagna', Browning writes:

No. I yearn upward, touch you close,
Then stand away. I kiss your cheek,
Catch your soul's warmth, – I pluck the rose
And love it more than tongue can speak –
Then the good minute goes.

We are left satisfied and unsatisfied, feeling pleasure but still longing, fulfilled and restless for more. In the obvious reality before us, each of us seems to go . . . beyond everything. Whatever it is that we experience, person or hope or a painting, the things themselves point to something further, hint at something past themselves, signal us on like a policeman at the cross-roads. In such a moment there seems to exist something unidentified, but inviting and real, the far side of the pebbles, shells and sand, like the ocean stretching away hauntingly.

Rahner sees that if we attempt to take hold of this mysterious experience, perhaps by thinking about it carefully, the experience seems to expand or recede like the horizon as we advance. If by an act of intelligence or imagination we appear to grasp this horizon, we find that it seems contained within another horizon. As human beings, we have the experience that we are always going further and never coming to a halt. In the questions which we ask about our lives and their meaning, the few answers we get never really satisfy us. No experience completely fulfils us. Our personality resembles a vast water tank waiting to be filled, which most of the time contains scarcely enough water to cover the bottom. Perhaps the problem is inside us as much as outside. Perhaps the problem relates to our tank's almost infinite capacity. Human beings, while inevitably remaining within the realm of the senses, seem also to go beyond the everyday material world, its objects, things and even other people, to . . . but that is the puzzle! To what? To God?

In Rahner's account, what such transcendental analysis reveals is that personality, in these special moments, seems almost to go beyond the empirical. And, for Rahner, what personality goes beyond the material world to is God. The horizon – to use our earlier image – is not to be identified with God; this would imply that God can be known. But in the act of reaching out to the horizon we seem to experience the existence of a mysterious absolute, and this absolute is what we call God. God is the mysterious goal that we are dimly aware of in certain timeless moments when, while remaining within the material world, we seem at the same time to go beyond the material world.

Rahner regards these special moments – wondering about the point of it all in the supermarket, being deeply moved in front of a Rembrandt – as exceptionally revealing. This to some extent is because these special moments have a particular self-awareness as part of the experience. The everyday goes wrong, and we are aware of ourselves depressed, feeling that everything is a waste of time. We are aware of ourselves deeply moved by music or poetry. We feel a loneliness that alienates us from the everyday; we experience grief for the death of someone we love; we see and accept the reality of our own future death. There are times when we are aware of great responsibility, like a parent watching over a seriously ill child. There are situations when we are confronted by our freedom: a woman attracted to a colleague at work is aware of the reality of a choice between staying faithful to her husband or the excitement of a new relationship. Human love produces many such moments. In a marriage ceremony the two people may suddenly be moved by a realization of the commitment they are about to make to one another. Prayer and religious worship sometimes produce such an awareness.

If we analyse these special moments we discover that they are . . .

difficult to analyse! What an examination of these special peak moments does reveal is that they seem to have more in them than categorial reality. My response to the Rembrandt has more in it than a sense of pleasure at lines and colours and a fine picture. The two people aware of their own and each other's love are aware of something beyond the finite loves of two human beings. The married woman torn between attraction to her colleague and the man she is married to is aware of something else that should be taken into account, beyond the immediate situation. Feeling low in the supermarket I really do feel there is more to me than shopping, everyday chores and staying alive.

According to Rahner, such special moments reveal that we do not simply experience categorial data. For a start, we constantly question categorial data; we often evaluate the experience; we question, evaluate and come to conclusions. Among our conclusions are that we are happy but know our happiness is inadequate, or that there is a greater happiness. Or we love another person and know our love for him or her is not enough. Or we are loved by another person and experience that being loved by him or her does not fully satisfy us, if for no other reason than that one day he or she will die, just as we will. In front of a painting, or listening to music, our pleasure and satisfaction are such as to leave us wanting more pleasure and satisfaction. The point is that in such experiences we experience limits . . . limits . . . limits. Limits to ourselves, to our experiences, to other people, to our loves and hopes and knowledge, to the whole world. But paradoxically this experience we have of boundaries implies something positive. The human experience of limits is not indicative of any limitation. Quite the reverse.

In all this we realize, perhaps not fully consciously, that we can only know that something is limited if at the same time we go further. The experience of a limit means that there is something in us that goes beyond what we have experienced as limited. The experience of a limit also means, even more startlingly, that we must have experienced something beyond the limit. How in a relationship can we experience the love received as wonderful but just not enough, unless we have an awareness of a greater love?

And Rahner holds that such self-aware moments, with their awareness of going further than mundane categorial reality, do not occur only exceptionally. Even when the shopping in the super-market is going smoothly, this element of beyond is present in our experience, even though we may have little conscious awareness of it being there. Whatever the activities – working on the car, reading, mending a plug, shopping, choosing to go to the cinema – all have this element of 'going beyond'. They share this with special peak moments of suddenly realizing one's love for another person, of standing moved before the Rembrandt, of wondering in the supermarket about the point of it all. What is common to all these moments is that in all of them we seem to go beyond the activity, the relationship, the knowledge, the enjoyment. And we go beyond because none of them are enough.

It is as if the experience of every pleasure, love, fulfilment and knowledge, takes place within a horizon of a greater pleasure, a greater love, a deeper fulfilment, a more comprehensive knowledge. Implicit in such experiences there seems more than we explicitly experience. In Browning's 'Two in the Campagna', the poet tells the beloved 'I would that you were all to me,/ You that are just so much, no more.' It is as if – to return to the earlier, rather too static metaphor – even in unexceptional, everyday and scarcely self-aware moments, the water tank of personality never contains more than a puddle of happiness, love, fulfilment, whatever.

Rahner stresses that the self-awareness particularly involved in special moments is with us most of the time, even in everyday life; it is just that we are scarcely aware of this awareness. In Joyce's fiction – *Ulysses* is an obvious example – we come to realize the presence of the extraordinary in everyday life. Nothing could be more ordinary than the day which Leopold Bloom lives through, but we recognize there the quality of an epic journey. Like Joyce, Rahner views the mundane everyday as full of epiphanies, of extraordinary revelations. For Rahner, what causes ordinary moments to be extraordinary, though for the most part scarcely recognized as such, is because even in the everyday we reach out beyond the categorial world. Like the curé in the Bernanos novel, *The Diary of a Country Priest*, in living our mundane life we often seem to go beyond ordinary experience.

Using Rahner's transcendental method we explore our everyday loving and knowing and choosing and thinking. We study these *a posteriori* categorial experiences. And what does our self-aware reflection on our everyday reveal? It reveals that not only in special timeless moments, but in everyday loving, thinking, choosing and knowing, human beings appear to go beyond ordinary experience. They must be doing so, since they are aware of the love with which they love, the thinking with which they think, the hoping with which they hope. They are like physicists observing and at the same time aware of the light by which they observe. And our self-aware reflection on our ordinary moments reveals that the objects, ideas and people we experience in everyday life fail to satisfy us fully. Even of everyday moments each of us can say, like Shakespeare's Cleopatra, 'I have immortal longings in me'. As in our special moments – peak moments, moments of being, timeless moments, epiphanies – so in the everyday we are always striving to go beyond. But to what? To God, according to Rahner.

For Rahner, the basis for what has just been described is not conjecture or hypothesis, but an account of common passive human experience. Rahner does not doubt the reality of such original experience; it would be difficult to do so, and such experience is almost a cliché in literature. In Scott Fitzgerald's novels, like *The Great Gatsby* and *Tender is the Night*, the young men and women have it all – wealth, youth, pleasure, leisure, intelligence, power, beauty, even human love. But like the rich young man in the Gospel, they are unhappy, empty, even desperate. Accepting the reality of such experience, we move on to ask what *a priori* transcendental structures must be present in human personality for such experiences to be possible. This is more difficult, and Rahner is aware of the problem. The difficulty is in deciding what these experiences reveal about the transcendental *a priori* structures of personality which make them possible. For Rahner there is inherent in these *a priori* transcendental human structures the possibility of a knowledge of God. As Aquinas states, 'All knowers know God implicitly in all they know.'

Rahner argues that the categorial, the pebbles and shells and sand on the shore, is not the limit of human knowledge. He is saying that in knowing something is a limit or finite, one has already gone beyond it. So there must be an *a priori* structure in personality that enables us to know this and to know how we know it. We could not know we are finite unless we had a concept of something more, beyond our limits. Quite simply, human personality anticipates infinite being. How can we say this? Because in our everyday experience and in more special moments we have, implicit in our awareness of the finite that confronts us, an awareness of something beyond.

It is because we have this awareness of something beyond and infinite that personality knows its own finiteness and the limited nature of all categorial reality. This sense of having experienced something just out of reach is particularly well expressed in the arts. In *The Great Gatsby*, Gatsby's memory of his earlier love for Daisy may be a fantasy, but the experience of the fantasy is real; a paradise has been glimpsed. Both the longing for and the awareness of a condition that fulfills our heart's desires seems rooted as a structure in human personality. Perhaps what is expressed in passages of the music of Elgar and Richard Strauss is not a nostalgia for some fictitious past, but a yearning for a real paradise that has tantalisingly been experienced.

The point is that knowledge and experience of what is finite, knowing it is finite, implies that we have knowledge and even experience of something infinite, against which we contrast the finite object. The same applies to freedom; we are aware of human freedom but also of the limits to our freedom in everyday reality. The same is true of happiness. If, as is our experience, we experience a variety of happinesses and find none of them enough, it suggests that we have an awareness of a happiness that is complete.

Rahner expresses all this by saying that human beings are open. Such openness is part of the structure of human personality, which the transcendental method reveals. Humans are open in the sense that nothing satisfies or fulfils them; no experience makes them feel complete in a way that lasts; whatever love they receive, it is never enough; when their hopes are fulfilled, they hope for something further; if they obtain a certain security and safety, it proves insufficient and they want still more; they continually ask questions, and having found an answer they ask more questions. Rahner is not proposing such openness as a theoretical hypothesis; he is suggesting it as a fact of human experience. Because of such openness, nothing, no other person, not even a wife or husband, no system of beliefs like science or even religion, no set of ideas or experiences like nationalism, no institution to which we belong like the organizations we spend our lives working for, will completely fulfil us.

With this open quality it is as if there are no boundaries to a human personality. Human beings, because they are open, cannot be contained within any definition. And Rahner, seeing human beings as the beings who ask questions, extends this to seeing human beings as themselves a question. Human personality itself constitutes a question, and at the beginning of *Christian at the Crossroads*, Rahner declares: 'Man is the question to which there is no answer.' It is as if – to return to Newton's metaphor – only the ocean and its mystery will satisfy us; but all we have is the shells, pebbles and sand on the shore. All we can do, since the sea stretches out beyond our grasp, is, like the character in Beckett, to move the pebbles around from one pocket to another to pass the time and alleviate the boredom. Eliot remarks in a letter that all great art originates in boredom.

What is the answer to the question 'to which there is no answer', which human personality asks by its existence? What is this mystery that the ocean expresses? What is the limitless, infinitely expanding horizon which contains our limited categorial knowledge within its horizons? For scientific materialism, the unanswered question or mystery or limitless horizon is simply the knowledge we do not yet have. The assumption of scientific materialism is that the advances of human knowledge will eventually explain what is as yet not understood.

Rahner expresses his dissatisfaction with materialism in the form of a question. How, he asks, can we talk of matter as the only thing that exists, if we have no knowledge of anything other than matter? If a fish lived at the bottom of the sea, we would not expect the fish to know about air or dry land. And in the absence of knowledge of air or land, the fish would have no appreciation of what sea is. Like the fish, we would not be able to talk about matter, nor have any notion of what matter is, unless we had experience of a reality other than matter.

Rahner regards spirit and matter as different. However, for Rahner, spirit and matter do not refer to two different areas of reality; spirit and matter refer to two different aspects of the same reality. Rahner holds that, in a human being, spirit and matter are part of the same reality, in close affinity and inseparable. In his monograph *Hominization: The Evolutionary Origin of Man as a Theological Problem*, Rahner adopts Aquinas' distinction between primary and secondary causes. Rahner sees spirit as the historical product of evolution, but at the same time he holds that the power of God made possible the emergence of complex matter and spirit through evolution. Similarly he regards human beings, both matter and spirit, as both the creations of God and as wholly the product of their parents.

Rahner uses the transcendental method to demonstrate further the shortcomings of scientific materialism. We have seen that if we examine ourselves and our lives we know that nothing in our everyday experience, no matter how improved, will satisfy us. Self-aware reflection on our depression in the supermarket, on our sad elation before a Rembrandt or a lovely landscape, tells us that nothing satisfies us. Rahner's point is that we know, reflecting on our everyday experience as well as occasional peak moments, that our ordinary material life in the categorial world will never be enough; we long for something more. We long for a paradise or utopia, knowing that they imply experience qualitatively different from our present experience. And we realize that in this world no society is ever going to produce any such paradise or utopia. How do we know this? We just do. There has never been a society fit for human beings; and, if for no other reason than death, we know there never will be. Things can be improved, but we know that there will never be a society on this material earth which will satisfy our deepest, and very real, 'immortal longings'. Nothing less than the mysterious ocean will do.

If we examine both self-aware everyday and peak experiences, there is something else, says Rahner, that we discover. We discover that though such experiences are part of us, they are not identical with human personality. Rahner again points out that in these experiences we seem to be aware of limits and that often we appear to experience something beyond the limits. Examining the *a priori* structure of personality, Rahner concludes, we discover in our experience a mysterious something that is not identical with us, but which is partly independent of human personality.

For Rahner, if we gave a name to this mysterious something it would be God. What if there were no word for God? What if someone who experienced this mysterious something did not know a word for God? Or, what if in some totalitarian atheistic state all words for God had been banned by thought-police? It would make no difference. It would make no difference because there will always be the experience. Whether we use the term God, mystery, self-actualization, or if we use no name, there remains the experience. Voltaire's 'If God did not exist, it would be necessary to invent him' is also true in a way slightly different from what Voltaire meant. Because of this human experience of . . . we could call it 'Mystery', here we will use the the more traditional term . . . 'God', if a word for God did not exist, it would be necessary to invent one. But human beings usually have no need to invent a word for God, in the way that they have needed to make up a word for telephone and computer. Usually, a word already exists. Rahner points out that even the atheist declaring that God is dead or claiming that the word 'God' has no meaning helps the word to survive. And perhaps the fact that a word for God usually exists and survives is significant. And the word for 'God' continues to survive, in spite of there being no obvious reality we can point at, as we can, for example, with 'tree'.

Rahner's point is that 'God-talk' expresses a real experience. The experience is real, regardless of what the experience refers to. And if we stopped using words relating to God, the experience would be unlikely to go away. The experience of some inexpressible mystery would always be there, disturbing us still.

In his affirmation of the reality of our experience of mystery, regardless of what it might signify, Rahner resembles Jung. Jung said that he was happy to use the term 'God' as a label for something which his therapeutic work suggested was central to human life, but which remained essentially mysterious. But by doing so, Jung commented, he was merely giving this mystery a label which made it even more mysterious. For both Rahner and Jung the fact that 'God' is a word that describes a human experience is unproblematic. More problematic is what this experience refers to. For the materialist psychologist, it might be the experience of unfulfilled sexuality; for the more psychoanalytically inclined, it might refer to a traumatic fear or to childhood awe of father lodged in the unconscious; for the humanistic psychologist it refers to human beings' experience of some aspect of their potential and of their self. For Rahner, this experience is certainly an experience of one's self, but is also an experience of a reality called God.

In humanistic psychology, the experience of self and of going beyond self is expressed in self-actualization, seen as a wholly psychological process within personality, unrelated to any external reality such as God. Rahner takes the Christian view that such experiences involve both the reality of the self and God. In Rahner's account, the experience of self and the experience of God are inseparable and make up a unity; but they are not identical.

For Rahner, God is something with which we are already familiar. One might say that God is so familiar, so much a matter of everyday experience that we are in danger of not noticing God's presence. The arts provide a useful analogy. In the poem 'The Daffodils', Wordsworth is not expressing the emotion which he felt when he saw the flowers. He is expressing a recollection of the emotion, which is not the original emotion. For Rahner, our experience within our self of mystery is also the experience of God. But thinking about our experience gives rise to uncertainty. Like the difference between the feeling in Wordsworth's poem and his original emotion at the sight of the daffodils, our subsequent reflection on the experience is not the experience itself. Any attempt after the event to identify this experience and definitively to conclude that God is present proves difficult. Once we move from the undeniable experience to a theoretical explanation of the experience, uncertainty arises.

Rahner's claim is that in our experiences, for example, of love, freedom, hope, there is the experience of God. Rahner sees God as present in our experience, and he claims that this remains true no matter how well we recognize the fact, if at all. Rahner distinguishes between the experience and the intellectual knowledge, obtained by intellectual analysis, of what it is an experience of. Jung placed an inscription on his house: 'Invited or uninvited, God is present'. Similarly, according to Rahner, in all truly human experience, recognized or unrecognized, God is present.

Two people read Eliot's *Four Quartets* and both acknowledge that they have experienced the timeless moments which the poem describes. One reader admits to ignorance of what such moments signify, while the other believes, as Eliot probably did, that such moments refer to the experience of God. Is the reader who has both the experience and who intellectually 'recognizes' that the moment is an experience of God, any better off than the reader who only has the experience? Rahner, like Jung, regards the experience itself as more important than the intellectual knowledge of what it is an experience of. So at one level it does not matter since, recognized or unrecognized, God is present. But Rahner also holds that at another level it does matter. Just as Wordsworth's interpretation of his feelings when he saw daffodils produced a poem, so reflection on our experience may result in intellectual knowledge of God, which is of value.

However, for Rahner, the original experience is more important than any conceptual knowledge which comes from reflection on the experience. After all, conclusions which we arrive at about experiences are often wrong; we think we are happy when we are depressed, or we think that we dislike someone to whom we are really attracted and whom we even love. So we may experience God with no intellectual awareness at all, or only with an attenuated awareness, that God is what we are experiencing.

Rahner does hold that the *a priori* transcendental structure of our knowledge and activity may be grasped by us in what he calls a non-explicit way – Jung would say unconsciously – while we have the experience. But Rahner believes that to have a complete intellectual grasp on this *a priori* transcendental structure is not possible. He argues that an understanding of one's own activity and knowing and experience can never adequately be put into words or concepts. It is the difference between experiencing a work of art and reading criticisms of the work of art. So though humans are always striving to reach beyond their experience, Rahner holds that what is involved in this reaching beyond can never be fully understood. Even though humans study their own nature and personality in a variety of sciences, people's experience can never be fully grasped intellectually. This seems particularly true of people's experience of themselves.

Rahner's position is that the experience of human beings can never be fully understood by scientific and non-scientific analysis. This existential notion, that human beings are more than they can rationally know about themselves, is rejected by much of modern reductionist psychology. But in Rahner's view, scientific or non-scientific accounts of human beings present only part of the picture, and possibly a less important part than the human experience itself.

There is the implication here in Rahner's thought that it is possible to have experience independently of language; some philosophers and psychologists would deny this. Some theologians argue that it is the inevitable confusion of experience and language which makes necessary an articulated revelation from God. For the Christian such a revelation comes in scripture, Christian tradition and the teaching church. And though Rahner regards the original experience as more important than the results of any conceptual understanding, he holds that a knowledge of the existence of God arrived at by intellect is also important. He sees a knowledge of God's existence as ultimately the intellectual basis for believing that human life has meaning and purpose.

The extraordinary increase in scientific and non-scientific knowledge over the past few hundred years has not revealed the meaning and purpose of human life and human personality. We continue to ask 'What's it all about?' and 'What is this quintessence of dust?' questions. Shakespeare's *Hamlet* has been described as a series of questions to which no answers are given, because none exist. The play captures Rahner's view of humans as beings who ask questions. Humans call everything into question, and as they do, they become aware of the further questions which the apparent answers endlessly raise.

In its questioning, human personality attempts to reach beyond the material world, and this suggests that personality refuses to accept this finite world as final. In doing so, personality is implicitly asserting the reality of an existence beyond the finite material world. Rahner expresses the human striving to go beyond the material world by the word 'transcendence' in the ordinary dictionary sense. The word is not used here to refer in Kant's sense to *a priori* transcendental structures of mind. Here, transcendence means that there exists, in human personality, an orientation directed at a reality not contained in the material world. This orientation is not the product of experience, but is itself innate, *a priori*, and transcendental in the Kantian sense. Rahner holds that what makes it possible for us to be fully human is our personality's transcendent relation to a transcendence which can never be fully understood, but which we call God.

And, as we have seen, not only for Shakespeare in *Hamlet* but for Rahner, too, it is also valid to regard human personality more existentially as itself posing a question. 'What is this quintessence of dust?' 'Man is the question to which there is no answer.' By our very existence, each of us poses a question. And Rahner holds that to this question no answer is forthcoming – unless the answer is God. But human personality remains utterly mysterious, even when directed towards the greater Mystery that is God.

And since God remains so hidden, it is not obvious how this Mystery, which is God, feels about us. God may be indifferent to us; God may feel maliciously disposed in the way that Shakespeare's Lear suggests: 'As flies to wanton boys, are we to the gods;/They kill us for their sport.' The tragedies of Aeschylus, Euripides and Sophocles suggest that the Greeks, when believing in God or the gods, were deeply puzzled as to how divine reality felt about human beings. For this reason, humans need God to tell them. Human beings are, in Rahner's expression, hearers of the word, waiting for a divine revelation, and waiting on the edge of their seats, since they have no means of knowing in advance what the message will be.

Rahner's exploration of personality using the transcendental method suggests that human beings are ready and waiting for some revelation. This can be illustrated with an example. A man loves a specific woman whom he met at a certain time and place. One could not have predicted in advance that it would be this particular woman he would meet, love and marry. But we could know in advance that this man, like most men and women, needed another human being in a loving sexual relationship for fulfilment. Before meeting this particular woman he was ready and waiting to meet someone suitable. We can only understand his fulfilment in this particular woman, met at a particular time and place, if we realize that his nature is such that it calls for a loving sexual relationship with another human being. The woman here stands as a metaphor for revelation; the man's predisposition for a loving sexual relationship is a metaphor for the human readiness and capacity for such a revelation.

Yeats, the poet, said that the whole of his life he had been waiting for an event which never happened. The tramps in *Waiting for Godot* also wait, hoping for someone to arrive. There is pain and despair in Beckett's play. The tramps' resigned disbelief that anyone might come is matched by the intensity of their desire that someone bringing hope will eventually arrive. Rahner examines the transcendental structure of human personality and concludes that humans are *a priori* ready for revelation, like Beckett's tramps. Rahner sees as part of the structure of personality what he terms the supernatural existential. Rahner's supernatural existential is God's presence within us, which means that humans are already orientated towards a revelation. The supernatural existential signifies that human beings are ready prepared for something significant to happen, in the way which Yeats suggested he was. Because of this divine presence within us, we are able to recognize God's self-revelation as a certain event at a specific time and place. When the event arrives the key fits, and we are able to acknowledge a specific historical event as God's revelation.

Rahner holds that if God intends some sort of revelation or self-communication to human beings, it would have to be at a particular time and place. After all, it is in history that humans live. Christians believe that revelation to have been made in Christ's life and death, recorded in the Gospels. And the news which humans have been waiting on the edge of their seats for is 'good news'; this is what the word gospel means. We can breathe a sigh of relief. The good news is that God loves us.

In a sermon Karl Barth, the Swiss theologian, tells the story of a traveller lost in ice and snow who comes to the edge of a forest. A large open area confronts him and he treks across. Shortly after, he meets a local inhabitant. Before guiding him on his way, the local asks how he got there. When the traveller describes the large open space which he had crossed, the local informs him that he has just walked over a lake. The Christian's terror is like the traveller's at the realization that he had been walking on ice over deep water. But the danger is past, since Christ has come and revealed that God is love and loves all human beings. Christianity sees Christ as the answer to the eternal questioning which human personality asks by its very existence. Christ also reveals that in some mysterious way God is in the quest.

Rahner sees Christianity as adding the data of Christian revelation to philosophical and psychological accounts of personality. The revelation of God in Christ provides the data for Rahner's second account of personality. We have outlined Rahner's philosophical and psychological theory of personality, which starts from human experience and is aimed at the non-believer. But Rahner also provides a theological account of personality, centred upon the person of Christ, and addressed specifically to the practising Christian.

But what, according to Rahner, is the core of Christian revelation? First, our lives are inextricably involved with the mystery of this loving God. Secondly, this loving God has been revealed to us in Jesus Christ as that which gives meaning to our existence and promises eternal life. Thirdly, this presence of God in Christ continues with us in the church.

Rahner's second, theological and specifically Christian account of personality sees life in terms of a personal relationship with God become human in Christ. God loves us and has revealed this love for us in the person of Christ. Since the creator's self-communication to creatures has been through Christ's human personality, we are not talking in terms of concepts or abstractions. We are talking of a relationship (normally called love) with God become a human being.

Rahner sees two aspects to this. First, the development of a unique relationship with Christ. The individual personality entrusts itself to the incomprehensible Mystery of God, which has communicated itself in the concrete and personal historical figure of Jesus Christ. The fulfilment of personality comes from discovering the right way to follow Christ and from following this way as the result of personal decision. By entering into Christ's life, we enter into the life of God. By finding God through our relationship with Christ, we become absolutely and uniquely ourselves.

Rahner's second aspect relates to our neighbour. We do not find God in some elevated way which leaves other human beings and the rest of the world behind. Rather, we find God in everything and above all in everybody. For Rahner, loving and serving others is an essential element in human existence and makes real what is involved in being a Christian. And the necessary partner in this relationship with our neighbour is God.

The irony of revelation for Christians is that it firmly returns them to the material world. Rahner holds that though humans have the capacity for going beyond the categorial world, the Christian revelation draws them back into the material world where the revelation occurred. Christianity is not only about discovering God's presence in the universe, though Rahner holds that humans are able to do this. Rahner sees Christianity as about finding God in the human words of the Bible, in humanly mediated sacraments using earthly materials such as bread and wine, in other human beings, in the community of the church, and in society generally. God becoming human in Christ means for the Christian that the world and, above all, other people have more than a provisional value. The world and other people have absolute value since they are loved unconditionally by God. When the love of my neighbour is contained within the love of God, death becomes irrelevant and my love for my neighbour becomes eternal. And in the love of another person we once again experience the mystery which is also the Mystery of God. Love of God and our neighbour cannot be separated. Rahner comments that for the Christian it is not God or the world, but God and the world. The more God, the more other people; the more other people, the more God. The world is of value in itself, but this value has an eternal value as something created and loved by God. The poet Blake comments: 'Eternity is in love with the productions of time.'

Rahner sees personality development in three stages. The first stage is the movement away from the created world to God; the second stage is the movement back to the human situation and to the love and service of others. But a third stage remains. In this third stage we find other human beings, their very selves, each in their dependency on the Creator and each at the same time an autonomous independent personality within God. The human self is fully realized only in relating to other human beings in God.

But the terror of walking on ice over a void is not easy to dissipate. And Rahner regards as partly valid existentialism's account of the human condition as an experience of meaninglessness. God's revelation in Christ cannot completely rid us of the terror or root out the meaninglessness, because God remains hidden. Between the finite human being that asks questions and the Infinite Being that is the Answer, there is a chasm. As we have seen, by experience and deduction from the experience, humans may attain a grasp of the Incomprehensible Mystery. And if, as Christians believe, Infinite Being is revealed to humans in Christ, then for Christians the existential void in personality can be filled through a relationship with Christ. But such is the divine nature that God remains incomprehensible and essentially mysterious. For human beings, the Infinite Being is at best the known unknown.

In *Christian at the Crossroads*, Rahner says: 'My Christianity is therefore, rightly understood, the act of letting myself go into the inconceivable mystery. My Christianity is consequently anything but an "explanation" of the world and my existence.' If, according to Christianity, the 'answer' involves committing oneself to an unknown and unknowable Mystery called God, then it is no wonder that we have difficulty in holding on to meaning in life and often live in fear. All questions end up eventually as a question about God, and to that there is no answer.

In the rationalist world of science, to conclude that something remains a mystery is a confession of failure. However, for Rahner, mystery is not a limitation; quite the reverse. Mystery does not mean that something obscure and confused will, when analysed scientifically, eventually yield up its secrets. For Rahner, mystery is positive, and here not-knowing is superior to knowing. In our rationalist world we account for everything in terms of reason, because we have refused from the start to accept the possibility of mystery. But, according to Rahner, humans exist orientated to mystery. And this orientation to mystery, and ultimately to the divine Mystery, in part constitutes personality. Our happiness after death, and even in this life, comes in surrender to a Mystery. For Rahner, Christianity consists in a loving surrender to the Mystery called God.

We return to Newton's metaphor. Like Newton, most of us realize that our knowledge is no more than a few pebbles, shells and grains of sand. For Rahner, the unexplored ocean beyond is God, but a God who is present here and now. Rahner regards any vagueness or haziness about God's presence in this life as originating in lack of faith or understanding. The reality of the sun and the sun's light continue even if we have joined the curtains. When death draws back the curtains, we will not only see God better but realize that God has been there all the time. But though we will see God more clearly after death, Rahner holds that the Mystery will remain incomprehensible. God is always beyond our imagining and understanding.

God will remain a Mystery, but in the experience of God after death there is perfect happiness. In our life on earth, the Mystery may be present but is distant and our experience indirect. After death the experience of the Mystery will be immediate and intimate. According to Rahner, in the experience of God after death, called the beatific vision, our knowledge of God will involve surrender, and this surrender is called the love of God. Union with God is what human personality is for. And Rahner holds that our happiness will also relate to the mystery of ourselves and others, who are all mysterious because we are grounded in the greater Mystery of God.

Rahner rejects the view of atheists that belief in God alienates. Their suggestion is that humans project the good within them on to God, and in doing so they alienate what is really their own. In the atheistic account, we ascribe to God the love, goodness, freedom and power which belong to ourselves. In this view, the only way to be rid of such alienation, and to return these qualities to our selfs where they really belong, is by consigning 'God' to history. Rahner holds the opposite: the more God, the more human personality. Human relationships do not diminish us; I become more in loving some other person, not less. Rahner sees the same to be true with regard to God. The more I lose myself in God, the greater becomes my autonomy, my reality and my being. In the vision of God after death, we will not only experience more immediately the Mystery of God, but we will more intimately experience the mystery of our own personality. In the Christian view, it is the absence of God which alienates us; it is in the experience of God that we discover our identity and fulfil our personality.

Human personality is always orientated to God. And, as we have seen, Rahner regards personality as existing in a state of readiness for revelation. However, for Rahner, to talk of a readiness for a revelation, as if humans, like the tramps in *Waiting for Godot*, wait for something which has not yet happened, is theoretical. Rahner, as a Christian, holds that a revelation has already occurred. Personality's readiness for such a revelation is part of what Rahner calls the supernatural existential.

In existentialism, an existential is a concrete circumstance of human existence, a unique characteristic which makes humans human. To put this the other way round, existential refers to a characteristic that a human being possesses simply as a consequence of being human. According to existential psychology, in contrast to the way in which an animal or an object like a table inhabits the world, an existential refers to the human way of being in the world. Similarly, Rahner sees certain existentials as characterizing human beings, and as a theologian Rahner explains personality partly in terms of one particular existential. This is the supernatural existential, which is God's grace on permanent offer. Grace is quite simply the presence of God within us, and because of this presence, human beings are always orientated towards God and a revelation from God.

The supernatural existential consists in the offer of grace to human beings, and human nature never exists without this offer. Rahner sees grace as always potentially present at the core of human personality. What the supernatural existential means is that this questioning and questing human nature is somehow united to the reality of God. The supernatural existential is God's presence within all human beings, enabling them to seek and find God. The supernatural existential means that human personality, from its beginning, has a desire for God. God is the cause of that desire and wants to satisfy that desire by giving us God's own self. God has, so to speak, graced the world before any human being has even begun to respond to God's invitation.

In Rahner's account, as a result of this supernatural existential, history has never been merely natural; human history has always been in a state of grace and supernatural. The world which we inhabit, and ourselves inhabiting that world, are the 'graced' creation of a God who wishes everyone to be saved. Rahner sees personality as never just natural. Always, in the *a priori* transcendental structure of every personality, God's grace is present to human beings; again this means that at a deep level the experience of ourself is also the experience of God. For Rahner, human action is never only natural, and all human actions are invariably raised by grace to a supernatural level. Rahner sees grace as always present in human knowledge and freedom. And Rahner holds that at the core of the personalities of all human beings they are called by God.

Rahner makes a distinction between nature and person. By nature he means human nature in the raw, the 'poor, bare, forked animal' of Shakespeare's *King Lear*. Nature in this sense, as opposed to person, is that part of a human being which is not under the control of freedom. Nature is what is given and passively received as a result of being human, and so constitutes human potential. Rahner sees a tension between what a human being is as nature and the person that a human being wishes to become by a decision. Rahner regards the person (as opposed to nature) in terms of freedom. Persons are what human beings make of themselves by free decision. It is only through the exercise of freedom that one becomes a person. Paradoxically, by making free choices one becomes a person, but only in being a person is one free. Whether freedom or being a person comes first is an enigma. In our nature we are born personal, but by our free choices truly become persons. This is the task of every human being – to become a person. Rahner sees God's offer of grace, the supernatural existential, as activating the potentialities of our nature and moving us to personhood and union with God. For Rahner, as in all Christian psychology, only in relation to God does one become a full human person.

Rahner follows an old tradition in distinguishing between nature and supernature. But, as we have seen, for Rahner the distinction is in a sense academic. Nature without God's grace is only a theoretical possibility. The supernatural existential implies that such a human nature has never existed. Because of the supernatural existential, the offer of grace is present in everyone as an offer from God which precedes a person's knowing, deciding, behaving. For Rahner, human personality never exists as pure nature but always in a supernatural dimension where it is acted upon by God.

The supernatural existential means that our capacity to search for God and to enjoy the beatific vision after death is a free gift of God. But since we are able to receive this gift, the supernatural existential also means that this capacity must be part of our nature. The supernatural existential signifies that we are always ready for God because that is our nature. We are made – one might say that we are ready-made – for participating in God's own life and for the vision of God. We all of us exist for one purpose, to see and enjoy the Mystery we call God.

The concept of supernatural existential reveals a chasm between scientific accounts of personality and Rahner's. In a scientific account there is only the natural human personality; for Rahner the purely natural personality is a theoretical construct and never exists, since human personality exists only with the supernatural existential. Rahner's view of personality differs from secular existential accounts in seeing personality as always acted upon and affected by God's offer of grace and as the constant target of God's saving will. As a result of the supernatural existential, of God's self-communication which we call grace, human personality participates in God's life. All of us are already participating in God's life, and all of us are always on the receiving end of God's efforts to bring us to do so more fully. 'In the human existence which You have made Your own for all eternity, You have never left us . . . the heart of all things is already transformed, because You have taken them all to Your heart' (*Encounters with Silence*). For Rahner, God has come, and as a result the world has already been transformed.

But Rahner also holds that our participation in God's life here and now is only the beginning. For Christians the significance of the incarnation, of God becoming a human being, does not end when life ends. The value of the created world, of other people and of God manifest in the person of Christ, is not temporary and insignificant beside the absolute of God. The world, other people and the humanity of Christ are loved unconditionally by God; for this reason they will be enjoyed by us for ever in eternal life. According to Rahner, even after death when God becomes all-in-all, we will find the world and other people in God. And through Christ we will find God, since Christ's created humanity is and will remain our path to God. The personality of Jesus is our way to God now and will remain the gateway which opens to God through all eternity.

'Behold, You come. And Your coming is neither past nor future, but the present, which has only to reach its fulfilment.' And when our life on earth ends, 'I shall gaze upon His human heart, O God of Our Lord Jesus Christ, and then I shall be sure that You love me.' All our days will 'finally empty into the one day of Your eternal Life . . .

Then, united with You, O God of my brothers, I shall really be able to be a brother to them . . . Then will begin the great silence, in which no other sound will be heard but You, O Word, resounding from eternity to eternity . . . No more human words, no more concepts, no more pictures will stand between us . . . You are the God of the one and only knowledge that is eternal, the knowledge that is bliss without end . . . Incomprehensible, even when I see You face to face . . . in the blissful hour of Your Eternity' (*Encounters with Silence*).

7

Scientific Psychological and Christian Personality Theory: Similarities and Differences

God (if there be a God), bless my soul (if I have a soul).
(Agnostic prayer)

Like the children in Arthur Clarke's *Childhood's End*, human personality seems to be on the way to something. Certainly, both scientific psychology and Christian theory take growth and development as central to personality. Erik Erikson goes so far as to say that we can never really speak of having a personality, since our personality is constantly in a state of developing. This emphasis on development in scientific and Christian accounts suggests that we are not so much human beings as human becomings. Besides development, three other dimensions of personality are considered here: important influences on personality, personality structure, motivation.

Development implies progress towards a goal or ideal. Parents usually prefer their children to grow into decent caring adults rather than into uncaring egotists. Such a preferred condition or goal becomes a criterion for deciding whether personality change is for the better or for the worse. Are the children now showing more concern for others? In theories of personality, development always has a direction and moves towards some goal or ideal.

In the different accounts of development given by scientific theories, the goals of development vary. In Freud's psychosexual stages, the genital personality, capable of true reciprocal relationships, of giving as well as receiving, is the ideal towards which development hopefully proceeds. For Jung, the goal of second-half-of-life individuation is the individuated self and a growth in consciousness. In humanistic psychology, the objective is self-actualization. In existential psychology, personality development is a movement from the inauthentic to the authentic, from living impersonally as one of the crowd to being an individual who accepts the reality of freedom and personal responsibility. In Piaget's cognitive theory, growth is developing a capacity for abstract thought; Kohlberg's account of moral stages moves in the direction of the individual's attaining personal ethical principles.

Christian theories regard development essentially in terms of progress towards God. Christian accounts see God become human in Christ as intimately involved in this progress and hold that the personality of Christ is the model for development. And always in Christian accounts, the growth towards God relates to the love and service of other people.

For Kierkegaard, development, stated negatively, is to rid us of our despair; stated positively, its goal is for the self to become transparent before God. Kierkegaard sees human development as a progress from the aesthetic to the ethical and, in a leap of faith, to the religious, where open before God we are cured of our despair. Augustine describes a three-step growth of withdrawal from the world, turning inward to the soul, and rising above the soul to God. For Merton, development involves a transformation from a superficial pseudo-self to our real identity in God. In Merton's account the goal of development is God, but in finding God we also discover our identity and true self. For Pascal, development is a movement through the physical and mental orders of experience to the third order of spirit. If personality achieves this order of spirit, of Pascal's supernatural heart and charity, then God becomes the centre of personality.

For Teresa, development is a journey through the castle to a centre where God is; the goal is union with God in the final room. This union in the final room may happen in this life or, as is more likely with most of us, after death. Rahner sees development in terms of a movement from the material world to God, followed by a return to the love and service of others in the world, and finally the discovery of other human beings within God. More specifically for

Rahner as a theologian, development is the growth of a unique and personal relationship, normally called love, with that Mystery which we call God, which has manifested itself in Jesus Christ.

To evaluate development, Christian accounts adopt various criteria. Among the criteria of Christian accounts are moral criteria, in the sense that they are overtly concerned with right and wrong. An example is Augustine's use of the two cities, Jerusalem and Babylon, as a metaphor for good and bad. In one city there is a concern for God and the things of God; in the other city there is preoccupation with money, power, prestige, sex, success.

Scientific theories of development do not use obviously moral criteria, and they avoid terms like goodness, sin, virtue, vice. In the behaviourist account, whether behaviour is 'good' or 'bad' depends on how it is reinforced by others. Behaviourism holds that good and bad, right and wrong, describe actions which are positively or negatively reinforced. In the Freudian account, morality is a set of rules enforced by society for our own and other people's benefit. Human beings, in Freud's view, are violent and potentially such a threat to themselves and others that life would be more dangerous if these rules were not obeyed. Good and bad, right and wrong, depend on whether the rules are being obeyed or broken. For Freud, morality is a form of enlightened self-interest; we treat others well because, in return, they will treat us well, and we do not treat others badly because, if we do, they will treat us badly. The relevant concepts of humanistic psychology, such as self-actualization and the fully functioning person, are a different sort of criteria and relate more to psychological health. Rogers, for example, refers to a human valuing process, valuing 'right and wrong' according to their potential to actualize the self.

Atheistic existentialism maintains that there are no values out there in the world or inherent in human nature, and that certainly no God has given us guide-lines to follow. The extreme atheist position is that humans have to create right and wrong, and values to live by, for themselves. Christian psychology takes the opposite view: since God exists, moral values do exist. According to Christian personality theory, there is right and wrong, good and bad, virtue and sin, though in the real world it is not always easy to decide which is which.

Where Christian theories tend to refer to right, wrong, sin, virtue, scientific accounts prefer terms like social disease, genital personality and fulfilment. But scientific accounts of personality are not value-free. The notion of 'oughtness', of how the individual ought to be and ought to act, is usually at least implicit in psychological theories. In humanistic psychology, the concept of self-actualization, though relating to psychological health, appears to acquire moral overtones. With humanistic psychology, notions of psychological health such as self-actualization, fulfilment, productive character and the individuated self, carry resonances of the good life and of what is right. The criteria of scientific accounts of personality usually have an implicit moral dimension, though one less obvious, and perhaps different, from the conventional moral criteria of Christian accounts.

But whether in the obvious moral terms of Christian psychology, or whether according to scientific psychology's concepts of the common good, society's safety and individual psychological health, one criterion consistently emerges. Our relationship with others is invariably seen as a criterion for evaluating personality development. Growth in love and concern for others exists in most theories as a measure of genuine development. In humanistic psychology, personality development is characterized by a growth in loving others, and by greater understanding, trust and acceptance of other people. Even in Freud, the genital personality is capable of giving and receiving in relationships. Merton stresses that the revelation of God in Christ returns us to the material world and to the love of others. The New Testament continually stresses the importance of loving one's neighbour as oneself and sees the whole of the law fulfilled in doing so. Teresa is emphatic that progress towards God, and ordinary or extraordinary experiences of God, move us back to service in the world and to our responsibilites with regard to other people. For Teresa, personality growth shows itself in 'the birth always of good works, good works'.

Implicit in many Christian accounts of development is the notion that we are not born fully human. Kierkegaard's spirit-self is not yet a self. For Augustine as well as Rahner, though our nature is given, a person is something which we each have to become, partly by free choice. Merton's true self has to be achieved, also by free decision. Some scientific accounts too, especially those of existential and humanistic psychologies, emphasize that being a wholly human person is not innate but something we have to make ourselves. The Jungian individuated self, Fromm's productive character, Maslow's actualized self and Rogers' fully functioning person are not supplied at birth; we have to achieve them. But in the materialist accounts of scientific psychology, personality development is wholly biological and social; in Christian theory, God too is involved in the process .

'Control' is another issue in development, whether God is regarded as involved in the process or as irrelevant. At some stage, according to both Christian and scientific accounts of development, letting go and relinquishing control are necessary. The change from active to passive prayer in Merton and Teresa illustrates this. Teresa specifically writes of the need to stop holding on to what is safe and of a willingness to take risks. Rahner, more generally, refers to Christianity in terms of a surrender to a Mystery. Scientific theories too, especially those concerned with therapy, suggest that significant development only occurs when we eventually stop clinging and trustfully let go. In Jungian psychology the difference is captured in the difference between first- and second-half-of-life individuation. At a certain stage, personality continues to develop and grow only if we surrender ourselves. In scientific materialist psychology, the surrender is to the collective unconscious, to the true self, to trustworthy other people, to the therapist, to life's changes, to the universe. In Christian accounts, the core surrender is to God.

One consequence of this loss of control is the experience of psychological distress. Both Christian and scientific accounts of development emphasize that relinquishing control, and opening up to the new, involve risk and loss of direction. Before the transformed soul emerges, as Teresa's butterfly, or Rogers' fully functioning person, or Merton's true self, there are invariably painful trials and conflicts.

Scientific and Christian theories agree on the value of everyday experience. The absence of any emphasis on the extraordinary is to be expected in scientific materialist psychology but is more surprising in Christian theory. But Teresa repeatedly stresses that though mystical experiences are wonderful, they remain inessential, and ordinary experiences which return us to the service of others are more important. If anything, Maslow would seem to stress the value of peak moments for human personality more than Teresa does consolations and spiritual delights.

Nevertheless, Christian psychology does recognize the importance for development both of special experiences and of those everyday moments which Rahner describes when personality reaches beyond the empirical. Rahner regards as significant this potential, which humans have, to breach the boundaries of experience while remaining in the material world. Augustine, too, acknowledging that life for the most part is lived on the horizontal, claims that moments exist when we move to the vertical and experience in time foretastes of the eternal. Merton particularly stresses human artistic experience as a form of active contemplation, where extraordinary moments are possible. Merton holds that aesthetic experiences, like Maslow's peak moments, can take us outside the everyday and provide illumination.

Scientific materialist theories regard such seemingly extraordinary experiences as sexual, or caused by the unconscious, or related to other biological or social processes such as self-actualization. Humanistic psychology holds that what is experienced in peak moments is an aspect of ourselves. Scientific psychologists generally, with the exception of William James and Jung, see all such experiences as wholly subjective in the sense that the experience relates to nothing external to personality. In contrast, Christian theories regard such experiences as relating ultimately to an objective reality called God. Jung takes an intermediate position that, though what is experienced resides in the collective unconscious, such an experience relates to a reality independent of the individual. Christ, for Jung, may be a symbol of the individuated self, but Jung holds that symbols relate to something external to the individual personality.

Christian and scientific accounts also differ, and agree, on the second dimension of personality to be considered, namely, important influences on personality. Since Christian psychology assumes that God exists and that human personality consists of more than the biology of traditional materialism, God and God's grace are held to affect our actions. So for the Christian, obvious influences on personality and personality development are prayer, worship, meditation, contemplation. Christian theories also see a relationship with Christ, through prayer and the sacraments, as a central influence. And since, according to Christian accounts, personality is not determined by cause and effect but is free, human actions are regarded as in part a product of free choice.

For Kierkegaard, it is free choice of commitment to God which cures our despair and enables us to achieve true selfhood. For Augustine and Rahner, by free decision one moves to God and becomes a human person. For Rahner, choice enables humans to move beyond immersion in the senses and, strengthened by the revelation of God's love in Christ, confront the void at the centre of human experience. Pascal and Merton agree with Rahner's existential view that a solution to the void and to life's apparent meaninglessness comes through the exercise of freedom. For Pascal, the decision for the Christian is between the void and God, specifically God become human in Christ. Christian accounts of personality hold that, however powerful the influences of biology, past experience and the present situation, human beings usually retain a degree of freedom.

But from early on Christian thinkers knew that freedom was limited. No one was more aware of this than Augustine, who stressed the pressures which 'the flesh' exercised on human freedom. Augustine, like Freud with regard to sexuality and violence, felt that at times human choice is almost overwhelmed by the body's demands. Because of this, Augustine, again like Freud, welcomed the constraining influence which family, state and social institutions exercise on the individual. But Augustine also stressed that human beings needed not only the help of God's grace, but also asceticism and self-discipline, to control their dangerous tendencies. In contrast to Augustine and Freud, humanistic psychologists like Maslow and Rogers inclined to a more optimistic view. They held that human beings are not inherently dangerous, though influences in the past might have damaged them and distorted their basically good tendencies.

Humanistic psychology's more optimistic account of personality has influenced Christian theorists such as Merton to redress the asceticism of thinkers like Augustine. A traditional Christian account sees sin as the cause of our unhappiness – we are unhappy because we have sinned. Humanistic psychology takes the opposite view – we do wrong because we are unhappy. Merton, while still valuing self-control and discipline, agrees with humanistic psychologists in regarding fulfilment and self-actualization as significant influences on personality development. If we are fulfilled and happy, we are less likely to do wrong or sin, and we are more likely to do good and be concerned for others.

Like Freud, Augustine recognized the influence of the past, including childhood, on apparently free actions. Augustine saw that past experience influenced our behaviour by means of acquired habits stored in the memory. Pascal, too, was aware of the importance of habit. But Pascal was also aware of the influence of pure chance. He saw, somewhat disturbingly, that contingent factors and fortuitous circumstances affect our personality and behaviour. In Pascal's account, if each of us were born not into this family, class, country, time, but into that family, class, country, time, our personalities would be very different.

With regard to freedom and determinism in human behaviour, scientific theories adopt a greater variety of positions than Christian psychology does. Christian theories invariably assert, to a greater or lesser degree, the existence of free choice. But on a continuum of scientific accounts, denials of human freedom from hard determinists, like Freud, are found at one end. At the other end of the continuum is existential psychology's emphatic and at times terrifying assertions of total free choice and responsibility. In between is Jung's assertion of purposes as well as causes in human behaviour, as well as the soft determinism of humanistic psychologists such as Rogers. Soft determinism maintains that humans, at one and the same time, are both free and determined in what they do.

For Freud, a powerful and dangerous influence on personality and behaviour is the personal unconscious. Jung also believed that humans are affected by an unconscious, but he was more interested in the collective unconscious, which he saw as containing the experience of the human species. And for Jung, this collective unconscious was only potentially dangerous, becoming an important influence for good when its contents became conscious. Central to Jungian psychology is the view that unconscious material, made conscious, becomes a source of creative energy and power.

Earlier, Augustine and Teresa had been aware that mental

processes, of which the individual is scarcely aware, influence behaviour. Certainly both Christian and scientific theories emphasize the importance of insight and self-knowledge for personality development. Pascal warned of the dangers of self-deception; Jourard stressed the importance of self-knowledge for personal growth; Augustine prayed: 'May I know Thee; may I know myself.'

The influence of other people is recognized by both scientific and Christian theories. Carl Rogers, the humanistic psychologist, emphasized the importance for personal growth of unconditional love by others. Personality's development, whether towards Freud's genital stage, or the self-actualization of humanistic psychology, or to God and the real self of Christian theory, involves other people. Christian and scientific accounts for the most part hold that personality can only develop through relationships with other human beings and human love. Object relations theorists such as Fairbairn, and symbolic interactionists like G.H.Mead, see human personality as created by such relationships.

Though aware of the importance of other people, and of external influences generally, humanistic psychology tends to regard development as a growing from within. Erik Erikson, the neo-Freudian humanistic psychologist, states that a ground-plan for personality is present at birth, and that personality develops largely according to this innate blueprint. In this view, the environment, particularly that of other people, has a significant influence, but only to the extent that it helps or hinders the unfolding of potential already there. According to Maslow, just as humans are born with a biological structure, so human personality has an innate core psychological structure, which in a good environment will develop healthily. This brings us to the third dimension of personality, namely, structure.

With regard to structure, behaviourism took a very different position from that of Erikson and Maslow. Behaviourism held that humans enter the world as blank slates, with no inborn ground-plan for personality. Behaviourism denied the existence of any blueprint or core and ignored the possibility of an innate structure called mind. But modern cognitive psychology now regards mind as central. Augustine, though emphasizing the influence of physical needs and habits on human behaviour, also stressed the importance of mind; Christian accounts have always done so. Rahner, like modern cognitive psychologists, emphasizes that mind is partly a pre-existing structure.

As well as mind, the self too now holds an important place in scientific accounts of personality structure. The self and self-actualization are at the core of modern existential and humanistic theories. In Christian theory, the notion of self goes back as far as Augustine and further, recurs in Teresa, Kierkegaard and others, and arrives in modern times with Merton and Rahner. For Christian theorists such as Merton, the search for God and the search for the true self are one and the same. Most Christian accounts of personality structure stress a mysterious inter-relatedness of the true self and God.

This inter-relatedness, and the centrality of self in Christian theory, weakens the view that belief in God is alienating. According to this view, just as in earlier times the Devil was a projection of our own nastier side, so too God's goodness, beauty and power are a projection of what is really within ourselves. Christian belief is accused of alienating us from the goodness, beauty and power which are really our own, by having us project them on to a fictitious God. We should first withdraw the projection, the view declares, and then accept our projections for what they really are, parts of ourselves. But the inter-relatedness of God and the self, in Merton, Rahner and other Christian accounts, suggests that belief in God does not necessarily cause any such alienation or impoverishment. The effect should be the reverse; more God should mean more of our true self. In the Christian account of personality structure, God is central to the self. For Jung the self-archetype relates to the God-archetype, but for the most part God has no place in the scientific accounts of the self of modern psychology.

In both Christian and scientific theories, the true self which we need to become is not usually regarded as something new, which we have to work at to make ourselves into. For Christian thinkers like Merton, and humanistic psychologists like Maslow and Rogers, the true self is something which we already are and have only to let ourselves be. But in Christian accounts, the wholeness and true self which we seek is possible only in union with God and the person of

Christ. Only God can reveal to us the self which deep down we really are.

Christian theories also differ from scientific psychological accounts of personality structure in asserting that humans are not just the physical matter of traditional materialism. For example, while Freud regards id, ego and super-ego as the stuff of biology, Kierkegaard sees the free human self as a synthesis of spirit and body. Augustine, a dualist, holds that human beings are in part spirit, and he believes that only spirit makes free choice possible. Rahner regards humans as always in a state of readiness for grace, which is God's presence within us, so humans are never just natural in the sense of being only biological beings.

With the fourth and last dimension of personality to be considered, namely, the motivation and causes of human actions, theories of personality can be categorized in two traditions. One tradition states that human beings are free, act according to reason, are aware of their reasons, make choices between right and wrong, and are responsible for their choices. Christian theories of personality and certain existential accounts are in this category. In the second tradition, the behaviour of humans is regarded as caused, being determined mainly by biology, past experience and current circumstances. As we have seen, according to this second tradition, since actions are caused and humans are often unaware of their causes, people's actions cannot be judged by conventional moral criteria of right and wrong. Psychoanalysis, behaviourism and most of materialist scientific psychology are usually placed in this second category. These two traditions are regarded as being in opposition, with Jung, humanistic and some existential psychologies, awkwardly positioned in between. But our examination of specific theories has suggested that the two traditions often have common ground and overlap.

The materialist theories of scientific psychology propose a variety of motives for human behaviour. For Freud, humans are motivated by pleasure from the satisfaction of their instincts. In Fairbairn's object relations account, people search for satisfying human relationships. In existential accounts, we seek to fulfil our personality by becoming authentic, and by finding meaning and purpose in our lives. Humanistic psychologists regard self-actualization as the key source of human motivation. Carl Rogers sees, beneath an apparent variety of motives, self-actualization as one master motive and the cause of all human behaviour.

In Christian accounts too there is one fundamental or master motive, the search for God. Human personality, according to Christian theory, is always seeking God. According to Kierkegaard, the hope to find God, which motivates all that we do, comes from our despair. Augustine holds that we want to be happy and that only God can make us happy. According to Augustine, what we seek is delight, and God is the ultimate delight; what motivates our actions is the delight which God gives. We occasionally experience this delight in our human loves, in the beauty of the world, in our earthly pleasures. But, according to Augustine, the delight will be fully enjoyed, and the restlessness which motivates us will cease, only when we possess and are possessed by God.

Merton writes of a positive force in personality, coming from God and moving us back to God and our true self. For Merton, our motivation is to find God, and in doing so to discover our true identity and self. The search for God and our real self, and the love and service of others, are the same motivation central to our lives; but, says Merton, the search for God comes first. According to Pascal, what we particularly experience in the absence of God is boredom. Besides boredom, Pascal, like modern existentialists, detects anxiety and lack of meaning in our experience of life, and together these motivate us to seek distraction. If sufficiently distracted by pleasure, sport, work or whatever, we may avoid having to acknowledge and confront the wretchedness of our situation. But Pascal held that humans are wretched only because they look for happiness in the wrong place. The happiness that we seek and that motivates us is only to be found in God.

Teresa expresses our value as human beings by asserting that God invites us to intimate friendship, which is a relation between equals. God needs our friendship, says Teresa, and the cause and motivation of human action is to arrive at a loving friendship with God. This friendship achieves its fulfilment in a spiritual marriage and vision of God, where in a union with God, our joy and happiness are complete. For Rahner, the underlying motivation and cause of human behaviour is experience of the Mystery which we call God. We are motivated to seek this Mystery, which is present in our everyday as well as in special moments; but as we reach out, the Mystery seems to elude us.

Scientific psychology concedes the reality of such mysterious experiences as Rahner, Teresa and other Christian accounts describe; but materialist psychology denies that the word 'God' captures what is being experienced. For materialist psychology, the mystery is identical with the self and what we experience is an aspect of our own personality. Freud provides an explanation of the mysterious experience in terms of childhood history; humanistic psychology explains the experience in terms of self-actualization.

Existential and humanistic accounts of personality recognize as central the motivation to find a meaning and purpose in life. Existentialist and humanistic psychologies, believing that God is dead, hold that there are no longer any absolute and objective meanings and purposes to life. Their solution is in some form of self-actualization, or in commitment to an earthly ideal or purpose which is larger than ourselves. In Rahner, Merton and other Christian accounts, the existential recognition of the world as apparently meaningless is seen as a start, but as only a start; it is the beginning of a search for a God who is not dead. Christian accounts of personality recognize the sources of motivation in biological needs such as hunger, thirst, sex, and in social needs such as love, esteem and other people's approval. But Christian theories contend that the search for God is a primary motive in human action, while recognizing that the search for God manifests itself in a variety of ways.

Scientific psychological and Christian theories of personality have common ground and overlap. But with regard to two basic assumptions they differ fundamentally. Scientific theories assume that God does not exist or is irrelevant, and that the human person can be accounted for by traditional materialism. But with regard to human development, is all personality growth biological and social, simply 'natural', and in no way related to the possibility of God? When it comes to important influences on personality, are there no influences other than those which are physical and social? With regard to structure, is personality constituted only of the biological matter of traditional materialism and nothing more? With regard to motivation, is there definitely no God which humans, whether they know it or not, seek? In short, are the scientific accounts of psychology, with their atheism or agnosticism with regard to God, and with their assertion that humans beings are no more than the matter of traditional materialism, adequate?

8

Personality and Science:
The Assumptions of Materialism

I have no need of that hypothesis.
  (Laplace, French astronomer and mathematician, referring to God)

My fundamental premise about the brain is that its workings – what we sometimes call 'mind' – are a consequence of its anatomy and physiology and nothing more.
  (Carl Sagan, *The Dragons of Eden*)

Traditional materialism, which is the basis of the natural sciences, and particularly of classical physics, dates from the sixteenth and seventeenth centuries, and is partly responsible for the success of science. According to scientific materialism, everything which exists is matter, and matter works by cause and effect; and matter operates according to consistent, enduring and discoverable laws. Matter is irreducible, and usually thought of as characterized by its being extended in space and time. Matter is the fundamental stuff of everything, and everything can largely be explained by reducing it to its material parts – though matter itself needs no explanation.

  Modern psychology extended traditional materialism to the study of human beings. Modern psychology for the most part has held that the actions of human personality can be explained by the laws of physical matter. Scientific psychology assumes, in accordance with evolutionary theory, that mind and its activities are part of the natural world and can be explained by the physical brain of traditional materialism. Cognitive psychology, like most of modern psychology, holds that mind and the brain of orthodox biology are the same. The attempt in philosophy to argue that mind is brain, and that mind can be accounted for in traditional materialist terms, is called identity theory.

There are several versions of identity theory, but all assert that mind is identical with brain. Identity theory says that mind and mental states exist, but that they are physical. Having a good idea, classifying objects as squares or triangles, feeling pain or softness, are physical processes of the brain, nothing more. Even complex workings of the mind, such as apparent freedom in decision-making, originality in language, and creativity in the arts and sciences, are the brain alone at work.

Modern psychology's materialist assertion, the 'mind equals brain' of identity theory, was questioned early on from within psychology by William James. In his *Principles of Psychology* (1890), James argued that there is a non-material dimension to personality. There is, says James, a 'self of all the other selves', a principle of personal identity, an active dimension in a human being which goes out to meet the content of thought. He hypothesized a 'non-phenomenal Thinker' independent of what is thought. This raises the question of who or what the thinker is. James concludes that we have to consider this thinker in terms of soul, spirit, or some other transcendental principle. At this point, for James, the problem becomes metaphysical, beyond the scope of a scientific psychology.

Science is concerned with material data and seeks to explain physical phenomena in terms of the material world. So James proposes an alternative view, that the identity of the human thinker consists in a stream of passing thoughts. Such an account of human identity is acceptable to scientific materialist psychology. James holds that a scientific psychology has to content itself with equating the thinker with this train of passing thoughts. But he points out that this does not square with human experience; our experience is that behind the passing thoughts is a thinker. Common experience suggests that thoughts and the thinker are not the same. Common experience suggests that there exists, independent of our thoughts, a thinker usually called consciousness or 'I'.

For James, explaining the thinker, consciousness or 'I', in terms of something like spirit or soul, is as valid as any materialist psychological explanation. He holds that scientific solutions, like his own stream of passing thoughts explanation, are not necessarily more true than spiritual and transcendental explanations. In holding this position, James is rejecting scientism, the view that a complete and adequate explanation of humans can be given using the methods of natural science. Implicitly James is touching on the nature of the different perspectives provided by religion and science.

As a science, psychology is concerned with the material world, with the physical cause of things, with events which can be observed or whose effects can be observed. In practice, modern psychology makes the materialist assumption that human actions can be reduced to physical laws which determine the behaviour of all inanimate and animate matter. But the question of whether matter as conceived by traditional materialism is enough to account for human personality remains unanswered. Whether brain as conceived by orthodox biology equals mind has not yet been demonstrated.

When it comes to the existence or non-existence of God, modern psychologists, apart from Freud and Jung, have little to say. Scientific personality theorists have by and large adopted the agnostic view that we cannot know whether God exists and should regard the question as irrelevant; or they have taken Freud's atheistic stance.

Freudian psychoanalytic theory points out that feelings about parents influence the view we have of God. But Freud goes further and declares that God is no more than an exalted father-figure and that religion in part derives from ambivalent feelings about Father. He notes that young people often abandon religious beliefs as they mature and reject the authority of parents. Freud regarded God as an infantile residue from childhood; he saw reason, education for reality and science as eventually replacing such infantile illusion.

Though Freud was a reductionist, he did not deny the reality of mind. As a therapist he was particularly aware of the reality of people's anxieties and phobias and fantasies; he saw mind as playing a part in all these. After all, the point of Freudian psychoanalytic therapy is to reduce anxiety and phobia and depression by working on mind. Freud would like to have demonstrated that mind was brain and that there was only the physical body and brain. In an early work, 'Project for a Scientific Psychology', he tried to do this. He never published the 'Project' and subsequently described the work as balderdash. So he asserted, while holding that there was only biological body and brain, that mind and its products, such as thoughts and memories as well as fantasies and phobias, are real enough.

By the end of the nineteenth and the beginning of the twentieth century, academic psychology had abandoned words like 'spirit' and 'soul' and was exploring mind by means of introspection. Early in the twentieth century, behaviourist psychologists largely stopped studying 'mind', which still seemed contaminated by its historical association with non-material soul and spirit. Behaviourism no longer regarded psychology as the study of mind, but rather as the study of of behaviour. Behaviourists chose to ignore, even to deny, the existence of mind and to concentrate on the study of actual behaviour which could be observed. Behaviourism was central to psychology for many decades and remains influential.

Behaviourism regards human beings as blank slates with a massive capacity for learning. This learning is not related to internal processes such as mind but is the result of external rewards and punishments. According to behaviourism, the rewards and punishments of the external environment shape our behaviour; what we do is the product of such conditioning. Mind does not enter into it – or, at least, we can ignore mind in the behaviourist account. Behaviourist psychology, seeing behaviour as responses to external stimuli, regards humans as being like any other animal, just better at learning, and not really free.

Behaviourism's attempt to account for human beings in terms of observable behaviour was a justifiable and worthy attempt to create a scientific psychology. Behaviourism was able to explain much human behaviour in terms of conditioning by reward and punishment. But behaviourism had difficulty in accounting for higher human activities such as language, abstract thought, culture, science, the arts, moral behaviour. These are very real activities, central to human beings. We usually regard such activities as the product of mind, which behaviourism ignored.

It seems that mind cannot be ignored for long or just left on the periphery of explanations of humans. If humans think that they think, the first 'think' seems to clinch it. Descartes' 'I think, therefore, I am' seems a reasonable basis on which to conclude not only that I exist but that, whatever ever else I am, I am a thinking thing. I may doubt the existence of others but I cannot doubt that I am doubting. Thinking, doubting, reasoning, remembering seem real enough in human experience. If they are real, they suggest the existence of mind. The difficulty for psychology has been that of observing mind at work, and until recently introspection had appeared the only way. This altered with the arrival of the computer.

In the 1960s, psychology changed direction. Cognitive psychology asserted that mind was central to human activities such as thinking, understanding, learning, language, reasoning, planning, creativity, recognizing patterns, remembering. According to cognitive psychology, behaviourism was misguided in ignoring mind and suggesting that mental processes do not exist or are irrelevant. According to cognitive psychology, at present a dominant force in psychology, mind is central to human behaviour. With the computer, there was now a method for studying mind scientifically which seemed superior to the earlier approach of introspection.

A digital computer is a machine which manipulates symbols according to rules, such as those contained in its programme. A digital computer takes in data, which it transforms, stores, retrieves, transmits. Isn't this what a human mind does? The computer takes information and processes this information according to certain rules. Doesn't the human mind work by logically processing information and manipulating symbols according to rules? There have certainly been philosophers who thought so. Hobbes, for example, regarded thinking as calculations using symbols instead of numbers; Hobbes' 'reasoning is but reckoning' view has been held by some for a long time.

Cognitive psychologists start from the position that the human mind is an information-processing system, like a computer; humans use mind to sort out information. Cognitive psychologists regard the human mind as a system that accepts, transforms and stores information, and retrieves, uses and transmits that information, just like a computer. In the cognitive account, activities of the mind such as thinking and remembering and recognizing are forms of processing information according to rules. Cognitive psychologists regard humans and computers as two kinds of information-processing systems; humans and computers are different sub-species of the species, information-processing systems.

This information-processing approach avoids problems of purpose and choice raised by other accounts of mind. The actions of a computer are caused; with the computer as model, a scientific mechanistic cause-and-effect explanation of mind is guaranteed. The distinction between the obviously caused behaviour of a computer and the apparently purposeful actions of humans is illusory, according to many cognitive psychologists. A central-heating system, turning itself on and off as the temperature falls and rises, appears just as purposive as the householder who turns the heating system on 'to warm the house up' and switches it off 'because it is now hot enough'. In the cognitive-psychology account, the actions of both heating system and householder are caused.

By producing apparently intelligent behaviour which resembles what humans do, the computer seems to lay to rest one of the oldest problems about human personality, that of the body-mind relationship. For traditional materialism, the body-mind question comes down to: how can mind be explained without resorting to a ghost in the machine? Behaviourism dealt with the problem by denying, or ignoring, the existence of mind. But, as I have said, the reality of mind cannot be denied for long. Once concede its existence, and the question returns of explaining mind without resorting to spirit or soul. If we adopt as a model the programmed computer, a machine apparently intelligent like a human, and certainly with no spirit or soul, the problem seems solved.

Cognitive psychology regards the relationship of mind to brain as resembling that of wired-in programme to computer. With a human being, this wired-in programme is the specific innate features of the human brain. If the brain is like a computer, then mind resembles the programme and is a kind of innate pre-programming. In the cognitive account, a human being is not a blank slate, as behaviourism alleged. Cognitive psychology adopts an innate position, holding that there is something already written on the slate when humans are born. To behaviourism's adage, taken from Locke, that 'there is nothing in the intellect that was not first in the senses', cognitive psychology following Leibniz adds, 'Nothing – save only the intellect itself.'

Cognitive psychologists have amassed a wealth of valuable data and understanding relating to mind and its activities. But there are now queries about whether the human mind does work as an information-processing system. Experts had predicted that in a short time computers would equal and even surpass what the human mind can do. But the achievements of artifical intelligence over a period of thirty years have proved much less successful than was predicted. Compared with humans, the competence of computers is (as yet) limited. This raises queries about whether the human mind is only an information-processing system. Perhaps we do not reason, remember, understand, recognize, in the way that computers do, by logically processing information and manipulating symbols according to rules. Or if we do, perhaps this is not only what we do, and the human mind reasons and remembers and understands and recognizes patterns by other means as well. If the human mind is an information-processing system, this is possibly not the sum total of what mind is. Perhaps cognitive psychology is too restrictive in taking the information-processing model, the equivalent of Pascal's mathematical mind, as the complete explanation. After all, Pascal goes on to suggest that human personality also works with an intuitive mind.

The doubt about whether humans operate as information-processing systems goes further. Computers handle information and data by reducing them to bits. But it seems that the human mind does not work with information and data in this reductionist way, first breaking them down into bits of knowledge, then building them up again. Gestalt psychology always emphasized that 'the whole is greater than the sum of its parts', and stressed that parts can be understood only in relation to the whole. Is human thinking, use of language, remembering, artistic and scientific creativity, built up from discrete elements in the way that a programmed computer works? Do people recognize the faces of friends by a building-block process of assembling parts of the face? Current evidence suggests that the answer to these questions is 'No'. And if the human mind does not work in a reductionist and additive way only, then the information-processing computer as a model of the human mind is inadequate.

Programmes have been written which enable computers to learn. But such programmes have equipped computers with a very limited capacity for learning, and only over a restricted area. There are, for example, programmes for playing draughts which improve by storing information from previous games. But the human capacity to learn remains superior to that of the computer and extends over a wide area. Humans have a capacity for learning which is general and not specific to draughts or language vocabulary or skills in a particular sport. Of course, it remains possible that in the future more powerful computers will equal the human mind's comprehensive capacity to learn.

It is also becoming clear that the human mind functions in terms of an everyday knowledge of the world. We know how we are expected to behave at meal times, to dress for work, to act when we go shopping. At present it is difficult to provide computers with programmes for how to operate in such everyday situations. Humans, as a result of childhood and adult experience, have an easy grasp of contexts in which everyday life takes place. Computers have to be specifically programmed for these, and this is a vast task which as yet has not been satisfactorily done. Humans can think and apply their cognitive processes not in one area only, but generally; human beings have a sort of general all-round intelligence. Computer programmes for thinking or problem-solving as yet operate only in specific areas, such as a particular kind of algebra or chess.

Certainly one area where the computer equals the achievement of the human mind is chess. Programmed computers now play chess at a level where they would win against nearly all human players. This serves to make a point about computer accounts of how the mind works. Cognitive psychology is concerned with understanding the human mind. What is really relevant for psychology is not whether a computer plays chess well, but how it plays. Does the computer decide moves in the way that a competent human player does? It now seems unlikely. The interest of serious chess players in analysing past games, like medical specialists recalling similar cases in the past when attempting a diagnosis, is perhaps significant. It seems clear that when faced with a problem the human mind does not always, perhaps does not usually, start from first principles. The research suggests that the human mind often starts by trying to find out what worked in the past. When the chess-playing computer wins, the rule-following information-processing computer is equalling and surpassing the achievement of the human mind, but it may not be replicating how the human mind works.

The cognitive-psychology account of humans as information-processing and rule-following systems may eventually prove inadequate. But the achievements of computers could still be taken to demonstrate that something completely physical, like a computer, thinks and understands. There is no ghost, spirit or soul in the computer machine, so if computers really think and understand, then the problem of the body-mind relationship seems solved. Whether or not computers exactly parallel the way in which the human mind works, the achievement of computers would appear to prove that a traditional materialist account of mind may eventually be possible. That a computer, something wholly material, apparently thinks, recognizes, remembers, understands, is regarded as very significant by many psychologists. Such psychologists, and some philosophers, see the computer as providing evidence for the traditional materialist position. Margaret Boden (1990) asks, 'So why shouldn't some future tin-can have feelings and sensations, too?'

But even with the advent of computers, there remain problems for the materialist position on mind. Cognitive psychology proposes that human minds resemble computers in that both operate by following rules. But the sense in which computers and humans follow rules seems different. The mechanical and electrical reactions of a clock are determined by its design; in a similar way, the actions of a computer are laid down and determined by its circuitry and programme. In this sense, clock and computer are both following rules. Is this what we mean when we say that the human mind operates by following rules?

A friend tells me how to get to his house. 'Once you have passed the railway station, go straight across the next three crossroads.' This rule, 'go straight across the next three crossroads', means something to me. The rule has meaning, which I understand. Humans follow rules the content of which has meaning that they understand; they are guided by the meaningful content of a rule. As I pass the station, and when I approach a crossroad, I will remind myself of this 'go straight across the next three crossroads' rule. But this is different from the rules that computers and, for example, planets follow. Planets do not say to themselves: 'The rule is, just keep on swinging to the left', or, 'I must follow an ellipse whose diameter is . . .' Similarly, computers do not tell themselves what to do, since they are not guided by the meaning-content of any rule. Computers, like planets, appear to 'follow rules' in a way that is very different from the way in which humans do.

The actions of computers are caused and determined, like the actions of any machine or planet. If we describe as rule-following the caused and determined reactions of the computer to its programme, it is only as a kind of metaphor. It does not imply that rules have any meaning for computers in the way that 'Go straight across all the traffic lights until you come to a bridge' means something to a human. A computer does not react to any understanding of rules. A programme mechanically determines that the computer will follow certain procedures; what the computer does is determined. Computers and humans do not 'follow rules' in the same way.

Cognitive psychology has provided much understanding by seeing the human mind as an information-processing rule-following system like a computer. But when it comes to computers (and planets), rather than speak of their following rules, it might be more correct to describe their behaviour as law-like. The human mind is usually responding to the meaning contained in rules, but a computer is not. A thought-experiment proposed by Searle (1984) makes this clear.

In Searle's thought-experiment a man sits in a room, with a set of rules in English and a box full of statements in Chinese. The man speaks English but not Chinese; so he has no understanding of the statements in the box. When messages in Chinese are posted into the room, he has no understanding of these either. The set of rules in English, which he understands, do not explain what these messages in the Chinese language mean, but they do tell him what to do when he receives one. So when the messages in Chinese are posted in, he looks at the rules. The rules instruct him that when a particular specified set of Chinese symbols is posted in, he should take from the box and post out another particular specified set of symbols. He picks up a message in Chinese posted in, and he posts out the statement in Chinese which the rules specify. He continues to do this, but neither what is posted in, nor what he posts out, means anything to him.

The people outside the room are posting in questions in Chinese. And what the man in the room unknowingly is doing, by following the set of rules in English, is posting out correct answers. Soon the man in the room is adept at processing what to him are meaningless symbols, but what to Chinese speakers outside are meaningful questions and answers. Those outside might conclude that inside the room there is someone who understands Chinese. But this is not the case. And no matter how long the man in the room processes these symbols, he will never in this way learn to understand a word of Chinese. He knows what to do with the symbols in front of him, because of his set of rules in English. What he does not know is the meaning of the questions and answers in Chinese.

The analogy is with the computer. A programme could be written which enables a computer to do what the man in the room does. A question in Chinese is fed in; the computer matches the question against its memory or data base; the computer produces an answer in Chinese. The man in the room, by following the rules, has given the impression to those outside that he understands Chinese, but he does not understand a word. Similarly, the computer running through its programme understands not a word. All a computer has is what the man in the room has, a set of rules called a programme, for processing Chinese words which mean nothing to him.

What Searle's thought-experiment illustrates is the difference between thinking which involves understanding and 'thinking' which involves no understanding. And normally thinking, remembering, perceiving and other human cognitive processes involve understanding; such processes have meaningful content for the mind. However, for the computer, just as for the man in the room, such processes have no meaningful content. What computers do, and they do very well, is to process symbols which mean nothing to them, in the way that the Chinese words are meaningless to the man in the room.

Searle underlines the difference by imagining the English-speaker in the room having questions in English posted in. Here the man understands the content of question and answer. The human mind may operate according to certain rules like a programme, but what human minds work on normally has meaningful content. Humans not only follow rules, but they also understand the meaning of the material which they are processing using rules. The human mind reacts to meaning (semantics) as well as to rules telling it what to do (syntax). Most activity of the human mind involves meaning and understanding in a way that the operations of a computer do not.

Even if in the future an improved computer provided answers as good as, even better than, those of someone who speaks Chinese, nothing would have changed; the computer's situation would still be no different from that of the non-Chinese speaker in the room. Should the technology of computers improve so that they achieve what human minds achieve, it would still be misleading to describe the machine as having understanding and intelligence. For intelligence and understanding, both syntax (rules) and semantics (meaning) are required. In the digital computer, or any machine, we have only the rules of syntax. The symbols in a computer programme can refer to anything – words, atoms, incidence of disease, nails; this illustrates how devoid of specific meaning they are. Searle's contention is that in no sense does a computer have understanding.

Another relevant scenario is where a computer-controlled train crashes, injuring passengers, because of some failure in the circuitry or program. Ought the public to demand that the computer be tried in a court of law? Would we now, or could we in the future, have a judicial trial of the computer for committing such a serious error? The differences between the mind of a human being and the 'mind' of a computer are real and are not dependent on the state of the art in computer technology.

Following the decline of behaviourism, with its emphasis on external behaviour, cognitive psychology emerged and, using the computer, has returned mind to psychology. Modern psychology reasserts the reality and centrality of mind. And according to cognitive psychology, human mind is characterized by innate preexisting structures. But the scientific materialism assumed by psychological accounts of mind and personality has yet to be demonstrated. Materialist assumptions, that personality and mind consist only of the body and brain of traditional materialism, and that God does not exist or is irrelevant to personality, remain unproven.

9

Personality and God:
The Assumptions of Christian Theory

We could discover all kinds of startling things about ourselves and our behaviour; but we cannot discover that we do not have minds, that they do not contain conscious, subjective, intentionalistic mental states; nor could we discover that we do not at least try to engage in voluntary, free, intentional actions.

(John Searle, *Minds, Brains and Science*, The 1984 Reith Lectures)

We know very well that the self is not a material substance.
(Karl Popper, *The Self and Its Brain*)

If, therefore, we speak of 'God' as an 'archetype', we are saying nothing about His real nature but are letting it be known that 'God' already has a place in that part of our psyche which is pre-existent to consciousness and that therefore He cannot be considered an invention of consciousness.

(Carl Jung, *Memories, Dreams, Reflections*)

There is a God: the most august of all conceivable truths.
(John Henry Newman)

Like cognitive psychology, Christian accounts of personality hold that mind exists and is characterized by pre-existing structures. But Christian theories reject the materialist view that mind and personality are identical with biological body and brain. Christian accounts of personality assume that there is more to a human being than the physical matter of traditional materialism.

The belief that something of human personality survives the body's death has existed throughout history and across human societies. According to scientific materialism, nothing survives of the individual personality, since there is nothing to survive; personality and mind are only the perishable matter of biological body and brain, nothing more. Though the complexity and power of the brain are astonishing, the materialist view that mind and brain are identical presents difficulties. Such an assumption creates problems for those who regard humans as being to some extent free. The material world of which the brain is part seems characterized by cause and effect. If humans are the matter of traditional materialism, their actions must be caused and determined, so humans cannot be free and capable of choice.

If humans are not free and are incapable of choice, human knowledge ends in a cul-de-sac, as a paradox proposed by Haldane suggests: 'If my mental processes are determined wholly by the motions of atoms in my brain, I have no reason to suppose that my beliefs are true . . . and hence I have no reason for supposing my brain to be composed of atoms.' The point which the paradox makes is that materialism as a theory cannot be supported by argument. If materialism is true, then everything (including mind) works by cause and effect. If mind works by cause and effect and is consequently determined, how can we know anything to be true, including materialism?

But most of us do not believe that we cannot know anything to be true. If we hold that Newtonian physics gives a better account of the real world than the physics of the ancient Greeks, we do so because we have seen the arguments. If materialism is true, then (as Haldane's paradox demonstrates) there are no such things as arguments, since everything, including the workings of mind, is determined.

Modern psychology, particularly humanistic psychology, attempts to resolve this problem by what is called soft determinism. Soft determinists, such as Carl Rogers, hold that though all behaviour is caused, some caused behaviour remains free. Soft determinism argues that there is no contradiction, and nothing incompatible, between holding that human behaviour is determined and believing that human behaviour is sometimes free. But soft determinists have yet to provide a satisfactory argument for how behaviour can at the same time be both determined and free.

Language also appears to pose a problem for materialist accounts of mind. The study of linguistics confirms that the number of combinations of words possible in constructing a sentence is very large. Linguistics suggests that young children speak sentences which they have never heard before. This is true not only of children; as adults we create sentences original to ourselves. We constantly create new and original sentences of our own, and we understand the new and original sentences of others. Language is certainly rule-based; and the rules of language which we acquire almost certainly have an innate basis in the brain. But human language, in spite of its rule-based nature, is characterized by originality. How do we explain such originality?

A materialist account of mind in terms only of brain and body seems inadequate to account for the originality of language. Quite simply, how can the physical be original and capable of the freedom which makes originality possible? How can the brain, which is material, come up with something new? The originality of language might suggest that there is more to the human mind than the brain of materialist psychology. Or if human beings are just matter, it is an odd sort of matter, and certainly not the matter of classical physics.

When we come to the arts, they too seem products of mind. Cognitive psychology suggests that following rules is one activity of mind involved in creativity. Mozart composing music had the rules of keys and chord structures and modulation and harmony to guide him. But would the creation of a melody, and deciding on key and key changes, and choosing harmony and chords, be done by Mozart on the basis of following rules? He did it by . . . if only we knew! He probably just based his choices on what sounded right and good. After the event the music critic can point out, 'By introducing A flat here Mozart has changed the key, and it is the slight discord of the key change that makes the sound exciting.' After the event, rules may in part explain why the music works – though usually only in part. It seems unlikely that Mozart when composing was guided only by rules. Creativity is involved in making, and in appreciating, a work of art.

Such creativity poses a problem for scientific materialism. How can what is purely physical be creative? A picture by Rembrandt may end as paint on canvas, but originates as an idea or image in the painter's mind. The creativity of the rest of us, appreciating painting, music or dance, may be less than that of Rembrandt but is none the less real. Great artists seem to know what they can leave to the creativity of their public. This is obvious in sketches and drawings where our mind builds on what is there, filling in the gaps, interpreting, reconstructing, extrapolating from the lines to make a complete and unified picture. It is difficult to see how mind, if it is solely the material brain of orthodox biology, can manage the creativity and the freedom involved in the creation and appreciation of the arts.

The same seems true of science, also in part the product of mind. Scientists look at water, salt, brass, zinc, copper, silver, gold, neon, oxygen, nitrogen, silicon, sulphur, and they categorize them as compounds or elements. The scientists can then look at the elements and break them down further into metals and non-metals. What scientists are doing, here and elsewhere, is mapping different classifications on to these objects. Since such a classification brings some objects together and separates others, the classification cannot arise from the objects themselves. Classifications come from the minds of the scientists. Mind decides the realities of science. Kant says: 'Our intellect does not draw its laws from nature but imposes its laws on nature.' Water, steam and ice seem different, but all are classified under the formula H_2O. Though computers can classify, as yet their capacity to develop, by themselves, their own categories remains limited.

Science, of course, is not wholly a creation of the human mind. A scientific theory comes up against external reality. And external empirical reality confirms whether the scientific theory is valid or whether it is wholly or in part wrong. But even the observations of reality are made by mind; mind, in part, chooses what it observes. Even the modification and changing of a theory when its predictions do not accord with external reality is done by mind. But how can mind – if it consists solely of matter as traditionally conceived – choose observations and alter its theories in the light of its observations? The material world, according to materialism, is characterized by determining cause and effect.

Science works also by asking questions and criticizing. Scientists adopt a category such as vertebrates to categorize and make sense of the data which they have on animals. But standing back, the scientists realize that a classification in terms of vertebrates is too general. As a result of criticizing their own classification they come up with mammals, birds, fish, reptiles and amphibia, and then finding this still too gross they sub-divide, for example, mammals into primates, carnivores and other orders. This illustrates the active nature of the human mind in science, frequently criticizing its own ideas.

Materialist cognitive psychology regards brain as like a computer and mind like the programme. But if humans can question and criticize their own ideas and revise them, then mind seems more like the programmer than the programme. Human mind in science is not tied down by the information given through the senses but, standing back, can evaluate, question, criticize and revise. In the self-criticism that characterizes science, mind reflects upon the catagories and hypotheses and theories that are its own product. The characteristics of the human mind at work in science do not seem those of matter as described by traditional materialism.

There are further difficulties with the materialist position on mind. When our mind is active, it is always active about something. When we think, use language, are creative or make criticisms, it is always about something. Philosophers refer to this 'being about something' as intentionality. I think about a glass of water, growing old, what is on T V this evening . . . always about something. The active mind invariably has a focus and direction. If mind consists only of the matter of traditional materialism, how can mind have direction and focus, and always be about something? Can something purely physical, like a stone, have intentionality and 'be about something'?

Intentionality characterizes certain activities of mind in an obvious way. The work of a painter is always about something – like sunflowers. There is nothing which determines that the painting should be about flowers; it could have been about vegetables or a man seated before a fire or the flowers could have been in a garden. But Van Gogh chooses to make a painting about flowers, not about roses or lilies, but about sunflowers in a vase on a table indoors. The activity of mind, whether in language or artistic creativity or scientific classification, is always about this and not that, or that and not this. But mind would seem to be incapable of this intentionality, if traditional materialism were true.

It is, of course, possible that as computers improve they will acquire intentionality, and be capable of free actions, originality in language, creativity in the arts, and new ideas in science. But at present this remains materialism on promise. And Searle's thought-experiment calls in question whether developments in computer technology will change the situation. Searle's thought-experiment proposes that, regardless of technological advances, nothing can ever mean anything to a computer. There seem to be inadequacies in the sort of traditional materialist explanations of mind, such as cognitive psychology has been trying to provide using the computer as model.

If we examine materialist identity theories which prefer biology to computers, we find that problems remain. Certain identity theorists claim that mind *emerges* from the brain's astonishing biological complexity. The word 'emerge', or some similar term, is used to explain how mind is the product of brain cell activity. But the word 'emerge' or similar concepts explain very little. Identity theorists believe that brain research will eventually solve the problem. They hope that brain science will eventually demonstrate that what goes on in the brain – its chemical and electrical impulses, the activity of its cells – is identical with mind and its activities. They may be right; and research may eventually show how mind both emerges from brain and is identical with brain.

But it is difficult to see how brain research will eventually solve the problem. If we compare the materialist 'mind is brain' view with a modernized version of a dualism like that of Augustine or Descartes, we find that both make similar predictions. They would all predict, for example, that the use of language and thinking will be accompanied by activity in the brain; and they are. Brain research confirms that, when there is cognitive activity such as remembering or problem-solving, specific parts of the brain are active. This is what materialist identity theorists would expect. But this is what anyone would expect who, while holding that there is more to mind than the matter of materialism, appreciates the importance of the brain. And it is hard to know what else of relevance that brain research might demonstrate, apart from this close parallel between mental activity and the physical activity of the brain.

Human freedom, creativity in language, originality in the arts and

sciences, and intentionality remain problems for traditional scientific materialism. Such problems are avoided by assuming either
that there exists a non-material dimension to mind, or that the
matter of brain and body is not the stuff of traditional materialism.

Two philosophical traditions have attempted to explain mind as
something other than the physical matter of traditional materialism.
There is the extreme or moderate dualism of Plato, Augustine and
Descartes. And there is the view of Aristotle and Aquinas,
intermediate between dualism and the materialist account of mind as
matter. Aristotle's and Aquinas' position is midway between
materialism's monist account of a human person as one physical
thing only, and the dualist account of the person as two substances,
matter and spirit.

Aristotle asks, what is it that makes anything what it is? The
answer, said Aristotle, is form. Form determines what something is,
and matter cannot exist without it. The form of an axe – form has
nothing to do with shape – is what makes it an axe. But certain things
such as vegetables, animals and humans are characterized by an
autonomous activity from within, which makes them unlike any
other kind of matter. This is explained by the sort of form they have,
which is soul. Animals, for example, besides having in common with
vegetables a vegetative soul, have – and this makes them animals –
what Aristotle calls a sensitive soul. With humans, too, it is the kind
of soul that informs which makes them human and different from
other living beings. Human soul, in addition to being vegetative like a
vegetable's and sensitive like an animal's, is rational. Rational soul is
what as form makes bodily matter into a human being.

In the Middle Ages, Aquinas followed Aristotle in regarding the
person as a composite of soul and body, but still one thing only. For
Aristotle and Aquinas, not only does body depend on soul for life,
but what the activities of a living being are depend on what sort of
soul informs the body. Humans can have abstract ideas and can
express concepts in language because the soul which informs them is
non-material. Self-consciousness and free choice are possible
because the soul informing humans is not entirely physical.

Aquinas' monist view of the human person as only one substance
is further qualified. He held that body and soul must be different,
since he believed that the human soul created by God survives the

body's death. Nevertheless, Aquinas' position remains that the person is one substance, since he also held that the soul is not a complete human when apart from the body. For the human being to be complete and whole in heaven, the resurrection of the body is necessary. So Aquinas regards the human person as one thing. And Aquinas' view, asserting the material aspect of the mind's activity, could accommodate without difficulty research confirming that brain activity accompanies cognitive activities such as thinking and imagining. But Aquinas is no identity theorist. He would have rejected the materialist assumption that humans are only body and brain and that the human mind (or soul) is just the physical brain at work.

This rational soul reasons, makes free choices, creates the arts and sciences, has intentionality. But, according to this philosophical tradition, the soul depends in part on the body's senses to do all this. Though the rational human soul in its higher activities goes beyond the physical, in this existence certainly the human soul for the most part relies for ordinary knowledge on the body's senses and on bodily experience. Humans are not body and soul; they are not two substances. Body and soul are two components that can be distinguished in a human being; but for Aquinas the human person remains one thing only. Without either soul or body we could not think, create, reason, use language, understand; the complete human being does all this. But Aquinas' assertion of the oneness of the substance of a person ultimately remains qualified because he holds that the soul does not rely completely on the body to exist.

The other philosophical tradition, outlined earlier with reference to Augustine, is dualism. According to the dualism of Plato, Augustine and Descartes, two things exist: non-material mind, which is spirit, and material body. In the extreme dualism of Plato, the spirit which constitutes mind is not only separate from the body but is more important than body and is really the human person. The spirit or soul is the captain of the ship; the body is the ship. Augustine, like Plato, believed that this immaterial dimension of soul is the real human being, the body being merely the soul's container. Augustine held that though the soul was attached to the body, it remained separate and complete in itself. But he also held that the whole human person consists of both body and soul. For Augustine, soul or mind is dominant and uses the body to achieve its aims and purposes. The later dualism of Descartes gives a different emphasis. According to Descartes, there are indeed two things, body and mind, and they are indeed different substances; but they depend on each other and interact, and only together do they constitute a human person.

Karl Popper, the philosopher of science, and John Eccles, the brain scientist, in *The Self and Its Brain* (1977), have come out in favour of Descartes' dualism: there are physical objects and states, and there are mental states, and these interact. Mind and mental states are not part of the physical world, though they relate to the physical world, since they liaise with parts of the brain. According to Popper and Eccles, the brain is the servant of the mind; what they call the self-conscious mind is in charge. I decide to move my hand and my hand moves; my hand moves because I, the self-conscious mind, have decided to move it.

These two philosophical traditions are in opposition to materialism, which holds that only matter, as traditionally conceived, exists. But the traditional materialist position has recently been slightly undermined by modern physics. Philosophers have always realized that if only matter exists, the nature of this matter remains problematic and puzzling. Philosophers have long been aware that it is not obvious what the stuff of matter consists in, nor self-evident what the properties of matter are. Modern physics has now demonstrated that the stuff of matter is odd.

Modern physics has discovered that, at the level of the very small, matter does not always act in the way which traditional materialism and classical physics had thought. Atoms once regarded as indivisible can now be split. At the sub-atomic level material events, once thought to operate invariably according to cause and effect, do not always appear to have causes; events sometimes just happen, apparently at random. Because of this, what happens at the atomic and sub-atomic level cannot always be predicted precisely, but only stated in terms of probabilities. The example frequently given is of an electron travelling at a known speed, whose actual position at a particular moment can be expressed only in terms of probability. Modern physics finds that at the sub-atomic and atomic level there is not the inevitable certainty of cause and effect, but indeterminacy and uncertainty. According to traditional materialism, the stuff of matter operated according to consistent, enduring and discoverable laws. But modern physics finds that, at the atomic and sub-atomic level, there seem to be basic problems in establishing consistent and exact material laws.

What matter is and how it operates had once seemed self-evident. Whatever existed, whether the matter of a brick or a human body, existed in one particular place, occupied space and persisted over time. Modern physics now reveals that the solid and supposedly irreducible stuff of matter can change into vague amorphous energy. Matter can be transformed into energy, and energy can be transformed into matter; matter and energy are interchangeable. When particles collide and fragment, the bits they break into may be bigger than the original particles; the energy from their collision has turned into matter. Modern physicists report that inside the atom traditional ideas on cause and effect, and matter, no longer apply.

According to modern physics, in the world of the very small, of the sub-atomic, single events occur in terms of probability, and not in a simple cause-and-effect way. In the world of the very small, of quantum theory, the relation between cause and effect is no longer clear-cut. Events may possibly still be determined, but not on a mechanical one-to-one basis. These probability-occurring events at the micro-level statistically produce law-like mechanistic events at the macro-level. For this reason the cause and effect of traditional materialism still operates at the level of classical physics, where millions of atoms are involved; such large numbers obscure the individual uncertainties.

But it remains the case that new physics presents a problem for traditional materialism as a philosophy, since the assumptions of materialism no longer hold over the whole range of the physical world. In this sense, matter has become slightly dematerialized. As a result, some physicists no longer regard traditional materialism as a respectable scientific philosophy. The stuff of matter is not as obvious and self-explanatory as was once thought, but requires some explanation.

When it comes to mind, the inadequacy of a traditional materialist explanation is suggested by the Popper and Eccles arguments for dualism. Popper and Eccles use optical illusions studied by psychologists to make their point. In a typical illusion we see either faces or a vase. Often with an effort we can see a vase, then faces, then back to a vase, and so on. This would seem to demonstrate that the human observer is not to be identified with the receptive physical brain. It suggests that the observer should be identified with something which chooses what is seen (faces or a vase), and which is apart from the brain. However, in many illusions, though with an effort we can choose to see one figure rather than another (a vase rather than faces or faces rather than a vase), the observer tends to revert to seeing one rather than another. This suggests that the structure of the brain limits or puts pressure on what the mind can do; body-mind interaction is two-way.

In their dualist account, Popper and Eccles see the self-conscious mind as an independent entity that reads out information from the brain. This self-conscious mind, which is not part of the material world, selects the information which it reads out. Though its power is limited, this mind controls and acts back on the brain. The control which the self-conscious mind can exert comes more from interpreting and being able to select from the information which the brain gives. It is self-conscious mind which provides the unity of consciousness and underlies the active agency of human thought and action. Popper likens it to a searchlight in the dark, sweeping the brain for information. I watch TV and see an actress and know that I have seen her in some other play and try to remember what play it was. I know what I want to say or write, and aware there is the right word to say it, I search for that word.

Such dualism, and the qualified monism of Aristotle and Aquinas, differ in their emphasis. Both philosophical traditions agree that human personality does not consist only of the matter of traditional materialism, common sense and classical physics. But both non-materialist traditions have difficulties.

First, what is this soul or spirit (or Popper's and Eccles' self-conscious mind) which is not part of nature? What does it consist of? But modern physics suggests that the same questions now have to be asked of matter, which seems to have become almost as puzzling as soul and spirit. However, at least we have conscious experience and knowledge of matter. The most we can claim with regard to soul or spirit is that our consciousness of matter seems to imply an awareness of a reality other than matter.

Secondly, there is the question of how this soul or spirit can have knowledge of the material world. And there is the more general problem of how soul or spirit can interact with matter. This is a particularly difficult problem for dualism. Popper and Eccles refer to the non-material self-conscious mind as reading out information from the brain; but this does not seem an explanation of how matter and spirit can interact. Dualism has also to address the problem of the location of this spirit. Where does this immaterial spirit reside? The reply that only matter has location and extension in space does not seem entirely satisfactory.

The same is true of Aristotle and Aquinas, who suggest that when soul takes a certain form in matter, then matter changes its nature. Aquinas holds that when the form of matter is vegetative, sensitive and rational soul, we have human beings liberated from material cause and effect and capable of making free choices. It may be that, in this 'ensouling' of body, matter becomes increasingly immaterial, in the way that matter becomes odd in the sub-atomic world of modern physics.

This notion of the 'ensouling' of body resembles modern materialist explanations of mind as 'emerging' from the increasing complexity of the physical brain. But the suggestion that mind is the product of 'ensouling', like the materialist suggestion that mind is an emerging product of the brain's complexity, does not seem a full explanation. Such 'ensouling' of brain, like modern psychology's materialist identification of brain with mind, becomes more plausible if we recognize matter as the odd and strangely immaterial stuff of modern physics.

The human brain's amazing complexity would certainly appear to be involved in humans being able to act freely, use language, create the arts and science, have intentionality. Because of the brain's amazing complexity, cognitive psychologists liken the human brain to a computer; the human mind is seen as a built-in programme. But even with computer and programme, a programmer is necessary to write the programme. In the Christian view, the human mind is not the programme but the programmer. And between programmed computers and programmers who programme them, there is a difference.

Christian personality theory can make the dualist assumption that a human being consists of two substances, body and spirit. Christian theory can make the alternative assumption of qualified monism, that the human person is one thing only, a composite of matter and soul. In spite of the shortcomings of both assumptions, either seems as reasonable as the contrasting assumption that mind and brain are identical, and that the stuff of brain is the matter of traditional materialism.

According to modern physics, matter is stranger than was originally thought. Quantum theory appears to have taken a step in the direction of partly 'dematerializing' matter. So it might become possible to reconcile scientific psychology's view that a human being consists only of matter with the contrasting Christian assumption; the behaviour of matter now seems sometimes to resemble the behaviour of soul or spirit in Christian accounts. If matter proves to be much stranger than was thought by traditional materialism and classical physics, an account of personality which embraces both scientific and Christian assumptions could become possible.

Among the exceptions to the agnosticism or atheism of modern psychology is William James. In *The Varieties of Religious Experience*, published in 1902, James concluded that he had grounds for believing in the existence of a supreme reality that Christians call God. In his study of experiences regarded as religious, mystical or prayerful, he detected a common factor. This was people's experience of their selfs as connected with something similar, but separate and independent. There seemed an awareness of a 'more' which is not the self, but to which the self felt related. The experience usually contained the feeling that an external power had been involved. James's interpretation was that in such experiences the human self encounters a more extensive self, which is the source of the experience. From this, James moved to the pragmatic conclusion that God must be real, since the effects that God produces are real.

Experiences and reports of such experiences are empirical data for the psychologist, but deciding their significance, in the way in which James does, involves a considerable degree of interpretation. An interpretation or assumption may have to be made when it comes to the question of God. On the basis of an interpretation of the data,

Christian accounts of personality assume that God exists, while atheism assumes that adequate explanations of human existence and experience are possible without God. If we hold solely to reason and logic, we are pushed in the direction of agnosticism. Adopting either atheism or belief involves making an assumption or an act of faith. Belief in God and atheism are not a matter of intellect alone; both are existential and involve making a choice, and coming to a decision.

The existential element in faith was emphasized by Augustine. We do not understand to help us believe, but the other way round – we believe to help us understand. Augustine saw that in part we believe in order to make sense of the world and human life. Similarly, atheists choose not to believe because for them disbelief makes more sense of things. If we accept only what the empirical data make conclusive, we will not decide whether God exists.

However, for some, the position with regard to God is resolved by experience. And Jung regards an experience of God as more valuable and useful than any assumption, argument or act of faith. He holds that the knowledge of God through experience makes intellectual decision, argument or act of faith unimportant. Jung concludes from his anthropological research that '"God" is a primordial experience of man . . .' (*Brother Klaus*, 1933). And on the basis of experience of helping patients in therapy, and probably of his own personal experience, Jung further concludes, 'Religious experience is absolute; it cannot be disputed. You can only say that you have never had such an experience, whereupon your opponent will reply: "Sorry, I have." And there your discussion will come to an end' (*Psychology and Religion*, 1938/1940).

Jung holds that religious experience is not always of an obvious God-archetype. In Jungian psychology, archetypes of the self, that is, of personal wholeness, of a centre to personality, are scarcely to be distinguished from God-archetypes. According to Jung, at the level of experience it is difficult to differentiate between God-archetypes and self-archetypes of wholeness. Jung is not saying that God-archetypes and self-archetypes are identical; he is saying that it is through archetypal contents of the unconscious, such as the self, that the experience usually comes in which God is found. In religious terms, this suggests that at the deepest level the human self in some way relates to the God within. This view, that the true human self is both separate from God and at the same time united to God, has recurred in Christian accounts of personality.

Jung holds that if we find this God within us, we are more likely to find the God outside us. He sees God-archetypes and self-archetypes as a way through which God is discovered. All such archetypes manifest themselves in powerful experiences, in dreams, in the images of the arts, and in symbols of human culture, especially those of religion. Such archetypes, of God or self, emerging from the unconscious and demanding fulfilment, confirm for Jung the reality of the religious experience. This means that personality – Jung prefers the term 'psyche' – by nature possesses a religious function.

Humanistic psychologists would agree with Jung that such experiences are empirically real. But humanistic psychologists question the appropriateness of labelling the experiences as religious, regarding the term 'religious' as too restrictive. Humanistic psychology sees the notion of God as redundant, except as a metaphor for wholeness. Humanistic psychology asserts that any 'God' within is not separate from us but is a symbol for personal wholeness, human fulfilment, self-actualization. And these may be achieved in ways which are not obviously religious, such as psychotherapy.

So the source of these experiences, which Jung regards as archetypal religious experiences, is an important question. Some Christian writers have taken Jung's position to what they regard as its logical conclusion: since there is a God-archetype experienced by humans, an external reality must exist which is the source of such experience – namely, a God without. Jung disliked religious writers using his work in this way, objecting to metaphysical conclusions being drawn from psychological data. Psychology, he held, could not establish philosophical or metaphysical truths. Jung argued that as a scientist he could justifiably concern himself with a God-archetype and people's ideas about God, since these were empirical. They were the data from the experience of people he had helped in therapy and from the different cultures he had studied in his anthropological work. But he held that as a scientist he could not deduce from them the reality of God.

In adopting this stance, Jung was in part defending himself against psychologists who accused him of using psychological data to try to prove the existence of God, and in the process becoming unscientific. So Jung carefully points out that when he speaks of the God-archetype, self or self-archetype, or when he says that God is an archetype, he is making no statement about external reality; he is speaking of the various effects and manifestations of 'God' in human personality. Jung is saying that there are certain experiences that humans have which are real and have their own validity. He contended that such 'religious' experiences cannot be completely reduced, in the manner of Freud, to something else such as sublimated sexuality or wish-fulfilment. Jung, rejecting the wholesale reductionism of scientific materialism, asserts the irreducible reality of the experience. But as a scientist he believed that he must stay with the facts of experience, making only interpretations that can be scientifically justified.

Jung is staying as close as he can to the data of experience and attempting to avoid unverifiable interpretation of the data. In holding that as a scientist he could not deduce, from the reality of the archetype, the reality of God, he takes a position similar to that of William James with regard to mind. James, while asserting that the reality of human thinking was undeniable, was reluctant to move from the reality of the thought to the reality of a thinker behind the thought. James regarded the idea of such a thinker as a metaphysical speculation beyond the scope of a scientific psychology.

In the same way, Jung is reluctant to move from empirical data about archetypes of God and the self to postulating the existence of God. But he asserts that there is nothing in his own account of personality that invalidates a belief in God. He rejects any suggestion that belief in God is invariably a symptom of neurosis, just as he holds that there is nothing in itself unhealthy about believing in a life after death. Contrary to Freud, he argues that psychology cannot prove the non-existence of God. But he also contends that no psychology, his own included, can prove the existence of God either. And though Jung objected to his observations being taken as evidence for a God, he was confident that his data confirmed the existence of a God-archetype in personality. He was also confident that his observations demonstrate the frequency with which such God-archetypes are found, their importance for human beings, their power in personality, and their numinosity.

So there remains the puzzling question of where God-archetypes and self-archetypes originate. Jung concludes that their origin is not known. But he points out that the 'type' of archetype derives from '*typos*', which means a 'blow' or 'imprint' (*Introduction to the Religious and Psychological Problems of Alchemy*, 1944). Jung sees such an idea as opening up for the scientist a method of investigating the basis of this supposedly religious experience. That is as far as it goes for the scientist, says Jung; scientific psychology must confine itself to studying the imprint, the empirical archetype.

But religious belief is partly the product of extrapolations from experience. Christianity, in its conclusions both about God and human personality, is placing a religious interpretation upon the data of human experience. And regarding an archetype as an imprint raises the question of an imprinter. Jung concedes that religious people, faced with the symbols and archetypes which his research reveals, are free to account for them with a religious or metaphysical explanation. In his late autobiography, *Memories, Dreams, Reflections*, Jung comments that all comprehension and everything comprehended is in itself psychic, 'and to that extent we are hopelessly cooped up in an exclusively psychic world'. But he continues: 'Nevertheless, we have good reason to suppose that behind this veil there exists the uncomprehended absolute object which affects and influences us.'

Christian personality theories hold that mind and personality are not explained completely by traditional materialist accounts of body and brain. Christian theories also assume that God exists. As yet, scientific psychology has not provided any adequate physical account of human mind and personality in traditional materialist terms. Nor has scientific psychology yet demonstrated God's non-existence or irrelevance in regard to human personality. For the present, both assumptions of Christian theories appear as reasonable as the opposite assumptions of materialist psychology.

Epilogue:
The Eternal Search

For always roaming with a hungry heart.
   (Tennyson, 'Ulysses')

God has given us eternal life.
   (*First Letter of St John*)

To the two assumptions of Christian theories, that personality consists of more than the matter of traditional materialism and that God exists, must be added a third. The third assumption is that human beings need God. In Christian accounts, only the possession of God completely fulfils personality and makes humans happy. Common observation suggests the unhappy, restless and incomplete character of human experience. Scientific theories of personality to some extent confirm this. Psychoanalytic and analytic treatment, psychotherapy and counselling, reveal a dissatisfied and searching dimension to human personality. According to Christian theories, this restless and dissatisfied dimension exists because humans seek God. In Christian accounts, to be fulfilled, happy and whole, human personality needs God.

   Freud was aware of the power of religion, but he regarded religious beliefs as illusions. Freud acknowledged that some people experience 'a sensation of "eternity", a feeling as of something limitless, unbounded - as it were "oceanic"' (*Civilization and its Discontents*). This 'oceanic' feeling is characterized by a sense of oneness with the world and of being related to all existence. Virginia Woolf seems to express this experience: 'that behind the cotton wool is hidden a pattern; that we - I mean all human beings - are connected with this; that the whole world is a work of art; that we are parts of the work of art' (*A Sketch of the Past*). William James refers to such experiences as mystical states. Freud, relating them to childhood, offers an explanation which is neither mystical, nor religious.

As adults, we are aware for the most part of the boundaries that exist between our ego or self and the external world. But, according to Freud, this was not always the case. Freud says that as infants we were unaware of these boundaries, especially of those between our ego and mother's breasts. In infancy, in the absence of such boundaries, our ego exists in a state of psychological union with the external world, and particularly with mother's breasts. As we grow up, we gradually become aware of this distinction between our ego and the external world. But sometimes, says Freud, we return to these childhood experiences of union, even after we have developed a reality-orientated ego and are aware of the boundaries between self and external reality. Freud holds that the oceanic feeling is merely a regression to the experience and false perception of the infant. Freud, while recognizing the psychological reality of the oceanic feeling, provides an explanation which denies that the experience is religious or related to some external being.

Freud saw religion as serving to justify the moral restraints which human beings have to place themselves under in all societies. But he held that religious needs originate in the helplessness of the infant. He regarded as particularly important the infant's feeling of helplessness and the child's longing and need for a father's protection. This, according to Freud, is the source of religion and its power. Even as adults, humans feel helpless in the face of illness, pain, accident, death. Confronted by these products of nature and chance, humans want protection from life's dangers, long for fairness and meaning in life, and desire the continuation of existence in a life beyond death. Freud regards religion as originating in such desires.

In *The Future of an Illusion*, Freud concludes that religious ideas are 'illusions, fulfilments of the oldest, strongest and most urgent wishes of mankind. The secret of their strength lies in the strength of those wishes.' He sees belief in God or gods, and accompanying religious practices, as reducing the terror of nature and chance, and as helping humans to reconcile themselves to death. According to Freud, the idea of God achieves for adults what fathers do for children; as helpless children we looked to father for reassurance, so as adults we look to a God for help. As adults, we project on to God what as children we sought and sometimes obtained from parents. In Freud's view, a longing for the omnipotent father is the explanation of our longing for God, and the oceanic feeling becomes associated with this need for a divine father-figure. The sense of oneness, unity and eternity gives substance and a framework to the need. But Freud concludes that all is illusion, God included, the product of childhood experience and wishful thinking.

Humanistic psychology is in some ways more sympathetic to the religious view. Humanistic psychologists regard God, and God's love, as concepts which enable individuals to make sense of the universe and to fulfil themselves - or as ideas which have done so in the past. But humanistic psychologists do not usually hold that these ideas relate to any objective and external reality, like God. They see such ideas as historically shaped, and now largely obsolete. Their view is that at a given stage of historical development, humans said something about themselves by means of religious ideas. By the concept of God, human beings expressed their awareness of their own potential, their longing for knowledge and understanding and truth, and their desire for a fulfilling relationship with themselves, with other humans and the world. Humanistic psychologists see the concept of God as expressing the human need for self-actualization.

The search for wholeness, identity, fulfilment and peak experiences are elements in the self-actualization of humanistic psychology. But humanistic psychologists regard self-actualization as wholly psychological, not connected with any external divine reality. Self-actualization is seen as largely the product of internal psychological processes that relate to ourselves, our own potential, and our relationships with others. In contrast to the Christian account, humanistic psychology sees self-actualization as something to be achieved without reference to any God.

According to psychoanalytic theory, biological instincts are ultimately the origin of behaviour. According to humanistic psychology, a self-actualizing tendency is the basic motive behind human behaviour. In the Christian account, at the core of human motivation is the desire for God.

Freud was right in suggesting that the way in which we see and experience God is shaped by our culture and childhood. But Christian theories regard this as an incomplete picture. What Freud saw as illusion and wishful thinking, in Christian theory relates to a reality, the reality of God. In the Christian account, the material world is real too, though its pleasures and achievements fail to satisfy completely, are transient, constantly threatened by death, and death eventually ends them. In the Christian view, the joys and achievements of the material world are genuine and valuable in themselves; but their reality and value also reflect the absolute reality and value of God.

Similarly, humanistic psychology is right in stressing our search for personal fulfilment. And the self-actualization which we experience in human love and relationships, in work, in the search for truth, in the enjoyment of arts and science, is partly the product of what is within us. But in the Christian view, self-actualization also relates to an external reality, the reality of God. For no matter how fortunate we are in finding love, friendship, beauty, joy and happiness in our lives, and though they prove deeply fulfilling, they never seem enough. According to Christian psychology, humans are made by God to be completely happy only in the possession of God. And in the Christian account, in possessing God we actualize our true self and achieve fulfilment in our relationships with other human beings.

Scientific theories of psychology add greatly to our understanding of personality. Christian theories also increase our knowledge of human beings and complement the explanations of modern psychology. But, according to Christian theory, even together they fail to provide a complete account. In the Christian view, we cannot yet know what human beings are, because the potential of personality will only be fully realized after death, when humans see God.

Sources

The following list includes works specifically cited in previous chapters and general sources for the chapter.

1. The Passionate Pilgrim: Augustine of Hippo's Restless Path

Augustine, *Confessions*, trans. R.S.Pine-Coffin, Penguin Books 1961
——, *The Trinity*, trans. Stephen McKenna CSSR, The Catholic University of America Press 1963
——, *The City of God*, trans. Gerald G.Walsh SJ and Daniel J.Honan, Fathers of the Church, Inc. 1954
Bourke, Vernon J., *The Essential Augustine*, selected and with commentary, Hackett Publishing Company 1964
——, *Wisdom from St Augustine*, Centre for Thomistic Studies: University of St Thomas, Texas 1984
Chomsky, N., 'Review of B.F.Skinner, *Verbal Behavior*', in *Language* 35, 1959, 26–58
——, *Language and Mind*, Harcourt Brace and Jovanovich 1972
Fairbairn, W.R.D., *Psychoanalytical Studies of the Personality*, Tavistock 1952
Guitton, Jean, *The Modernity of Saint Augustine*, trans. A.V.Littledale, Geoffrey Chapman 1959
Jaspers, Karl, *The Great Philosophers*, trans. Ralph Manheim, Harcourt, Brace and World Inc. 1962
Meagher, Robert E., *An Introduction to Augustine*, New York University Press 1978
Skinner, B.F. *Verbal Behavior*, Appleton-Century-Crofts 1957

2. The Despairing Self: Søren Kierkegaard's Christian Existentialism

Erikson, E.H., *Identity and the Life Cycle*, Psychological Issues, Monograph 1, 1, International Universities Press 1959
Freud, Sigmund, *New Introductory Lectures on Psycho-Analysis, Complete Works*, Vol.22, Hogarth Press 1933

——— , *An Outline of Psycho-Analysis, Complete Works*, Vol.23, Hogarth Press 1940

Fromm, Erich, *Man for Himself*, Routledge and Kegan Paul 1949

Grimsley, Ronald, *Kierkegaard*, Studio Vista 1973

Hannay, Alastair, *Kierkegaard*, Routledge and Kegan Paul 1982

Jourard, Sidney M., *The Transparent Self*, Revised edition, Van Nostrand Reinhold Company 1971

Kierkegaard, Søren, *The Sickness unto Death*, trans. Alastair Hannay, Penguin Books 1989

——— , *Either/Or* Parts 1 and 2, ed. and trans. Howard V.Hong and Edna H.Hong, Princeton University Press 1987

——— , *Fear and Trembling*, trans. Alastair Hannay, Penguin Books 1985

Kohlberg, L., 'Stage and Sequence: The Cognitive-Developmental Approach to Socialization', in D.A. Goslin (ed.), *Handbook of Socialization Theory and Research*, Rand McNally 1969

Roberts, David E., *Existentialism and Religious Belief*, Oxford University Press 1957

Rogers, Carl, *On Becoming a Person*, Constable 1961

3. *A Seeker of Identity: Thomas Merton's Christian Self-Actualization*

Alland, Alexander, *The Artistic Animal: An Inquiry into the Biological Roots of Art*, Doubleday 1977

Finley, James, *Merton's Palace of Nowhere: A Search for God through Awareness of the True Self*, Ave Maria Press 1978

James, William, *The Principles of Psychology*, Vol 1, Dover Publications Inc. 1918

Koestler, Arthur, *The Act of Creation*, Macmillan 1964

Maslow, Abraham H., *Toward a Psychology of Being*, Van Nostrand Reinhold [2]1968

——— , *The Farther Reaches of Human Nature*, Penguin Books 1973

——— , *Motivation and Personality*, Harper and Row [3]1987

Merton, Thomas, *Raids on the Unspeakable*, Burns & Oates 1961

——— , *Seeds of Contemplation* (originally published as *New Seeds of Contemplation*), Anthony Clarke 1972

——— , *The New Man*, Burns and Oates 1962

——— , *No Man is an Island*, Harcourt, Brace & World, Inc. 1955

McDonnell, Thomas P., *A Thomas Merton Reader*, Revised Edition, Doubleday 1989

Rogers, Carl, *Client-Centered Therapy*. Houghton Mifflin 1951

——— , *On Becoming a Person*, Constable 1961

Shannon, William H., 'Thomas Merton and the Discovery of the Real Self',
in *The Message of Thomas Merton*, ed. Brother Patrick Hart, Cistercian
Studies Series 42, Cistercian Publications 1981
—— , *Thomas Merton's Dark Path*, Farrar, Straus, Giroux 1981
Winnicott, D.W., *Playing and Reality*, Tavistock 1971

4. *A Distracted Searcher: Blaise Pascal's Religion of the Heart*

All quotations from Pascal are from the *Pensées* in the translation by
A.J.Krailsheimer. The number given after the quotation is that in the
Krailsheimer translation.

Barrett, William, *Irrational Man: A Study in Existential Philosophy*, Mercury
Books 1964
Cruickshank, John, *Pascal: Pensées*, Grant and Cutler 1983
Hazelton, Roger, *Blaise Pascal. The Genius of His Thought*, Westminster
Press 1974
Krailsheimer, Alban, *Pascal*, Oxford University Press 1980
Pascal, *Pensées*, trans. A.J.Krailsheimer, Penguin Books 1966
Steinmann, Jean, *Pascal*, Burns & Oates 1965

5. *The Resolute Traveller: Teresa of Avila's Inward Journey*

Jung, Carl, 'Psychotherapists or the Clergy', in *Collected Works*, Vol.11,
Psychology and Religion, trans R.F.C.Hull, Routledge and Kegan Paul
1958
Teresa of Avila, *The Interior Castle*, trans. Kieran Kavanagh OCD and
Otilio Rodriguez OCD, Paulist Press 1979
—— , *Way of Perfection*, trans. E.Allison Peers, Sheed & Ward 1946
—— , *The Life of the Holy Mother Teresa of Jesus, The Complete Works*, Vol.1,
trans. and ed. E.Allison Peers, Sheed & Ward 1946
Welch, John, *Spiritual Pilgrims: Carl Jung and Teresa of Avila*, Paulist Press
1982
Williams, Rowan, *Teresa of Avila*, Geoffrey Chapman 1991

6. *A Questioning Theologian: Karl Rahner's Transcendental Christianity*

Kress, Robert, *A Rahner Handbook*, John Knox Press 1982
Popper, Karl, *Conjectures and Refutations: The Growth of Scientific Knowledge*,
Routledge and Kegan Paul [3]1969

Rahner, Karl, *Hominization: the Evolutionary Origin of Man as a Theological Problem*, trans. W.T.O'Hara, Burns & Oates 1965

—, 'The Eternal Significance of the Humanity of Jesus for our Relationship with God', in *Theological Investigations*, Vol.3, *The Theology of the Spiritual Life*, Helicon Press and Darton, Longman and Todd 1967

—, 'The Concept of Mystery in Catholic Theology', in *Theological Investigations*, Vol.4, *More Recent Writings*. Helicon Press and Darton, Longman and Todd 1974

—, *Hearers of the Word*, extracts in *A Rahner Reader*, ed. Gerald A.McCool, Seabury Press and Darton, Longman and Todd 1975

—, *Encounters with Silence*, trans. James M.Demske, Burns & Oates 1975

—, *Christian at the Crossroads*, trans. V.Green, Burns & Oates 1975

—, *Foundations of Christian Faith: An Introduction to the Idea of Christianity*, trans. William V.Dych, Darton, Longman and Todd 1978

Vass, George, *A Theologian in Search of a Philosophy: Understanding Karl Rahner*, Vol.1, Christian Classics and Sheed & Ward 1985

—, *The Mystery of Man and the Foundations of a Theological System: Understanding Karl Rahner*, Vol.2, Christian Classics and Sheed & Ward 1985

Weger, Karl-Heinz, *Karl Rahner: An Introduction to His Theology*, trans. David Smith, Burns & Oates 1980

8 Personality and Science: The Assumptions of Materialism

Boden, Margaret A., *The Creative Mind: Myths and Mechanisms*, Weidenfeld and Nicholson 1990

Dreyfus, Hubert L., *What Computers Can't Do*, Harper and Row 1972

—, and Dreyfus, S.E., *Mind Over Machine*, Basil Blackwell 1986

Searle, John, *Minds, Brains and Science, The 1984 Reith Lectures*, British Broadcasting Corporation 1984

Weizenbaum, Joseph, *Computer Power and Human Reason*, Penguin Books 1984

9. Personality and God: The Assumptions of Christian Theory

Barrett, William, *Death of the Soul: From Descartes to the Computer*, Oxford University Press 1987

Bryant, Christopher, *Jung and the Christian Way*, Darton, Longman and Todd 1983

Hostie, Raymond, *Religion and the Psychology of Jung*, trans. G.R.Lamb, Sheed & Ward 1957

Jung, C.G., 'Psychology and Religion', 'Brother Klaus', 'Answer to Job', in *Psychology and Religion: West and East, Collected Works*, Vol.11, Routledge and Kegan Paul 1958

——, 'Introduction to the Religious and Psychological Problems of Alchemy', in *Psychology and Alchemy, Collected Works* Vol.12, Routledge and Kegan Paul 1944

——, *Memories, Dreams, Reflections*, trans. Richard and Clara Winston, Collins 1962

Madell, Geoffrey, *Mind and Materialism*, Edinburgh University Press 1988

Popper, Karl R., *Conjectures and Refutations: The Growth of Scientific Knowledge*, Routledge and Kegan Paul [3]1969

——, and Eccles, John C., *The Self and Its Brain: An Argument for Interactionism*, Routledge and Kegan Paul 1977

Presley, C.F. (ed), *The Identity Theory of Mind*, University of Queensland Press [2]1971

Searle, John, *Minds, Brains and Science, The 1984 Reith Lectures*, British Broadcasting Corporation 1984

Wilson, Edgar, *The Mental as Physical*, Routledge and Kegan Paul 1979

Name Index

228 *In Search of Personality*

Subject Index